*For my sons,
and for Willy's and Larry's*

CITIZEN NADER

Charles McCarry

Saturday Review Press

NEW YORK

Published simultaneously in Canada by Doubleday Canada Ltd., Toronto.

Library of Congress Catalog Card Number: 70–182488

ISBN 0–8415–0163–7

SATURDAY REVIEW PRESS

230 Park Avenue

New York, New York 10017

PRINTED IN THE UNITED STATES OF AMERICA

Design by Tere LoPrete

CITIZEN NADER

Contents

The most glorious exploits do not always furnish us with the clearest discoveries of virtue or vice in men; sometimes a matter of less moment, an expression or a jest, informs us better of their characters and inclinations, than the most famous sieges, the greatest armaments, or the bloodiest battles whatsoever.

PLUTARCH (Alexander)

Quis custodiet ipsos / Custodes?

JUVENAL (Satires vi. 347)

A Selective Chronology

1912	Nathra Nader emigrates to the United States from Lebanon
1924	Nathra Nader and Rose Bouziane married at Zahle, Lebanon
1934 (*February 27*)	Ralph Nader, youngest of Nathra and Rose Nader's four children, born at Winsted, Connecticut
1951	Ralph Nader graduates from the Gilbert School in Winsted and enters Princeton
1955	Graduates *magna cum laude* from Princeton
1958	Graduates from Harvard Law School
1958–1959	Serves six months in the Army as a cook at Fort Dix, New Jersey
1959	Publishes first article on auto safety in *The Nation*
1959	Establishes law practice at Hartford, Connecticut
1961–1964	Travels in Europe, USSR, Africa, and Latin America as a free-lance journalist

1964–1965   Serves as a consultant under Assistant Secretary of Labor Daniel Patrick Moynihan and writes an official critique of the federal highway and traffic safety program

1965
(*November 29*)   *Unsafe at Any Speed* published

1966
(*January 25*)   Vincent Gillen, a private detective, commences his investigation of Nader on behalf of General Motors Corporation

1966
(*March 22*)   General Motors officials summoned before the Ribicoff subcommittee to explain the corporation's investigation. GM President James M. Roche publicly apologizes; Nader vindicated by the subcommittee

1966
(*September 9*)   President Johnson signs the National Traffic and Motor Vehicle Safety and Highway Safety acts, bringing the design of motor vehicles under federal regulation

1966
(*November 16*)   Nader sues GM for $26 million, charging invasion of privacy

1967
(*December 6*)   Congress passes Wholesome Meat Act

1968   Congress passes Natural Gas Pipeline Safety Act, Radiation Control for Health and Safety Act, and Wholesome Poultry Act, all advocated by Nader

1968   First Group of "Nader's Raiders" investigates the Federal Trade Commission, publishes a critical report on the commission's activities

1968
(*June 28*)   Nader establishes Center for Study of Responsive Law in Washington

1969
(*May 3*)   Nader, in secret meeting, urges Joseph A. Yablonski to oppose W. A. ("Tony") Boyle for the presidency of the United Mine Workers of America

1969
(*May 12*)   GM halts production of the Chevrolet Corvair

1969
(*May 29*)   Yablonski announces candidacy for presidency of United Mine Workers

1969   Coal Mine Health and Safety Act, advocated by Nader, passes Congress

1970   Nader's Raiders investigate Interstate Commerce Commission, Food and Drug Administration, air pollution, airline safety, nursing homes, medical profession, and other activities of public and private agencies

1970
(*July*)   Public Interest Research Group founded in Washington with $280,000 proceeds of the settlement of Nader's suit against General Motors

1970   Campaign GM, advised by Nader, advances proposals for the reform of General Motors at the corporation's stockholders' meeting in May and is defeated

1970   Public interest research groups, funded by student contributions, established in Oregon and Minnesota

1970   Comprehensive Occupational Health and Safety Act, advocated by Nader, passed by Congress. He denounces as inadequate a bill to establish a federal agency to protect the consumer

1970   Nader assistants begin campaign against pollution by the Union Carbide Corporation

1971   Government orders Union Carbide to correct conditions producing excessive pollution at some of its plants

1971   Nader etsablishes Public Citizen to raise funds for his activities and those of the dozen organizations he has founded to seek reform

1971   Nader announces plans to investigate Congress

CITIZEN NADER

1

Brains and Anger

How much has this nation lost because there are men walking around today with invisible chains?

RALPH NADER

Let us suppose that it is a summer afternoon during the Eisenhower years, that long baseball season when the American elms were still alive, when the sound of our country's name evoked images of sweet air, living streams and lakes, intelligent industry, and a generous people at peace with their history. Let us suppose, further, that the president of General Motors is for some reason driving through Winsted, Connecticut, in a Cadillac that breaks down owing to a design fault. While waiting for the local mechanic to fix the car, our imaginary auto magnate strolls toward the sound of youthful voices and finds himself watching a sandlot baseball game.

American boys, gabby and freckled, drop bunts and field grounders and slide joyously into second base. For the president of General Motors, the cares of high position drop away. For a few moments in this common little town—neither ugly nor beautiful with its brick mills beside a spoiled river and its decent frame houses on the hillsides—the eminent man is happy. His eye falls carelessly, if at all, upon a spindly youth—darker than the American ideal, disfigured by the nose of a prophet—who plays first base the way the president of General Motors makes small talk, through concentration rather than talent.

This fictional scene illustrates our national mystery. You never know who is going to leap out of the crowd, holding your doom in his hands. The skinny first baseman, as the reader will have guessed, was Ralph Nader, who would grow up to believe, and to convince a very large segment of the population, that General Motors is symbolic of almost everything that is wrong with life in the United States.

Nader came to the attention of General Motors in real life on November 29, 1965, with the publication of his book, *Unsafe at Any Speed*. The book was a passionate attack on the American automobile and its makers. Its central argument was that automobile manufacturers routinely marketed vehicles they knew to be unsafe out of a lust for profits. This was a colorful accusation, but not a new one. What distinguished Nader's book, in addition to an illumination of the most obscure details of automotive design, was the unjaded quality of his anger. Nader may have been, as a GM executive who read a prepublication copy of the book thought, a clumsy writer. But his voice came out of the tangle of highway wrecks as clearly as Saint Augustine's from the thornbush.

Nevertheless, publication of the book ought to have been a quiet event. Automobile safety, as Nader knew after several years of trying to interest people in it, lacked sex. The author, a thirty-one-year-old graduate of Princeton and Harvard Law School, had neither a name nor connections. To one of the people who knew him, Nader looked a little like Franz Kafka. There was something faintly foreign about

him, as if he might be not just in the wrong country, but in
the wrong time. "He had the eyes of a reformer," says his
friend Paul Sitton of the National Academy of Sciences.
"Ralph would have fitted right in in the Middle Ages." He
lived in a rooming house alone and owned almost nothing.
His drab clothes did not quite fit his spare body; he seemed
to own only one necktie. His speech was fluent, the
vocabulary a mixture of literary flourishes and technical jargon. The intonation was proletarian, with the elusive echo of
an accent, as if he had learned English from someone to
whom it was not a native language. The effect was something
like George Raft reading Shakespeare. He had abandoned a
desultory law practice in Hartford, worked as a consultant
for the U.S. Department of Labor and as an unpaid adviser
to a Senate subcommittee, written freelance articles for *The
Nation* and *The Christian Science Monitor* and a few unsigned pieces for *The Atlantic Monthly*.

Because of his interest in a new theory of auto safety—
one that blamed the design of vehicles rather than human
folly for most accidents—he was known in Washington
chiefly to a few specialists who were themselves hidden in the
lower bureaucracy. Nader's zeal puzzled and amused some of
these people. "The impression I got," remembers John
Walsh, a speechwriter for Mrs. Esther Peterson, President
Johnson's special assistant for consumer affairs, "was of a tremendous loner, a guy you'd never expect to become a national figure. He was alone and intense and dark, always
wearing wrinkled dark suits, with dark eyes and dark skin."

Status, in what was still Kennedy's Washington, belonged
to those who had secrets to tell, or anecdotes about the famous. Nader, then as now, had only information to impart.
So remote was he from the effervescence of the era, in fact,
that his superior at the Labor Department, Daniel Patrick
Moynihan, thought for a long time that he must be a Republican. "I just couldn't conceive," Moynihan says, "how a man

could be working for that administration and never make a single reference to politics." Moynihan's wife, who was Nader's hostess at a number of dinner parties, eventually stopped inviting girls to keep him company. Nader ignored them and talked of nothing but cars. He thought that the nation should be in a rage because the automobile had killed almost three times as many Americans as all the wars in U.S. history. Instead, like the girls across Elizabeth Moynihan's table, the nation was bored.

It is Nader's chief gift, as his subsequent career has shown, never to be bored by the obvious. "Every time I see something terrible, it's like I see it at age nineteen," he says. "I keep a freshness that way." The companion gift, which is the explanation for his fame, involves his ability to free others of their indifference. This has something to do with his eccentric use of language. A Nader sentence is like the footprints of a rhinoceros on a glacier: unmistakable in its meaning but very queer in its choice of ground. He assigns no order of importance to his issues, being as much moved by a recitation of the ingredients of a hot dog as by the imminent pollution of the Earth. In another man this mingling of the trivial and the tragic might be laughable. In Nader it is convincing. But this was not always true. Before the publication of *Unsafe at Any Speed* and the bizarre conflict it provoked, Nader had not been able to put his gifts together. "He was such a solitary figure, always alone," says Elizabeth Moynihan. "I thought it was sad."

Unsafe at Any Speed was commissioned as an untitled work on auto safety in September, 1964, by Richard Grossman of Grossman Publishers in New York. The advance against royalties was about $2,000. Grossman had never heard of Nader. He first approached James Ridgeway, who had written an article in *The New Republic* about the General Motors Corvair, a rear-engine compact car that its critics said had a tendency to overturn because of a faulty rear suspension system and other flaws in its design. Ridgeway, who was busy with other projects, turned down Grossman's proposal to write a book about dangerous cars. But he told him about Nader, who had been the source of some of the material in Ridgeway's article.

At the time, Nader was writing a report for Moynihan on the role of the federal government in highway safety. This job paid him fifty dollars a day—when he was physically present at the Labor Department, which was about half the time and almost always at night. He wrote some articles for *The Christian Science Monitor,* including an exposé of inaccurate odometers that, in the course of his research for the Labor Department, he had discovered were being installed in some American cars. In a matter of months, Nader was to become an unpaid and indeed secret adviser to the Senate Subcommittee on Executive Reorganization, which was preparing hearings on the federal role in traffic safety.

Grossman and Nader, during a three-hour lunch in New York, established the ground rules for the book. "We decided," Grossman recalls, "that we were not going for gore, that there would be no pictures of accident victims, that we would stay away from maudlin human interest." Grossman advertised the work for publication on Memorial Day, 1965, but the manuscript was not ready for that deadline. Grossman went to Washington in the summer of 1965, rented a room in the Gramercy Motor Inn, and went to work with his author. He found him, despite a weakness for compound words, esoteric terms, and tortuous ironic humor, easy enough to edit. "It wasn't as if he was a technical writer and I was translating him into English," Grossman says. "I wasn't polishing zircons—we were going for quality together." The book was finished around the first of October and published, with remarkable dispatch, less than sixty days later. The title was Grossman's. Nader had misgivings about it, as did several of Grossman's professional friends, who warned him that no book with the word *safe* or *unsafe* in its title had ever sold. The whole phrase was lifted by Grossman out of a sentence in another book about automobiles, John Keats's *Insolent Chariots*. When the book came back from the printer, Grossman's partner—one half of the two-man firm, which operated out of a basement office in lower Manhattan—delivered copies in his own station wagon to bookstores in New York.

This combination of an unknown writer and a tiny publishing house, bringing out a book that another publisher had told Nader would be of interest to nobody except insurance men, was not one to make Detroit tremble. Grossman, after exposure to what he calls "the full Nader education," was at a point somewhere between fear and hope about the reaction of the auto companies. He traveled to about a dozen cities in the West and the South, urging book reviewers not to give in to industry pressure, if they received any. In New York, Grossman says, a reviewer for *Life* magazine told him, "I wouldn't touch this book with a ten-foot pole." He got a similar reaction from a forthright newspaperman in Houston. "With all our automobile advertising?" asked the Texan. "You must be crazy."

There was some reason for caution. Nader, in the first line of his preface, placed the blame for "death, injury, and the most inestimable sorrow" on the automobile itself—not, as conventional wisdom then had it, on the driver. The first chapter, entitled "The Sporty Corvair" with the irony Grossman had noticed in his author, was a devastating description of the handling characteristics of the popular GM compact car. Nader marshaled evidence, ranging from engineering data in the original jargon to clinical descriptions of severed arms lying on the highway, to make the point that the design of the Corvair was responsible for its tendency to overturn or skid out of control without warning.

Nader charged that the Corvair had been placed on the

market with a rear suspension system that caused the back wheels to change camber by as much as eleven degrees on curves, "a horrifying shift causing violent skidding, rear-end breakaway or vehicle roll-over. The change occurs without warning and in an instant." Other design factors, such as the need to maintain precise but different tire pressures front and rear, were described as contributing to a loss of control under normal driving conditions.

Nader, in his bludgeoning prose, called the Corvair design "one of the greatest acts of industrial irresponsibility in the present century." General Motors engineers, he wrote, "did not have the professional stamina to defend their engineering principles from the predatory clutches of the cost cutters and the stylists." Nader's thesis was that General Motors had marketed a car its executives knew to be unsafe, and that GM had done so for the controlling purpose of making money. This was, of course, very close to an accusation against the corporation of negligent homicide.

General Motors has defended the design of the 1960–63 Corvair on grounds that it was as safe as any comparable car of the same period. Frank J. Winchell, Chevrolet's chief research and development engineer, testifying before the Highway Committee of the Michigan Senate in 1966, said that "the Corvair's capabilities are greater than the capabilities of [its] drivers and the highways on which [it] is driven." [1]

1. Winchell maintained that the swing-axle rear suspension used on the Corvair during the first four years of production was "the most reliable and widely used rear suspension system known at the time." With the 1964 models, General Motors introduced improvements to both front and rear suspension systems that had the effect of transferring, in Winchell's words, "more cornering force to the outside front wheel." In other words, some of the strain was taken off the outside rear wheel, which Nader maintained had a tendency to "tuck under."
On the problem of "tuck-under," Winchell testified as follows:

Our tests prove that up to and including 0.6g the outside rear wheel does not "tuck under." On the contrary, the suspension is compressed. . . . Even at 0.75g's lateral acceleration, the suspension [i.e., camber] has dropped only one degree below its normal straight-ahead course. . . .

Until recently, there have been no figures from independent sources on the tendency of the Corvair to become involved in single-car crashes of the kind Nader described as being typical. But in 1971 the Highway Safety Research Center of the University of North Carolina, working under a grant from the Insurance Institute for Highway Safety, produced a study that can be interpreted as confirming Nader's view of the question. Researchers studied accidents involving 90,000 cars on North Carolina highways during 1966 and 1968.

The accident rate in single-car crashes for 1960–1963 Corvairs was found to be markedly higher than that of the Ford Falcon, Chrysler Valiant, and Volkswagen of the same vintage. The 1960 Corvair was involved in 2.16 single-car crashes per million miles, compared to 1.94 for the Volkswagen and 1.60 for the Falcon (the Valiant was not manufactured in 1960). For 1961, 1962, and 1963 models, the average rate of single-car crashes involving the Corvair was 2.44; the rate for the Volkswagen was 1.61, for the Falcon 1.09, and for the Valiant 1.00.

In 1964, the rate for the Corvair dropped to 1.66, and declined steadily in the following three years until, in the 1967 models, it recorded 0.16 single-car crashes per million miles—

Photographs of tire distortions with the car sliding sideways will show no significant difference between the proximity of the rim to the pavement of the Corvair and any other automobile.

Winchell pointed out that "0.6g [lateral acceleration] is the limit of control for all American passenger cars of that date." He agreed that the Corvair was essentially uncontrollable above 0.6g—but insisted that all other American cars were too. He added that "our experience is that in the emergency situation [e.g., skidding] few motorists have the capacity to control any car on public roads at much in excess of 0.3g at 30 mph and 0.2g at 60 mph." In the 1964 models, Winchell said, "the limit of control was extended to approximately 0.7g lateral acceleration. . . ." In a press release dated May 26, 1971, General Motors said: "General Motors has never denied that the 1960—1963 model Corvair may be rolled over after it substantially exceeds its limit of control, which is equal to or better than the limit of control of competitive cars of the same era."

a lower figure than that achieved by the Volkswagen (0.56), the Falcon (0.55), or the Valiant (0.24).

To Grossman's chagrin, there was no immediate public response from General Motors or any of the other manufacturers attacked in Nader's book. He had expected pressure. "Sometimes," he says, "I prayed for it." By January, 1966, Grossman says, "I was annoyed that the auto companies had not come out to fight." He decided to drive them from cover with a press conference in Detroit. In addition to alerting the newspapers, Grossman sent telegrams to all the automobile manufacturers, inviting them to ask Nader any question they liked, in public and in the presence of reporters and television cameras. "I made sure," Grossman says, "that I held the press conference in the hotel with Cadillac's name in it, the Sheraton-Cadillac. I was going for everything." Not surprisingly, no representative of the auto companies showed up to contribute to the promotion of *Unsafe at Any Speed*.

Despite Detroit's lack of cooperation, the book was not doing badly. The first printing of nine thousand copies sold out, and by the end of February, 1966, almost twenty-two thousand copies had been purchased. In July, after General Motors finally made its frontal assault on Nader, the book made the best-seller lists. "Then," says Grossman, "it sort of stopped dead. By that time it had been in the papers so much that people could go to a cocktail party and talk about the detective story without reading the book. I think, too, that there was an innate feeling that people didn't want to know the truth about auto safety." Eventually, *Unsafe at Any Speed* sold about seventy thousand copies in hard covers. The paperback edition sold about a quarter of a million copies of a press run of four hundred thousand.

Until what Grossman calls "the detective story" was broken in *The New Republic*'s issue for March 12, 1966, under James Ridgeway's by-line, *Unsafe at Any Speed* had generated only a modest amount of publicity. Few national publications had reviewed the book, except for such specialized magazines as *Science* and *Scientific American*. An adaptation of the Corvair chapter appeared in *The Nation* and was picked up by the Charleston, West Virginia, *Gazette*. The *Nation* article caused concern in Detroit, as did a letter from the American Trial Lawyers Association recommending Nader as a source of information for lawyers involved in the hundred or more lawsuits pending against General Motors as a result of Corvair accidents.

Even before the book's publication, General Motors had commissioned a private investigator named William F. O'Neill to look into Nader's qualifications as an expert witness. Aloysius Power, the general counsel at General Motors, afterward said that one of the purposes of the O'Neill investigation was to determine if Nader had a financial interest in the Corvair litigation, in which the corporation was being sued for a total of about forty million dollars. If it turned out that he did, Power said, the information could have been used to discredit Nader's testimony as a witness in any of the suits, and to provide a basis for filing charges against him with the bar association for a violation of legal ethics.

O'Neill's report, handed to General Motors on November 21, 1965, turned up little except the fact that Nader was probably in Washington. General Motors' legal staff decided to authorize a more thorough investigation. On December 22, Miss Eileen Murphy, a onetime Justice Department employee who had become a member of Power's staff, phoned Richard Danner of the Washington law firm of Alvord & Alvord and asked if he could recommend someone to do a complete background investigation of Nader. Danner put Miss Murphy in touch with a former FBI agent named Vincent Gillen, who had his own detective agency, Vincent Gillen Associates, in New York.

Under the pretext of a preemployment inquiry, Gillen began his investigation of Nader on January 25, 1966. "Our job," he told his agents, "is to check his life and current activities to determine what makes him tick, such as his real interest in safety, his supporters, if any, his politics, his marital status, his friends, his women, his boys, and so forth, drinking, dope, jobs—in fact all facets of his life." Gillen had not quite fulfilled this mission when Ridgeway's story broke in *The New Republic,* spilled over into *The Washington Post* and most other newspapers, and brought the president of General Motors before a Senate subcommittee. The subcommittee did something for Nader that the Senate had never done for an individual in the history of the nation. It certified his virtue, gave birth to him as a public figure, and equipped him with an image that has remained a combination of the best qualities of Lincoln of Illinois and David of 1 Samuel 17.

If General Motors had hired a novelist to create a character whose investigation would produce maximum embarrassment to the corporation, he probably could not have imagined a figure better suited to the role than Ralph Nader. As a child in Winsted he had learned from his father—a Lebanese immigrant whose intense patriotism included a reflexive anger over the injustices of society—not to trust power. "Not only to a child," says Nader's father, "do things seem upside down, if you judge by what is right." Nader's brief manhood had confirmed his father's teachings. After years spent in libraries, and a few sorties into the world, Nader believed in his bones that corporations were, by their nature, ruthless. In his own life he rejected all the things that corporations produced: he owned no machines, ate no processed foods, and shunned money. One of Nader's protégés, Larry J. Silver-

man, told him in later years that Nader reminded him of
Cato the Elder, who had made virtue unattractive. Nader
flinched. "All that," he replied, "is unimportant."

Nader was, besides, a natural-born secret agent. When he
worked at the Labor Department, he repeatedly warned
Moynihan, a man who is notably unguarded about what he
says, that the departmental telephones might be tapped.
Nader was as guarded as a spy about the most trivial aspects
of his life. He never talked about himself, never admitted to
an emotion, never invited anyone into the room where he
lived, never discussed his movements or his plans. "Ralph
would vanish," says his Harvard Law School classmate Joseph A. Page, "and then I'd get a postcard from Helsinki."
He detested the gossipy publicity that surrounds public
figures. Shortly after his book was published, a wire service
photograph showed Nader tobogganing with some children
in Winsted; he regarded the picture as a violation of his privacy. "Even something as humanizing as sliding downhill
with some kids," says Page, "is an invasion to Ralph." When,
speaking with rehearsed precision before the Senate subcommittee, Nader characterized the General Motors investigation,
he called it "an invasion of the self."

Gillen's agents had not been trying for long to puncture
the hymen of Nader's privacy before he detected them. According to Gillen, Nader detected them before they even
started to follow him. He felt his first shiver of suspicion on
January 10, 1966, in the Kirkwood Hotel in Des Moines. He
had gone to Iowa to testify before a safety inquiry by the
state attorney general. Nader noticed a man, twice in the
lobby and once in the corridor outside his room, who seemed
to be watching him. In late February, he flew to Philadelphia
to appear on the Mike Douglas Show and had his suspicions
aroused again. Nader does not like to waste time in airports;
his system for taking planes involves a sprint through the terminal, an impatient pause at the gate to have his ticket torn

off, and a plunge through the door of the aircraft into the
last empty seat. At 3:25 P.M. on February 21, Nader came
loping up to the gate for his return flight to Washington. All
the other passengers had already boarded the plane, except
two men who were still in the waiting area. The men followed Nader aboard his United Air Lines flight and took
seats near him. He thought that they were taking an unusual
interest in him during the flight. On arrival at National Airport, Nader hurried into the terminal, nipped in and out of
several doors, and leaped into a taxi. Looking out the back
window as the cab approached the Potomac bridges, he was
satisfied that he was no longer being followed. Gillen testified that his men had not begun their surveillance until
February 4, and that Nader was not followed in Philadelphia.

At about this time, Nader stopped in on Paul Sitton, then
an official of the Department of Commerce, and confided
that he was being followed. "I don't doubt it," Sitton told
him, "but if you go around saying so, people will think
you're nuts." At least one person did think so, at any rate for
a few moments. Nader had called a friend from a public
phone booth and was invited to dinner. A heavy snow was
falling, and Nader arrived soaking wet at his hostess's door.
He explained that he had left his cab at the corner and
walked in through the storm. He did this, he explained, because he believed he was being followed. "I thought this was
some kind of nut," his hostess recalls. "It seemed a very neu-
rotic sort of reaction." After a talk before the fireplace lasting until two o'clock in the morning, Nader's friend and her
husband thought that his apprehensions were saner than
they had seemed.

Other things were happening to Nader. On February 20,
while he was looking over the magazine rack in a drugstore
near his boardinghouse, a pretty girl with dark hair approached him. Excusing her boldness, she invited Nader to

join her and some friends for a discussion of foreign policy. Nader, failing to discourage her with polite excuses, turned his back on her. Three days later, while Nader was buying a package of cookies in a Safeway supermarket in Washington, another young woman—this one a blonde wearing trousers— asked him to help her move a heavy object in her apartment. Nader refused. The girl persisted, and he ended by being rude to her, too. During this period Nader received a number of telephone calls, usually hearing a voice that identified itself as Pan American Airways or Railway Express. "Is Mr. Nader there?" the voice would ask. When Nader identified himself, the connection would be broken. One caller, using a rougher tone, asked, "Why don't you go back to Connecticut, buddy boy?"

Nader was not amused by these events. "There was always," he says, "the question of who was doing it to keep you from being amused. Sometimes it got pretty close." He suspected that the auto industry was involved. He still suspects that the girl in the drugstore and the blonde in the supermarket were sexual lures. Had he responded to their advances, one supposes, the next step would have been motion pictures taken through a one-way glass.

On February 21, a man who identified himself on the telephone as "Mr. Warren" made an appointment with a young lawyer named Frederick H. Condon, who worked for an insurance company in Concord, New Hampshire. Nader had dedicated *Unsafe at Any Speed* to Condon, a classmate at Harvard Law School who had been crippled in an automobile accident. When "Mr. Warren" arrived, he introduced himself as Vincent Gillen. He told Condon that he was carrying out a preemployment check on behalf of a client who was considering Nader for a job. During his interview with Condon, Gillen held a tan attaché case on his lap. "The case," Condon wrote in a memorandum of the encounter,

"could easily have held a miniature tape recorder, or a bug
with the recorder in his car." Gillen asked a number of questions, taking notes on blue-lined notepaper in what Condon
thought was "a peculiar scrawl." He asked about the origins
of Nader's interest in auto safety, about his politics, about his
sexual preferences, about his travels. He asked whether there
was any possibility that Nader was anti-Semitic; he mentioned that Nader was of "Syrian ancestry." Condon corrected him, pointing out that Nader's parents were immi-
grants from Lebanon. "Well," Gillen replied, "it's about the
same thing. We just want to know if there is any anti-Semitic
feeling there."

Condon wrote a lengthy account of his half-hour talk with
Gillen for his own files and sent a telegram to Nader informing him of the detective's visit. Nader had meanwhile heard
from other acquaintances, who congratulated him on the job
he was about to receive. Gillen and his operatives, using the
preemployment investigation as a cover story, had taken
their inquiries into at least three states and the District of
Columbia. Everywhere they went, they asked about anti-
Semitism, about sex, about the history of Nader's interest in
auto safety. Few questions were addressed to what General
Motors later said was the basic purpose of the investigation—
to determine if Nader had any connection with the Corvair lawsuits. Nader assured friends he had not applied for
employment with anyone, and had no idea of taking a
position. Except for his brief Hartford law practice, Nader has
not, at any time in his life, held a full-time job.

In 1966 Jerome Sonosky was staff director and general
counsel of the Senate Subcommittee on Executive Reorganization. He was one half of the staff that, working behind
Chairman Abraham Ribicoff and Robert F. Kennedy and

the other senators who were members of the subcommittee, drafted the laws to bring auto safety under federal regulation. The other half of the team was Ralph Nader.

Nader had stopped in on Sonosky in January, 1965, less than a month after Ribicoff had decided to hold hearings on the federal role in highway safety. Nader, wandering in with a stack of *The Congressional Record* under his arm, had three things to recommend him to Sonosky: he was from Connecticut, which made him a constituent of Ribicoff's; he was a lawyer like Sonosky, and he worked for Moynihan, who was, in addition to being an Assistant Secretary of Labor and a Kennedy confidant, the most famous proponent of the new theories of auto safety that Nader was shortly to transform into a national issue. Nader had another important quality: he was willing to work in obscurity and let senators take credit for what he did.

After a three-hour conversation, Sonosky called Ribicoff and said, "We've just struck gold." Nader began to spend a good deal of his time in the subcommittee's offices in the basement of the Old Senate Office Building. Almost no one knew what Nader was doing. Nader was unpaid. He did not appear on any roster of Senate employees. He never met Ribicoff or any of the other senators on the subcommittee except, possibly, Robert Kennedy. He worked at night a good deal, spreading his charts and documents over any desk that happened to be empty. He kept no regular schedule and would sometimes vanish for days at a time. When he was present, he was feeding Sonosky the ideas and questions and technical material that determined the character of the subcommittee's hearings and, subsequently, the content of the new traffic and highway safety laws. Sonosky, in turn, gave the material to Ribicoff and Kennedy and other well-disposed Democrats on the subcommittee. "Nader was my prime resource, period," Sonosky says. "I didn't need anyone else. He had everything."

Nader's conversation with Sonosky was all business. "Sometimes," Sonosky says, "I had to shut him up. He was fixated on auto safety." There is something comic in the combination of Sonosky and Nader. Each makes sparing use of the pronoun "I": Nader because he talks of nothing except issues, Sonosky because he calls himself, in ordinary conversation, "Sonosky" or "this kid from northern Minnesota." Sonosky is a short, rubicund man, so charged with humors he seems to be darting around the room even when he is sitting behind a desk. He belongs to that breed of assistants which loves to tinker with the famous. Historical figures he has touched or telephoned—Martin Luther King, Robert Kennedy, Lyndon Johnson—tumble through his sentences like ghostly acrobats. Sonosky had a premonition that, in Nader, he was dealing with something more than a backroom resource: "I said to Ralph once, 'You'll be one of the biggest things that ever happened in this country. I'll tell my kids that I knew you.' Ralph's reply was, 'Hmmm.' "

Nader likes to keep the parts of his life separated and the people he knows in compartments. At the height of their relationship, Sonosky suggested to Nader that he ought to write a book. Nader was, at the time, working on *Unsafe at Any Speed*. "Old Ralph didn't say he was writing a book," Sonosky says. "He just gave me one of those smiles that means he's got another secret." When the book came out, Sonosky was surprised that the author was described on the jacket as being connected with the subcommittee. "Maybe I was even disturbed," Sonosky says. "He was not with the subcommittee, officially."

In January and February, 1966, Nader included Sonosky among those in whom he confided his belief that he was being watched and harassed. "Ralph used to say to me," Sonosky recalls, " 'Some very strange things are happening.' I'd say, 'Come *on*, Ralph!' " On February 11, according to Sonosky, a Capitol policeman named Brian McGovern rushed into Sonosky's office and cried, "Two private eyes have just followed Ralph Nader into the New Senate Office Building!" Sonosky picked up the phone, called Ribicoff, and said, "A strong auto safety bill has just passed."

Two detectives from the Arundel Investigative Agency of Severna Park, Maryland, who had been watching Nader as subcontractors to Gillen, had followed a man they thought to be Nader into the New Senate Office Building. Only the day before, Nader had testified before the Ribicoff subcommittee; with the publication of his book, he had materialized out of Sonosky's back room and become a witness in the hearings designed by himself. Certainly nothing could have been better calculated to annoy Ribicoff than having one of his witnesses tailed on Capitol Hill.

There is some question that the man the investigators were following was, in fact, Nader. A reporter for *The Washington Post* named Bryce Nelson, who, like Nader, is tall and dark and lanky, had entered the building at about 1:30 P.M. for an interview with Ribicoff. When he emerged from Ribicoff's office, he was told by Senate guards that two men had been following him in the belief that he was Nader. The guards saw the detectives loitering, questioned them, and ordered them to leave the building. Nelson went back to the *Post,* told his editor of the incident, and began to write up his interview with Ribicoff. Soon Nader arrived in the city room and told a reporter named Morton Mintz that the Senate guards had told him how he was being tailed by the detectives. Mintz, who was subsequently to become Washington's chief chronicler of Nader, did not at that time know him well. He did not quickly believe his story. "By God," says Mintz, "you have to be skeptical in this business." He began calling the Capitol police. After a few moments, the national editor, Laurence Stern, stopped at Mintz's desk to tell him about the incident involving Bryce Nelson. Nelson confirmed it. Mintz wrote a straight-faced little story, which appeared on an inside page.

"After the cops blew the whistle on the private eyes I was scared to death," Sonosky says. "We couldn't run out in the street and cry, 'GM, you did this!'" Nader, who at last had witnesses to confirm his own certainty that he was the subject of an investigation, was ready for cries in the street. He gave his story to Ridgeway and made himself available to other reporters. "The story popped," Sonosky says, "and we reacted." Part of the story was a General Motors press release on March 9 acknowledging that its general counsel had "authorized a routine investigation . . . to determine if Ralph Nader was acting on behalf of litigants or attorneys in Corvair design cases pending against General Motors. The investigation was prompted by Mr. Nader's extreme criticism of Corvair. . . ."

Ribicoff's reaction was to summon James M. Roche, then the president of General Motors, together with others connected with the investigation, to testify under oath at a subcommittee hearing on March 22. "It appears that General Motors," Ribicoff said, "is seeking to justify its investigation of Mr. Nader by impugning his motives as a witness before my subcommittee." Aloysius Power and an assistant, who had flown to Washington, were not admitted to Ribicoff's office until two hours after he had spoken on the floor of the Senate.

"Ted Sorensen," says a member of the subcommittee staff, "was worth whatever GM paid him, because he gave Roche the right advice: apologize. The GM lawyers maybe wanted to back off from that. If they'd tried it, we'd still be wiping blood off the walls of the Senate Caucus Room." There was blood enough, as things turned out.

Roche, flanked by the former presidential speechwriter, whom General Motors had hired as counsel for the hearings, testified first. Nader, who had been scheduled as the first witness, was late. "It was like a wedding," says Mrs. Ellen Broderick, a former assistant of Moynihan's at the Labor Department. "There were reserved seats on one side for Ralph's friends, and on the other side all those automobile executives in gray flannel suits." As Roche took the oath, Nader was standing on a street corner near his boardinghouse, trying in vain to hail a taxi. "I usually take no more than twelve minutes to come down to the Capitol from my residence by cab," Nader explained that afternoon in his apology to the subcommittee. "In this instance I gave myself twenty minutes. And as I waited and waited and waited to get a cab, and as my frustration mounted, I almost felt like going out and buying a Chevrolet."

James Roche had gone to work for General Motors when he was twenty-one years old, in 1927, the year he left La Salle University. He became president of the corporation, which in terms of its wealth is the sixth largest country in the world, in June, 1965, and was elected chairman of the board in 1967. His lifelong association with the corporation that is the key element of the American economy has given him a rewarded air and a reputation for that single-minded workmanship which is called, in men like Ralph Nader, genius. He lost no time in acting on Sorensen's advice, because he saw immediately that he was dealing with a first-class crisis.

"Let me make it clear at the outset," Roche told the subcommittee, "that I deplore the kind of harassment to which Mr. Nader has apparently been subjected. . . . While there can be no disagreement over General Motors' legal right to ascertain certain facts preparatory to litigation . . . I am not here to excuse, condone, or justify in any way our investigation of Mr. Nader. To the extent that General Motors bears responsibility, I want to apologize here and now to the members of this subcommittee and Mr. Nader."

Roche was facing senators Ribicoff, Robert Kennedy, Fred Harris of Oklahoma, Henry M. Jackson of Washington, and Milward L. Simpson of Wyoming, the only Republican present. Senator Carl T. Curtis, Republican of Nebraska, who had suggested at an earlier subcommittee hearing that Nader was using his testimony "to sell books," was not present. Curtis had asked Nader about his connection with the subcommittee. In the printed record, it seems an innocent enough question, but Nader evidently was stung by Curtis's tone of voice. "I am intrigued by the implication, Senator," Nader replied, "that this endeavor is somewhat suspect. I think it is a rather noble expression of citizenship."

Curtis's questioning was belligerent enough for Ribicoff to interrupt to defend the propriety of the situation. "The first time I ever saw Mr. Nader," Ribicoff said, "was when he walked into this room today." Curtis's approach to Nader jostled the instincts of Robert Kennedy as well. "As I hear the questioning of Mr. Nader," Kennedy said, "it sounds like he is a criminal of some sort or is guilty of some crime. . . . I am surprised, if I may say so, there seems to be a concerted effort to prevent Mr. Nader from giving his testimony before this committee."

Roche, as the man responsible, in theory, for everything that General Motors does, came before the subcommittee to explain what its chairman had publicly said might be a criminal act. "I am calling this hearing because a General Motors statement issued yesterday [the press release of March 9] raises issues," Ribicoff had said, "which go beyond the question of witness harassment and a violation of the U.S. Criminal Code." Roche did not receive easy treatment from Ribicoff, who reminded him that he, Ribicoff, had said on February 10 that he had never seen Nader before; eleven days later, Gillen was in New Hampshire asking Frederick Condon if Nader and Ribicoff were acquainted. Ribicoff wanted to know whether Roche was aware that the investigator had, in effect, asked "whether the chairman was telling the truth when he said that he had never seen Nader before." Roche said he was not.

Ribicoff told Roche that there was no doubt in his mind that Roche was an honorable man. Robert Kennedy, however, did not pause for the niceties. "Bobby had a way of showing his outrage," Sonosky says. "Maybe Abe didn't—but he was outraged." Ribicoff's outrage was directed to the idea that the privacy of individuals should not be violated. "There is," he told Roche, "too much snooping going on in this country. . . . Before you know it, you have a man who has led a private and honorable life having reflections cast upon his entire character, and that of his family, because of these questions that detectives, who basically aren't very sensitive, ask . . . and this must be happening all over America with many other Ralph Naders."

Roche testified that he knew nothing of the investigation until he read about it in the newspapers. He denied that General Motors had caused Nader to be followed in Iowa and Pennsylvania, had used girls to entice him, or had harassed him on the telephone late at night. In its press release, General Motors maintained that the incidents of harassment mentioned in the newspaper stories were not connected with its investigation.

Robert Kennedy told Roche that he believed the press release was an attempt to mislead the American people and the Congress of the United States. "That statement," Kennedy said in his opening series of questions, "really, Mr. Roche, . . . is not accurate." Roche conceded that it might have been worded differently, but he defended the intentions of the people at General Motors who had put out the press release. "I like my General Motors car," Kennedy said, "but you shake me up a little bit."

United States senators, as a Senate staffer said several years after the Nader hearings, do not mind being seen as avenging angels. Ribicoff, in his owlish, gentlemanly way, and Kennedy, with his gift for transforming himself into a falcon on the wrist of Liberty, did not spare Aloysius Power, or his assistant, Louis G. Bridenstine. Both men, prodded by questions, joined in Roche's apologies to Nader and the Senate. Neither would concede that the press release was intended to mislead Congress, and Kennedy kept insisting it had been misled. Power found himself, under questioning by Kennedy, saying that he didn't agree with some of the things Roche had said a few moments before about the meaning of the surveillance of Nader. Bridenstine, when he said he could not remember when he had first read one of Gillen's reports, was advised by Kennedy to be candid. "I don't imagine . . ." Ribicoff said to Power, "you are very proud of your activities."

Vincent Gillen was sworn in as the last witness late in the afternoon. Throughout the proceedings he had been snapping pictures of the senators and witnesses with a miniature camera of the kind used by spies in movies to photograph secret documents. Gillen was not in awe of the subcommittee. His testimony suggests that he may have thought he could speak the senators' language. He had forty years' experience as an investigator. He had spent about three years as an FBI agent before launching a career as a private investigator. He went through Fordham and Brooklyn Law School at night and was elected president of his class at both places. In his opening statement, he gave the subcommittee a great deal of autobiographical detail, including the information that he had been elected president of the PTA at his daughter's high school in Brooklyn. Gillen told the senators that he resented some of the things that Senator Gaylord Nelson had said about him on the floor of the Senate. "I have even," he said, "been accused of being engaged in a 'seamy trade.' "

Gillen had the flair of his trade for conveying outrageous information in prim language. He said he hadn't had Nader followed in Des Moines on January 10; indeed, he'd never heard of him until January 13. He had not used women to entice Nader, nor had "any of my former FBI colleagues." There had been no recorder in the attaché case that he had held on his knees while speaking to Condon, but he wished there had been, "because some of my questions have been characterized as 'lurid.' " He disliked being interrupted while reading his prepared statement; when Ribicoff broke in to ask a question, Gillen said that he hoped the chairman was reading and listening carefully. "I sure am," said Ribicoff.

Gillen, with the air of a professional explaining the elementary principles of his job, justified the questions that had been asked about Nader's sex life, his politics, and his suspected prejudices, on grounds that the detectives were carrying out their investigation under the pretext of a preemployment check. Therefore the questions were normal. Kennedy objected that the investigation wasn't, in fact, a preemployment check. "When you conduct an investigation under a pretext," Gillen replied, "you carry it out completely, sir. . . . If you do anything less or inject extraneous matters, you run the risk of losing the pretext."

"But you were lying," Kennedy said. "What you mean was that you were conducting an investigation under a lie and you had to carry the lie out completely." Gillen asked if that had never happened while Kennedy was Attorney General. Gillen returned several times in his colloquy with Kennedy to the point that all investigators, including the FBI, did their work under a pretext as a matter of course. He seemed genuinely annoyed that his questioners could not grant what

they so obviously knew to be true. "If you wish every investigator to conduct everything openly and honestly," he told
Ribicoff, "I don't think you'd get much information." Gillen
said he thought he might well have come up with some information linking Nader with the Corvair litigants if he had
been able to follow up one of his leads. "I never had the
slightest dream about the cookies and the girls things coming
up," Gillen said. "It was one of the strangest coincidences in
the world, if you want to look at it frankly and honestly."

Ribicoff countered that there was nothing to show Nader
had any such connection. "Your entire investigation, Mr.
Gillen, had to do with trying to smear a man, the question of
his sex life, whether he belonged to any left-wing organizations, whether he was anti-Semitic, whether he was an odd-
ball, whether he liked boys instead of girls. The whole investigation was to smear an individual, and I can't find anything
of any substance in your entire investigation that had anything to do basically with whether or not he was tied up with
plaintiff's attorneys that had to do with Corvair cars."

As Gillen's testimony proceeded, Ribicoff and Kennedy
began, in their questions, to call Nader "Ralph." Gillen continued to give Kennedy unreciprocated verbal winks about
the methods of the FBI and the Justice Department. "Oh,
Senator, come on, come on," he said. "For goodness' sake,
where did I learn to do this? In the FBI." In a final burst of
exasperation, Gillen told Kennedy that he had had to follow
up his questions about Nader's personal life "in fairness to
Ralph."

"What is 'fairness to Ralph'?" Kennedy wanted to know.
"You keep proving that he is not anti-Semitic and he is not
queer. In fairness to Ralph? Ralph is doing all right. You
were just a fair-minded citizen rushing around the country
in fairness to Ralph?" Gillen said he was just doing a job,
"and I still think it was a good one."

Gillen's job cost General Motors $6,700 in fees and ex-

penses. Subsequently it cost the corporation $425,000 to set-
tle a suit for invasion of privacy in which Nader had asked
for a total of $26 million in damages. The principal cost was
foreseen by Vincent Gillen, in his instruction to his agents.
"We must be careful," Gillen wrote, "not to arouse the ire of
Nader. Keep in mind that he is a brilliant fellow and a good
writer and he could, no matter how unjustly, write something about us which would be rather damaging."

Nader, in his own testimony, said, "I am responsible for
my actions, but who is responsible for those of General Motors? An individual's capital is basically his integrity. He can
lose only once. A corporation can lose many times and not be
affected."

That dictum, in the light of Nader's career since 1966, has
not quite held up. The Corvair, after a decline of 93 percent
in sales, was taken off the market in 1969. As Jerry Sonosky
predicted, in the first exhilaration of unmasking the private
detectives, a strong auto safety bill passed, with the result
that the manufacturers have had to install some of the safety
equipment that they had consistently demeaned. With the
passage of the legislation, the automobile industry lost for-
ever the power to decide, without outside interference, all
questions of vehicle safety. The industry exercised that
unchecked power from its infancy in 1899, when the first
American was killed in New York by a horseless carriage,
until September 9, 1966, when President Johnson signed the
National Traffic and Motor Vehicle Safety Act. In the inter-
vening years, more than 1,500,000 persons died in automobile accidents in the United States.

Nader, more than any other human being, was responsible
for that loss of power—not only because he wrote much of
the bill, but because he provided the occasion to establish
the need for it. General Motors proceeded with its investigation on the assumption that there must be something wrong
with Nader. "You have come out," Ribicoff told him at the

hearing, "with a complete clean bill of health and character, with nothing derogatory having been adduced."

Ribicoff and his colleagues certified Nader to be what most people thought had vanished from the American scene: a man of flawless virtue. Nader drew the contrast between himself and his adversaries. "General Motors executives," he told the subcommittee, "continue to be blinded by their own corporate mirror-image that it's 'the buck' that moves the man. They simply cannot understand that the prevention of cruelty to humans can be a sufficient motivation. . . ."

All Nader had, when he walked into the hearing room, was brains and anger. When he walked out, he had a constituency. In the years that followed, the constituency would hear from Nader the unremitting contention that General Motors and the pall of smoke and poison and mayhem that Nader has chosen General Motors to symbolize were acts of institutional cruelty that threatened to destroy life, and that had already pillaged life of much of its meaning.

Ribicoff's hearings, in creating Nader as a public figure, changed America, or perhaps merely reminded it of its powers for concern. People were stirred. As in Shakespeare one hears, behind the blank verse of the king, the murmur of a whole invisible people, so, behind Nader's eloquent argot that is the poetry of the technological age, the senators and the executives might have heard a mutter of discovery. One man, after all, could win because he was right.

2

A Very Good Storage Place

When I went past the Statue of Liberty I took it seriously.

NATHRA NADER

When Nathra Nader was born in the Lebanon in 1893, the
country had been for twenty-nine years an autonomous province ruled by an Ottoman governor. The chief executive was
not a Lebanese, but he was a Christian. Half his subjects, including the Naders, were descendants of the primitive Chris-
tians who in the sixth century fled out of North Syria before the persecution of Byzantine orthodoxy. Through most
of their history the Lebanese had been ruled by other people; the rulers, in order to accommodate the religious passion
and the intelligence of their subjects, frequently wore what
might be called pious disguises. The Turk who was a Christian, administering a Christian province on behalf of the
most powerful and extensive Moslem empire in history, was

the disguise that obtained throughout Nathra Nader's boyhood.

Nathra Nader's father died when he was six months old.
His mother raised him, he says, to love people. "Once a man
came into my restaurant in Winsted," he says. "He was mad
about something. He said, 'Mr. Nader, I hate you!' I said,
'That's your hard luck—I *love* you!' "

Nathra came to the United States in 1912, when he was
nineteen years old. "It was the old story," his son Ralph was
to say, "twenty bucks in the pocket." Nathra worked at a variety of jobs, mostly in New Jersey. He saved his money and,
with the celebrated acumen of his people, invested it slowly
and wisely. By the time he went back to Lebanon in 1924, he
had a bank account and some property in the United States.
In the town of Zahle he married a nineteen-year-old girl
named Rose Bouziane. In 1925 they returned to the United
States together, in search of a quiet place with good air
where they could raise a family. Nathra had some business in
Connecticut. They liked the countryside and chose as their
home the village of Winsted, which lies in the foothills of the
Berkshires, near the Massachusetts line, about thirty miles
northwest of Hartford.

Nathra was by this time a convinced American, a student
of U.S. history and an avid reader of newspapers. He liked
the way people discussed the nation's flaws, and he saw no
reason, because he was a new American, why the charter of
patriotic critic should not extend to him, too. "When I went
past the Statue of Liberty," he says, "I took it seriously." In
the beginning, he was exhilarated by the individualism of
America, but gradually he began to wonder about what lay
beneath the surface. "For the first ten years," he says, "I
loved this expression, Live and let live. Then I thought,
What is that? To hell with the rest is what that means."

The Naders opened a restaurant, the Highland Arms,

shortly after their arrival in Winsted. Nathra brought it through the Depression and the Second World War only to see it destroyed in 1955 when Mad River, in a freakish flood, wiped out most of the businesses on Main Street. The town never completely recovered from the devastation, but the Highland Arms, with the help of a disaster loan from the government, was rebuilt and remained open until the late sixties.

The Naders lived in a large white house on Hillside Avenue, above the main street and out of the reach of Mad River. The home resounded with discussion, conducted in a mixture of Arabic and English. There was a mixture of themes as well—the father perpetually angry over injustice, the mother joyful over human possibility. "I felt enriched by two cultures," Mrs. Nader says. "I always thought the children should be too, from infant up." The parents shared the idea that a citizen owed a debt to society, which must be freely paid. The way to pay the debt was through an honest life, lived with courage. "Never tip your hat," Nathra Nader would repeat, "and never look down on anyone." Everything could be questioned except the family. The Naders, Greek Orthodox Catholics who went to the Methodist Sunday school, property owners who did not belong to the Yankee establishment, foreigners even to the town's large Italian population, were closely bound together because there was no other family quite like them. "They weren't part of the usual world," says a Winsted man, "so they never feared the world. You could maybe say they just went ahead because they didn't know what couldn't be done."

Nathra Nader dispensed not only food in the Highland Arms, but also a kind of impassioned conversation that, in a small American town, verges on the insufferable. "The Highland Arms was no place to go and eat in peace," says Mrs. Claire Vreeland, who still lives in Winsted. "Mr. Nader would always try to heat everybody up about wrongs and iniquities. If someone strange was in town you'd send them there because it was nearby and decent. They'd come back with indigestion and berate you. Mr. Nader would never let anything alone." The Naders continually reminded their children that some things could not be left alone. "Conditions in the country were always talked over by us, and we talked it over with the children," Nathra Nader says. "We asked why; we expected them to ask why, too."

Ralph, the youngest of the Nader children, was born on February 27, 1934. Before him came Shafik, the only child to be given an Arabic name, and two girls, Laura and Claire. Nathra and the Highland Arms sent all but Shafik, who worked in the business, through college and graduate school. "The children," Nathra says, "were made to understand that the family was a bank. They put in work, duty, trust. Then they could take out what a child must have—education."

The whole family looks like Ralph: dark, bony, comely. Nathra, at seventy-eight, is an aged version of his son— a little shorter, the hair white, but with the same mien of focused zeal. His wife, with her fine dark eyes and nobly arched nose, is a handsome woman still. Parents and sisters speak of Ralph with the jollity, filled with echoes of his mischief and his uniqueness, that is reserved for a favorite child. "Ralph used to force his sisters to laugh, always," says Mrs. Nader. Asked whether her son's fame surprised her, Mrs. Nader shakes her head calmly and, with a smile taking control of her lips, says, "No."

When Ralph was almost four, the family sailed to Lebanon for a visit. En route, Ralph showed the first flash of the protectiveness that still marks his relationship with his family. "The dining room steward," Claire says, "took a shine to Laura. One day she was sick, and the steward asked about her and said he'd take something to her cabin. In a flash Ralph was down from the table. He ran down to the stateroom and barred the door with his body, arms outspread. 'You can't go into the room where my sister is!' he shouted."

Ralph and his mother remained in Zahle for a year with his grandparents. Even in Winsted, the Naders spoke Arabic at home. When Mrs. Nader and Ralph returned to Connecticut, he had spoken nothing but Arabic for a quarter of his life. The school authorities doubted that his English was good enough for the first grade. As far as Nader remembers, he spoke English as well as any five-year-old. His mother pleaded that he be given a chance. He had no trouble getting through the first grade, or in understanding considerably more complex English than is usually spoken to primary school students. As Nader remembers it, he used to wander into the courthouse at the age of four and listen to cases being tried. Since he spent most of that year in Lebanon, this must have happened, as his mother believes, somewhat later. "He'd come home a little late," she says, "and I'd ask where he'd been. 'In court.' 'What were you doing there?' 'I like to listen to the arguments.' He'd sit on the floor and listen if he didn't like the movie that was on that day."

Nader, as a boy, was a memorizer of batting averages and a New York Yankees fan. His attachment to the overlords of major league baseball began, he says, when Mickey Owen of the Dodgers dropped Tommy Henrich's third strike in the 1941 World Series. The Yankees went on to win. Nader, in his innocence, thought that Joe DiMaggio and his teammates were underdogs. By the time he learned the true nature of the Yankee dynasty, it was too late. Nader had been captivated, and not for the last time, by the romance of pure technique.

Nader remembers himself in boyhood as a long ball hitter and a classy first baseman. This is not the way his childhood friend David Halberstam recalls it. "Ralph was the kind of kid," Halberstam says, "who if you threw the ball at him he couldn't catch it." Halberstam and Nader and another boy were the only three males in the "A" class for their grade in grammar school. There was competition between them. "Ralph was, I guess the word you would use is argumentative," Halberstam says. "You can't talk about a pedantic nine-year-old kid, but that was the quality he had. He would make you define your terms outside the windows of the fourth grade. He was not a young person; he was disputatious." In a playground argument in 1944 over the policies of Halberstam's hero, Franklin D. Roosevelt, some hint of Nader's views came out that bemuses Halberstam to this day. "Ralph was, I'm quite sure, for the Republicans," Halberstam says. "I mean he was a *Republican*. You were used to Republicans in Winsted, but the idea that a Republican could get as good marks as Ralph did—I was astounded." Nader was just as astounded, more than twenty-five years later, that Halberstam could have got the idea that he was a right-winger. Nader remembered the argument clearly, and the fact that the wind was blowing snow into their faces. "I bet it was because I was critical of the New Deal," Nader said, eager to clear up the misunderstanding. "I thought that FDR had put through some merely cosmetic policies. Dave didn't agree."

Nothing in the General Motors investigation disturbed Nader so much as the suggestion that his father and his older brother were anti-Semitic. When he testified before the Ribicoff subcommittee, he called the charge, with evident emotion, "scurrilous gossip." In private, he spoke earnestly to a Jewish couple in Washington who had befriended him, asking them if they had any doubts about his own feelings. They did their best to reassure him. Nader thought that the question arose simply because the Naders are Arabs. Arab public opposition to the establishment of a Jewish homeland in the Near East was, as David Halberstam recalls, a large issue in the minds of Winsted's Jews. "There was a certain amount of tension between the Arabs and the Jews in

Winsted when we were kids," Halberstam says. "It was a different generation. The Jews felt that the Arabs of the town were anti-Semitic, not feeling that they, the Jews, might be anti-Arab." The Naders lived next door to a Jewish family named Gaber, who ran the dry-cleaning establishment that is now located on the premises of the old Highland Arms Restaurant. "I remember," Halberstam says, "that the Gabers had a big party. We sort of looked over next door to see if the Naders were watching us. And we were watching them. There were no Naders invited to the party, not a Nader there."

Whatever the apprehensions of the two communities may have been, they had little effect on the youngsters. "You should show Mr. Nader respect," Halberstam's uncle used to tell him. "He's worked hard, by God—he's really worked hard." Halberstam thinks that the Arabs and the Jews in Winsted had more in common than they realized. "We both had this enormous belief in education," he says, "and were at the same time aware of the prejudices of the country, that all was not as it was said to be. You grew up a little tougher, a little more skeptical about the ideal and the reality of the situation." Halberstam, of course, grew up to be one of the earliest and most powerful skeptics about the Vietnam War, and his dispatches from Saigon to *The New York Times* won the Pulitzer Prize.

The misunderstanding was due to the distemper of the times. The Arab position may have been a political, not a racial one; but, as Halberstam says, newspaper discussion on the subject of Palestine evoked, for the Jews of the town, all the things that had been done to Jews in the name of politics. The principles at the center of the Naders' life as a family excluded hatred. "We did what we did, always, because we loved life," Nathra Nader says in another context. "We tried to show the children that the wealth of the nation was people, not the dollar. So if you want a rich nation, you should love and help each other."

Laura Nader Milleron says that people write her letters asking what her family discussed around the dinner table. They want to talk about the same things with their own children. She thinks that her correspondents miss the point. "It wasn't a study course," she says, "it was an atmosphere, a sense of entity. A family that was not molded from the outside, that had its own values." When Laura's own daughter goes to school, bringing a lunch of raw carrots and other things that do not look like a lunch, she is sometimes teased. But, true to the Nader blood, she defends the principle behind raw vegetables. "You don't know how nourishing it is," she tells her schoolmates. "Besides, I think my mother has some idea in her head about it."

"I believe how to bring up a child is to give the child self-confidence and courage," Mrs. Nader says. "He must speak up when it's time to do so. The child should also listen; you must teach him how to listen." The Naders, especially Nathra and Shafik, did not hesitate to speak up in Winsted. They were as colorful at town meetings as Ralph was later to be on national television, and their theme was the same: improve, improve. Shafik was instrumental in bringing a community college to Winsted; he campaigned for the construction of a heliport to stimulate the town's moribund economy.

The Naders were not exercising their powers of citizenship in an atmosphere where the opinions of foreigners—a term, in New England, that embraces people from the next town as well as those from Asia Minor—are enthusiastically welcomed. If they had been a little quieter they might have been less controversial. "The family could have been popular in town," says Robert J. McCarthy, managing editor of the Winsted *Evening Citizen,* "except they always had something to say about everything. Lots of times they were right, of course." Had there been a World Anti-Hypocrisy Association, Nathra Nader would have been secretary-general. A local doctor, sipping a martini in the Highland Arms, told him that he charged fees according to the patient's income. "I like that idea!" Nathra said. "For you the martini is five dollars. For a poor man, it's ten cents."

When Ralph Nader returned to Winsted in 1970 to deliver the high school commencement address, he told the senior class, "When I grew up in Winsted, active citizenship was considered kind of bizarre. . . . Plunge in. Involve yourself. Almost every significant breakthrough has come from the spark, the drive, the initiative of one person. You must believe this." One of Nader's old teachers thought, at first, that he was doing a little subtle boasting. "Then I saw him looking at his father—and, of course, Ralph was just repeating, as a famous person, what old Mr. Nader had drummed into him years and years ago."

The *Evening Citizen,* with a longer experience of the Nader idealism than any other publication, had something to say about the town's most celebrated son in its issue of March 30, 1971. In an editorial, the newspaper commended James M. Roche for a speech he gave on the meaning of Naderism. "They crusade," Roche was quoted as saying of industry's critics, "for radical changes in our system of corporate ownership, changes so drastic that they would all but destroy free enterprise as we know it." To which the *Evening Citizen* added, "We commend Ralph Nader for having accomplished much good but we now stand at the point where we wonder if all this hasn't gone to his head. We would welcome some relief." The paper received twenty letters about its editorial, which was picked up by the wire services. All but three supported Nader. Only two came from Winsted.

Until Ralph Nader, the most important figure in Winsted's history was a nineteenth-century clockmaker named

William L. Gilbert. Gilbert did good in the world and perpetuated his own name at the same time. He founded the Gilbert Institute for Colored Children in Winsted, Louisiana, as well as the Gilbert Home for orphans and indigent children in his own town. His most important gift to Winsted was the Gilbert School, an institution that until 1948 gave a secondary education to every Winsted child at no cost to the taxpayers. The proceeds from Gilbert's bequest still pay 20 percent of the costs of the new Gilbert School, a large structure of contemporary brick and glass standing on the site of the former Gilbert Home, on the western edge of the town.

Ralph Nader graduated in 1951 from the old Gilbert School, a yellow-brick Victorian building on the town common now occupied by Shafik's community college. In *The Miracle,* his high school yearbook, a seventeen-year-old Ralph Nader, skinny and unsmiling, stands in the back row of the group photograph of the dramatic club. This was his only extracurricular activity. Mrs. Mary Nix Nalette, whose picture is next to Nader's in the yearbook, was an officer of the dramatic club; she was a vivacious girl, in school, as she says, for the social life. "If there was a play," Mrs. Nalette says, "I was in it. But Ralph was always out back, doing things behind the scenes. That's the way Ralph was." In the tone of the yearbook banter about Nader there is a suggestion that its authors were reaching for something to say about a boy they did not know very well. Under his photograph, the italic line that sums up their impression reads, in one of the more delicious ironies of a genre noted for them: *"Anything for peace."* Nader was called "quiet—smart—can be found either at home or at the restaurant—woman hater." In the Class Will, "Ralph Nader bequeaths his briefcase to Nancy Bronson." That was very likely the closest Nader ever got to Miss Bronson. "He never dated," recalls Mrs. Nalette.

"As far as I know he never went to a dance or anything. He wasn't *against* girls—if you walked up to him he'd talk to you, but he was not what you'd call aggressive."

In class, Nader had the answers. "You have a very good storage place," his mother told him, touching his forehead. "You should fill it up and take it out when you need it." There was never enough in school to fill up Nader's head. In his first year of high school he came home with a large stack of *The Congressional Record.* The principal, saying that no one ever read them, had given the papers to Nader. The insights into life that the printed speeches of members of Congress could give him seemed to Nader, even at fourteen, more rewarding than works of the imagination. He felt little attraction to poetry, and after an adolescent binge of novel reading, he gave up on fiction. The last novel he read, Nader believes, must have been one of the works of Zane Grey or Thomas B. Costain. The whole of literature, except for the books he was required to read in school and college, is outside his experience. To Nader, information is truth.

This estrangement from art renders him, sometimes, a little deaf to the resonances of human events. Last year in Cleveland, he was discussing the troubles in Northern Ireland. A companion remarked that it said little for the rationality of the human race that a people that was ethnically identical should tear itself apart over a religious question. Nader was amazed that the man should think the historic hatred between Irish Catholics and Protestants was at the roots of the upheaval in Ulster. "No, no," he said. "It's a struggle for social equality, pure and simple." Joyce or Yeats would have told him differently, but there are no graphs in *Ulysses,* no statistics in *The Land of Heart's Desire.*

Princeton in the fifties, when the tradition of flippancy was still in flower there, seems a strange place for Nader. There would appear to be material for a Fitzgerald short story in the arrival of this stringy dark youth on the aristocratic campus, except that Nader lacked the one quality a Fitzgerald protagonist must have: he did not care what the rich thought of him. "The education was there to get if you wanted it," Nader says. The scholastic reason that Nader chose Princeton was its strong department of oriental languages. As his major he chose Far East politics and languages—Russian and Chinese. In late adolescence he was greatly interested, too, in foreign affairs, and Princeton's Woodrow Wilson School of Public and International Affairs attracted him. His sister Claire describes another reason that, in the context of his character, was probably equally important. "I think it had a lot to do with the clean air in Princeton," Claire says. "The choice in his mind was between Princeton and Dartmouth. I remember his telling me that the air was cleaner in New Hampshire, but it was almost as good in Princeton. The language department at Princeton must have tipped the balance."

Nader probably could have qualified for a scholarship at Princeton. Nathra Nader forbade his son to apply for financial assistance. He could afford to pay the tuition himself, and he assumed that scholarships were reserved for boys who really needed them. Ralph became acquainted with a good many scholarship students whose fathers seemed to be better off than his own, but this did nothing to change the older Nader's mind; he continued to pay all the bills for the three children he was sending simultaneously to eastern colleges.

Nader, on his arrival as a freshman, was placed in a remedial English class. The reasons for this step, if they were ever communicated to Nader, have escaped his memory. He just took it for granted that the university singled out a certain proportion of every incoming class to improve its word power. He did so with a vengeance, and his extraordinary vo-

cabulary may have its origins in this experience. It is part of
Nader's character, as his friend Joseph Page says, always to
have the last word. Nader's last word is usually something
like *fungible* or *metastasis*. A man who has been frequently
attacked by Nader believes that his tormentor does not really
understand English, in the sense that he does not hear the
emotive nuances of the language. It is certainly true that
English words are full of echoes, some of which are heard
only by poets. If to a poet words are tuning forks, then to
Nader they are hammers and chisels. He is always saying
pretty much the same thing while changing his terms; when
the tools grow dull, he finds new ones. There is in his use of
language a violent quality, a relish for hyperbole, a determi-
nation to astound. It is useless to speculate how much of this
comes out of a childhood dazzled by Arabic, but it is argua-
ble that in societies like those of the Near East, where people
are largely illiterate and mostly devout, language strikes the
ear and the heart rather than the eye and the mind.

Nader loved Princeton. He has fond recollections of battles royal between raiding parties of freshmen and sopho-
mores. "Rocks, boiling hot water, bottles—in my day it was
really something." As a freshman, Nader paid thirty-five
dollars a month for the cheapest room on the campus. He
liked it because it was on the ground floor and he could step
out the window onto the grass and walk to class. There was
no advantage in this system, except that it was a larky way to
start the day. Nader thinks he is the uncrowned champion
Princeton hitchhiker; in his four years there, he never once
left town or returned on public transportation.

The contemporary uniform for Princetonians of the Silent
Generation was scuffed white bucks, open white shirt, rum-
pled khaki trousers, and a blazer or a tweed jacket from J.
Press or Brooks Brothers. Nader was never known to wear
this outfit on campus, but once, while visiting Claire at
Smith College, he turned up dressed in the ideal fashion.

"You look wonderful from the waist up," Claire said, "but why did you go to all that trouble with the blazer and necktie if you were going to keep on those dirty pants and shoes?" Nader replied, "What you do not understand, sister dear, is that I am now the perfect Princetonian." In protest over conformist clothing, Nader once went to classes in his bathrobe.

Theodore Jacobs, Nader's classmate at Princeton and Harvard Law School, does not remember his best friend protesting very much at Princeton. Jacobs and Nader were both, as Jacobs says, out of things. They were studious, drunk with discussion, uninterested in athletics in the heyday of the great Dick Kazmaier. They belonged to the Prospect Club, the only undergraduate eating club to employ no servants. The members did the waiting on tables and the dishwashing themselves, and, in violation of hallowed tradition, invited members of the faculty to dine with them. Nader and Jacobs spent hours in discussion. "Ralph was fascinated by the ethnic quality of our lives," Jacobs says. "I was a Jewish boy from the Bronx, and Ralph was Lebanese, and very much Lebanese. We would trade long stories about our ethnic backgrounds." Nader was a voracious reader who filled all empty moments with print. Jacobs remembers him excusing himself in the middle of a conversation; when he returned from the john an hour later, he had read the entire contents of a book on Brazil and wanted to discuss it.

When Nader returns for a visit to Princeton, he glows with nostalgia. One spring night, a few minutes before midnight, he led a companion into the Harvey S. Firestone Memorial Library. "This was my paradise when I went to Princeton," he said. The library has open stacks, so that students can wander freely among the shelves, taking whatever books they want. As an undergraduate Nader spent so much time in the stacks that he became a joke to the Princeton Charlies. "They used to walk by while I was studying," Nader said, "and hiss at me, '*Greasy grind!*' There was hostility to study in a lot of them." He liked to read forgotten books of social history, old copies of intellectual magazines, studies of industrial relations. He fell in love with Chinese. "Behind this door," he said, putting his hand flat on the wood, "is probably the finest oriental collection in the country. I used to love to spend time in there." Nader never used his knowledge of Chinese, and he has forgotten most of the hundreds of ideograms he memorized.

Afterward, in a walk across the campus, he came upon a boy and a girl kissing by a fountain. "That was a rare sight in my day," Nader said, and passed on. Behind the kissing students was the new building of the Woodrow Wilson School, an airy structure of marble, supported by slender fluted columns. Nader was lost in admiration. "That could last for a thousand years," he said, "like a Greek building. There's nothing fake about that." In the dormitory where he spent his freshman year, he peered through the mail slot of his old room, No. 404. No one was home; he wanted to see it again and lifted his fist to knock on the door of the room next to it. He hesitated when he saw the handwritten sign on the door: "Girl in Room," and went away. Outside, he stopped and said to his companion, "There was a guy killed in an auto accident from right down the hall. And then more. I don't really have a firm figure, but I think that about seventy of my classmates out of seven hundred and fifty have been killed in cars. I'd like to know exactly, but no one keeps track, that kind of death is so accepted."

Nader led his companion along a path. There used to be elms overhead, which have been removed to make room for a new building; there is much less open space now on the campus, the grass and the trees gradually disappearing beneath new piles of masonry. Walking under the elms in his junior year, Nader found the paving stones littered with dead songbirds. They had been killed by DDT when the trees were sprayed. Nader wrote a letter of protest to the *Daily Prince-*

tonian. It was not printed, and when he called at the offices
of the newspaper to find out why, he discovered that the
editors could not take seriously his concern over a few dead
sparrows. "I said, 'If that's what it does to the birds, what do
you think it's doing to *us*?' Guys used to walk through this
fog, this cloudburst of DDT; the workmen sprayed it into
the trees with great big hoses. We were breathing it in. I
couldn't get them to understand. DDT kills bugs was the way
they looked at it. Maybe the birds—but not *us*. If it was
harmful 'they' wouldn't do it. A perfect case of the insults
men will tolerate if they're conditioned to trust the system."
Nader passed the dormitory where he had lived as a sopho-
more. He stopped and took a few steps toward it, shaking his
head and smiling as if he might give the building an affec-
tionate pat on its stone flank. "It's been twenty years," he
said, in a tone of wonder. "That's a lot of years." Nader
watched a group of students, all with long hair, almost all
wearing dungarees and chambray work shirts. "How
conformist these kids are," he said. "Look, they all have to
have sideburns and funny clothes. True children of the
white bucks, if they only realized."

Nader is always prepared to discover something unex-
pected lurking in the commonplace. He can be electrified by
new information about an old situation, especially if it involves the casual acceptance of violence, or damage to the
body. Although Nader did not go to see the documentary
movie *Derby* when it came out, he was keenly interested in
all the information it contained about roller-skating derbies.
An acquaintance mentioned to him that some of the women
skaters had had their breasts removed because of damage
done by the elbows of competitors. He wanted to know all
the details, fascinated as always by what goes on beneath the
surface of human activities.

In Nader's last year at Princeton, he was trapped one night
by a bit of random violence as he was taking a shower. A

drunken classmate, the son of a famous man, wandered by the shower room window. He began throwing empty beer bottles through the window. "He terrorized me for about two hours," Nader said. "The idea that he had a naked, dripping person in a room with broken glass all over the floor did something for him. He kept going to get more bottles. *Crash* against the wall." The drunk finally tired of his sport, and Nader cleared a path through the smashed glass and escaped unhurt.

Nader's position at Princeton was something like that of a skindiver swimming through schools of fish. He adapted to the social element rather than becoming part of it. Where studies were concerned it was Nader who was suited to the environment. "He is the best undergraduate I have known in five years," one of his teachers said. In his four years, he made a below-average mark only twice—in classics and philosophy when he was a freshman, and in a sociology course in his junior year. His scholastic average in his junior and senior years was 1.56, the equivalent of a low "A" in the Princeton marking system, and he graduated with honors, in the top 9 percent of his class.

He was a natural scholar, with his combination of zeal and intellectual wonder, and a number of his professors tried to persuade him to take a Ph.D. and follow an academic career. He could not be moved from the idea of studying law. One of his professors, in a recommendation, wrote that Nader was, in his view, "a natural leader. He is not the kind of man one laughs at, no matter how different from one's own 'style' he appears to be. Ralph is a man of possible 'greatness.' I think he is going to be one of the most distinguished men in our country in years to come."

3

A Rational Panic

The icons were Holmes and Cardozo and Learned Hand.
Who the hell says a lawyer has to be like that?

RALPH NADER

It is said by Nader's friends and family that nothing has ever
changed him. "There was no turning point, no climactic
event," says his sister Laura. "Ralph's life is all of a piece."
There are, however, points of change in any life. In Nader's
case, the Ribicoff hearings were obviously a climactic event.
Something subtler happened to Nader at Harvard Law
School. When he began his study of law he was twenty-one
years old, and he was, more than most people his age, a
stranger to disillusion. Most people by twenty-one have lost a
girl or failed to make a team or flunked an examination, but
none of these things had happened to Nader because he had
had no commerce with the ordinary American experience.
His family, and Princeton, had made it possible for him to

live almost wholly in his mind. At Harvard he found himself in the world.

Yet Nader arrived in Cambridge in the fall of 1955 with some reason to be, for the first time, a little unsure of himself. During the summer, while he was working in a supermarket in Yosemite National Park, the Winsted flood took place. He saw a picture of his town's devastated Main Street—and the sign over the gutted Highland Arms—on the front page of a California newspaper and tried to call his parents. The telephone lines had been washed away, and he was unable to get through. He started east, and in Chicago he finally reached his mother by telephone. The family was unhurt, but their business was destroyed. "He was for the first time, and one of the few times," Theodore Jacobs says, "really depressed about the insanity of it all. He was very much influenced by this crazy happening." The loss of the restaurant took away some of Nathra Nader's independence. In all three years of law school, Ralph applied for student loans to meet his tuition payments. He had been disappointed, too, with the results of his law school admission test, on which he had scored a mediocre 494. Despite assurances from the admissions office that it was not necessary to try again, he had himself reexamined and raised his score by more than one hundred points. He was admitted without difficulty, as probably he would have been anyway on the basis of his record at Princeton.

Nader found Harvard uncongenial. He had liked the pastoral atmosphere of Princeton, the low stone buildings, the unhurried and courteous ambience that lends to undergraduate life the illusion of an endless weekend in the country. Harvard is an urban place, with the noise and smell of a great city spilling over its walls. Cambridge, which is really a big neighborhood of Boston, does not exist for Harvard as Princeton does for its university. "It was there that I first saw what a difference the arrangement of space makes to a human being," Nader says. "Everything was towers, vertical, cramped. It was very uncomfortable."

There were more significant discomforts. At Harvard, Nader was confronted for the first time with the impersonal. It is a place that tolerates, but does not flatter, eccentricity. This too was something new for a boy who had made an art of disdain: sorting through each new situation, as a friend said, to see what he wanted and rejecting the rest. Nader has a strong contrary streak. At Princeton he had been a student among the idle; at Harvard he became an idler among the studious. He berated Ted Jacobs as a stick-in-the-mud. He urged his friends to waste a little time in the interests of the spirit. One evening, emerging from the Commons with a couple of friends, he heard a favorite piece, Ravel's *Bolero*, playing over the loudspeaker system and urged his companions to sit down and listen. They wouldn't consider it, he recalls; they wanted to study.

"Within five weeks of the first year," Nader says, "I saw what was happening to students and opted out of their attitudes. They were taught the freedom to roam in their cages—an achievement unparalleled in mandarin China." He opted out so thoroughly that he, the natural student, ranked a great deal lower academically than might have been expected in view of his gifts and graduated in the lower half of the class of 1958. Because of his record, and, as he might say, because of the nature of the place, Nader is not vividly remembered at Harvard Law School, but one of his professors, Harold J. Berman, does not recall thinking of him as a rebel. "If he was in a cage," Berman says, "he liked the cage. [His] rhetoric has to be discounted. I think he was grateful then for what Harvard Law School gave him."

In Nader's eyes, the school chose its heroes badly and described moral options not at all. If any professional mood was communicated, that mood was the one most alien to Nader's nature—equanimity. "Harvard Law School," he says, "never raised the question of sacrifice. Nothing! The icons were not those who had sacrificed at all. They were Brandeis, who took a few briefs for child labor after he had made a million dollars and so became 'the people's lawyer.' The icons were Holmes and Cardozo and Learned Hand. Those were the heroes—the staid, the dry, those who were respected by the power structure. Who the hell says a lawyer has to be like that?" Professor Berman believes that the faculty made great efforts to instill the idea of service. "Students in the fifties," Berman says, "resisted this concept. They were very anxious to get out and make money."

Nader doubts that the goals of young lawyers have changed a great deal despite the transformation of the social climate since the fifties. He does not think Harvard has changed very much, either. "To say that the law school has been blind to the social injustices of the last half century," he said in a Boston press conference in 1969, "is to engage in understatement." When he speaks before law school audiences, he likes to mock their ambitions: "How many of you would do good in the world for fifteen thousand dollars a year? How many for ten thousand? How many for five? For nothing?" As hands are lowered after each figure, Nader shrugs, having illuminated the problem. The young "public-interest lawyers," many of them from Harvard, who have gone to work for him in the last couple of years are paid $4,500 a year and little recognition in return for long days and a depth of commitment that Nader in many cases deems barely adequate.

It was at Harvard that Nader began to speak about public-interest lawyers—in his later phrase, "offensive lawyers, lawyers without clients, lawyers who are primary human beings." But there was no interest among his contemporaries in representing the human race on a nonprofit basis. It has been said that Nader was not a member of his own generation. He has never really been a member of anything. In Winsted, despite his enchanted membership in his family, he was not a member of the community. At Princeton, despite his success as a student, he chose not to succumb to the mystique of the institution. At Harvard he became, on the surface at least, the complete outsider. A childhood filled with precepts and an adolescence filled with books had trained him as a believer. Harvard may have given him the greater gift: the occasion for irreverence.

Nader's goal, Ted Jacobs thinks, was to gain his law degree without being brainwashed. He flirted with the patience of the administration, cutting classes, disappearing for days at a time, devoting himself to outside interests. "He would vanish and come back with a suntan," Jacobs says. "He had been to Mexico, which only enraged those of us who were sticking it out." One professor complained that Nader had missed eight consecutive work sessions and threatened to flunk him. Nader, called in for an explanation, said he had been visiting his sick mother. In his last year, he sat in the wrong class of a course in commercial law for an entire semester because he found the professor more interesting than the one to whom he had been assigned. There was some question as a result of this escapade whether he would get his degree, but he found a politic way of explaining the mistake. Nader's contempt for institutions is mixed with a respect for their powers, and when his career in law school was in real danger, he was capable of worry. Once, suspecting he had done badly in an examination, he wrote the professor a humble letter, saying that he had been the victim of a severe headache: "I was subject to such sharp pain that fully half the time I was rendered totally useless with the remainder constituting weak incoherent dabblings." Ted Jacobs recalls that Nader usually did as well on exams as more diligent students.

Nader held a variety of part-time jobs while at Harvard. He typed term papers for fellow students and for a while was manager of a bowling alley. Soon after his arrival in Cambridge he sold the only automobile he has ever owned, a 1949 Studebaker. He developed a reputation as a trencher-man. His classmate Joe Page remembers that there were un-limited servings in the law school cafeteria, and Nader took full advantage. "It could be kind of awesome," Page says, "this thin, angular guy stoking it away as he did." He won a twenty-dollar bet by eating two twelve-inch strawberry short-cakes at the Durgin-Park Restaurant in Boston. Nader lived, even then, mostly at night, reading or writing until dawn and sleeping through the morning. His sister Laura, then at Har-vard, used to hear a shout under her window at 5 A.M. and look out to find her brother in the street below, ready for breakfast. She is herself a night owl, and she would leave her books and join him for ham and eggs in an all-night restau-rant. Nader was as likely to eat roast beef for breakfast, but there was a certain logic in that because he had reversed the clock.

In Nader's zest to restore the original humanism of Amer-ica, there is an element of time travel, an impulse to return to more virtuous days. "Ralph's philosophy," says one of the original Raiders, Robert Fellmeth, "is ninth grade civics—just as defined by our forefathers and in the *Weekly Reader*." At Harvard, Nader began to articulate his idea that the time for a general shriving had arrived, and he lost pa-tience once and for all with those who thought purification was either unneeded or impossible. Ted Jacobs once la-mented, in Harvard days, that all the good causes had been fought and wished that he had been alive in the thirties. "Ralph roared with laughter," Jacobs reports, "and said, 'You're out of your mind. *Now*'s the time! *Now* there are causes!'" The steady pursuit of that conviction led a later generation of students to describe him in the student news-paper as the most important man ever to graduate from Har-vard Law School. This was not a judgment that would have been predicted by many of his own classmates and teachers.

The faculty has perhaps remained unconvinced; when Nader was proposed in 1970 as a visiting lecturer, the idea was defeated on grounds that he was not a resident of Cambridge.

If Nader left any visible, as opposed to mystical, mark on Harvard Law School, it was on the *Record*, the student newspaper. He joined the staff early in his first year and became department editor soon afterward. The *Record*, when Nader began to work on it, faithfully reflected the tranquil surface of the law school. He tried immediately to change that. "The *Record* to Ralph was an opportunity to do some muckraking," says Ted Jacobs. Circumstances apparently caused Nader to go slowly. His first signed article, published in the spring of his first year, was an unremarkable piece on capital punishment, written in collaboration with a student named William G. Langston. It ended with an early Naderism: "Capital punishment is a blatant and ironically ineffective hypocrisy." In his second year, Nader became editorial manager and shook off whatever constraint he had felt in a lower position on the masthead. The preceding summer he had visited a number of Indian reservations on a hitchhiking trip through the West. At Princeton he had acquired an abiding interest in anthropology, and with it a fascination with the Indians. He had a ready resource in Laura Nader, then an apprentice specialist in Indian culture and later a professor of anthropology at Berkeley. Even with this background, what he saw and heard on the reservations left him shaken.

The article Nader wrote on the Indian for the *Record* must be the earliest example in print of that combination of invective and arcane information which is his style. The piece had another Nader characteristic: it was tremendously long, filling almost all the space in a six-page issue. It was, like almost everything he was to write later, not so much an effort to reconsider a situation as a command to his readers to reunderstand it in the light of an emotional arrangement

of neglected facts. "There developed a voluminous history of
the American idea of the Indian as a savage," he wrote, "a
concept indispensable to a righteous and ethnocentric people
appropriating a continent. . . . Jack Schaefer, the author of
Shane, said, 'These natives, on the whole, were not as savage
as the Europeans who called them savage. . . .' Four-
sevenths of our national farm produce consists of plants
domesticated by Indian botanists of pre-Columbian times.
. . . In the four hundred years that physicians and botanists
have been examining and analyzing the flora of America,
they have not yet discovered a medicine or herb unknown to
the Indians." Nader argued that the Indians were the authors of the concept of federalism, owing to their "habit of
treating chiefs as servants of the people instead of masters,
and the insistence that the community must respect the di-
versity of men and their dreams." The breakfast-food tycoons
of Battle Creek, one day to be denounced by Nader for the
low nutrition of their products, were listed as among the
beneficiaries of Indian ingenuity. "Not long ago," Nader
wrote, "an old Indian dish, toasted cornflakes, revolutionized
the breakfast routine of American families." "Moral satisfac-
tion and a healthy and vigorous Indian people will be the
fruits of equitable treatment of the Indian," Nader concluded. "That is why the Indian is our greatest challenge."

The article was quickly recognized by partisans of the
Indian for the brilliant propaganda that it was, and several
hundred reprints were sold through an organization in Colorado. The governing board of the *Record,* euphoric about
turning a profit, made the mistake a little later of reprinting
an even longer article of Nader's on Puerto Rico. This piece
was a legalistic and, for Nader, an objective treatment of the
problem of the island's commonwealth status. It pleased neither side in the controversy, and the unsold reprints are still
gathering dust in a closet at the law school.

In the fall of Nader's third year in law school, he was

elected president, or editor-in-chief, of the *Record,* and the
euphoria of the governing board quickly disappeared. Nader
had done his best, as a junior editor, to nudge the paper toward controversy. He wrote signed articles on subjects ranging from the mistreatment of migrant workers to Boston's
blue laws. He scoured the campus and canvassed the alumni
for writers who might be willing to explode myths that annoyed him, such as the theory of the inherent inferiority of
the Negro.

Nader took control of the *Record* with the expansive idea
of turning it into a national journal that would forage ahead
of what then passed for radical opinion. He had persuaded
such figures as Ashley Montagu to write for the paper, and
he was convinced that he could find other distinguished con-
tributors. All that was required was to alter the entire nature
of the *Record;* it would be changed from the conformist
"Bugle," unread even by the students who had given it its
mundane nickname, into a trumpet of reform. In speaking
for Nader's causes, of course, the paper would be speaking in
Harvard's name. This proposition frightened Nader's fellow
editors, and the ensuing conflict left an aftereffect. Some people at the law school still believe Nader was fired from the
Record; in fact, the question was resolved, in the best Establishment style, on a side issue. As a means of freeing funds
for his muckraking operation, Nader wanted to print the
Record on newsprint instead of the traditional slick paper.
When the matter came to a vote, the governing board tied.
The tie was broken by Joe Page, who voted against Nader.
Discerning the mood behind this minor defeat, Nader resigned before his name ever appeared on the masthead as
president. When new elections were held, Page was named
president. Nader, after an absence of three months, rejoined
the staff as senior editor—the last case on record of his joining those whom he could not beat.

If Nader had a spiritual home at Harvard, it was the office

at the *Record,* insulated by tradition from the intrusion of the administration. The paper gave him an outlet for his rhetoric and a ready audience of fellow editors on whom ideas could be tested. To veterans of those impromptu lectures there is something delicious in the fact that Nader's enthusiasms, which were old to them fifteen years ago, should now move the nation. Jacobs and Page, after watching Nader on a television talk show last year, caught each other's eyes and burst into laughter. "In the old days," Jacobs said, "Ralph would sit up in the *Record* office and we'd have to listen. Now it's the whole world."

At Harvard, the central issue of Nader's early career, auto safety, had begun to take shape from a combination of academic experience and direct observation that was sometimes sickening. On his hitchhiking trips he had seen a good many wrecks. He was bemused by the nonchalance with which torn bodies were viewed by highway veterans, and he learned something about the state of public awareness of hazards. He pointed out to one truck driver that the sharp hook on which he hung his coat was only two inches from his head. "Doesn't that worry you?" Nader asked. "It could pierce your skull if you had to stop and got thrown around." The truck driver said he had never thought of it. Sometime in 1954 or 1955, while thumbing between Winsted and Cambridge, Nader came upon a wreck in which a very young child had been decapitated when her parents' car struck another vehicle. The child's small body was thrown forward by the sudden stop, and the door of the glove compartment, snapping open under the impact, cut through her neck like a cleaver. The child's death was one example among millions of the "second collision" that occurs when the passenger in a wrecked car smashes into its interior.

Nader learned more about the effect of smashed machines upon the human body in a medical-legal seminar. The connection between blood and the design of automobiles was made clearer to him in 1956, when Congressman Kenneth Roberts of Alabama, chairman of the House subcommittee on traffic safety, held the first open hearings to make reference to the design question. Nader showed the printed record of the Roberts hearings to friends, but they could not see their significance. "For a student at Harvard that was crazy stuff," Nader says. "You didn't have anything in your hands except *Fuller on Contracts*. But to me, it was very symbolic. To me, that was the law, it was the whole thing." The whole thing, approached in those days mostly through innuendo, was the relationship between death and faults in the machine; to be impaled on a steering column or to be bled like a steer on a fragment of steel or glass was, after all, the ultimate invasion of the self.

In 1955, Harold A. Katz published an article in the *Harvard Law Review* arguing that automobile manufacturers might be held liable for injuries caused by the negligent design of their vehicles. Nader does not like to fix his ideas in time, or attach them to other persons, and he is casual in discussing the influence of the Katz article on his later work. But his friends remember his excitement, amounting to the elation of discovery, on seeing in print what he had apparently been feeling in his viscera: that there must be a legal and moral bridge between the horror and the makers of cars. He wrote his third-year paper on the subject and received an "A"—mostly, he feels in retrospect, because the school did not understand the implications of his argument.

Nader took his argument to the public, at least to that small public of the convinced who read *The Nation* magazine, soon after he left law school. The magazine published his article, which he believes was the first in a national publication to link automobile design with the causes of accidents, as Nader was awaiting a decision from his draft board. Friends remember that he was doubtful he could pass the physical examination; he complained of a twisted neck and a sore foot. Six months after his graduation from law school, Nader resolved the dilemma of his military obligation by joining the Army. He enlisted under a reserve program requiring him to serve six months on active duty, followed by five years in the inactive reserve. He was sent to Fort Dix, New Jersey, for basic infantry training and was afterward assigned as a cook. With his gift for disappointing the predictable occasions of drama, Nader went through his military service unscathed. He was happy with his work in the kitchen, admiring the quality of the food the Army purchased and, with his attraction to the mysteries of technique, deeply interested in the methods used by mess sergeants to prepare meals for thousands of men. One of the proudest moments of his life, he says, occurred in the Fort Dix mess hall when, substituting for an absent baker, he prepared banana bread for two thousand troops. He liked the whole process—getting up before dawn, mixing sacks of flour and crates of bananas in gargantuan pots, and having the recipe turn out well enough for the soldiers to take it for granted.

There is, in the seven years that elapsed between Nader's release from the Army and his emergence into the public eye, a quality of grayness. He was always at the edges of things, never in the center of an event. He returned to Connecticut and opened a law office in Hartford, but never really practiced law. He taught a course in government, off and on, at the University of Hartford. He wrote an article with a man named Arthur Train II for the *Reader's Digest* on Roscoe Pound, and a few pieces for *The Christian Science Monitor* and *The Atlantic Monthly*. He involved himself in auto safety and consumer bills in the Connecticut legislature. He kept himself to himself, drifting in and out of touch with his friends. "He was always a figure of mystery," Joe Page says, "now you see Nader and now you don't. He'd go off once a year and never say anything about it." Few people knew his address, practically no one his telephone number. The life he lived was very much like that of the sort of agent who is called, in intelligence work, a "fictitious"—someone who is sent to another country with instructions to build an identity while awaiting orders. Nader, of course, was his own secret service, and he was not awaiting orders but forming ideas whose time had not yet come.

But there was enough of the unexplained in his occupation, and enough of the mysterious in his manner, to arouse the suspicions of at least one sensitive observer. David Halberstam, just back from Vietnam, lunched with Nader in a Washington restaurant, together with Halberstam's brother Michael, a physician who lives in Washington. Michael Halberstam had kept in touch with Nader for old time's sake, and David was grateful to him because he had been kind to their mother while David was in Saigon. "He went out of his way," David Halberstam says, "to see her, to talk to her, to call her, and just to let her know that he knew what I was doing and he was impressed." Most of the lunch was devoted to a discussion of Halberstam's adventures in Indochina, but the talk eventually came around to Nader and what he had been doing. Nader was just back from Latin America, and he discussed other travels in Europe and the Soviet Union but avoided, in his usual way, questions about himself. "He really was very knowledgeable," Halberstam says, "he knew names and numbers." It was a strange combination of brilliance and evasiveness. When Nader had left, Halberstam's brother asked him what he thought of their childhood friend. "Jesus Christ," David said, "he's a CIA man!" Michael Halberstam regards his brother's suspicions, natural perhaps in a man who had just come from Vietnam and was on his way to Poland, as an example of the perils of an excess of sophistication.

David Halberstam did not think Nathra Nader was suffering from that particular malady when he met him at a party in Winsted given by his mother to celebrate his Pulitzer Prize. "Mr. Nader was there," Halberstam recalls, "and he was very excited. He kept saying, 'It's you, young people like you, people like you and Ralph who are going to crusade. You and Ralph.' I thought, what the hell has Ralph got to do with it? I love you and you're great—but Ralph? What has he done? Mr. Nader kept talking about the big interests and the big forces that thwart the little man. You had a sense of his stern pride—'You and Ralph, what you're going to do against them.' "

Ralph was finding few enough occasions to smite the big interests. In a highly organized society like the United States, there tends to be a lack of regard for individuals who have no auspices. Behind Nader stood his diplomas and his law practice. The diplomas meant little enough, and the law practice bored him. He kept the office open for a period of several years, but it never brought in a substantial income, and he was seldom in it. There were other disappointments. He regarded the sale of his article to the *Reader's Digest* as an upward turn of fortune, imagining that he could use the magazine for his campaigns. But the editors soon made it plain they were not interested in his material on auto safety. His other writings attracted little attention; he was an advocate, living through the twilight of objective reporting. His kind of journalism, requiring heated advocacy in the writer and instinctive belief in the reader, was not quite respectable.

Among the shards of accomplishment remaining from this underground period in Nader's life is the word *ombudsman,* which he believes he may have introduced into American usage. Nader brought the word back with him from a tour of the Scandinavian countries in the summer of 1961. Early in the following year, a state representative named Nicholas Eddy introduced the nation's first ombudsman bill in the

Connecticut legislature. Nader, who worked with Eddy and others in the drafting of the bill, overcame considerable resistance to the strange Nordic word among his collaborators. "They didn't like the use of the word," Nader says, "because it was a foreign word. I said, 'Then why don't we abolish *admiral* and *chef,* and like half the dictionary?' " Out of his association with the Connecticut ombudsman bill, Nader became a sort of expert, a member of another network of unknown enthusiasts. The Center for the Study of Democratic Institutions in Santa Barbara asked him to write a paper on the ombudsman system, and he sent off one hundred pages. "I talked it up and wrote a few articles and interested a legislator in Illinois. It went in in California and now we have one in Hawaii," Nader says. "It was one of my main projects, but I just dropped it when the auto thing came up." In 1963 Nader persuaded some Connecticut legislators to introduce a bill that would have required rudimentary safety equipment in cars registered in the state. He testified at hearings on the bill, but to an empty hall. "Everyone except the chairman walked out," Nader says. "This was seat belts and they weren't interested. Their reaction told me that we had to do a lot more."

Nader's tour of Scandinavia took him to Copenhagen and Stockholm for interviews with the Danish and Swedish ombudsmen and their staffs. He went next to Helsinki and from Finland crossed into the Soviet Union for a two-week tour. He gave the Intourist guides the slip and roamed the streets of Moscow and the countryside on his own. His Princeton Russian held up well enough for him to wander into the offices of *Krokodil,* the Soviet humor magazine, and have a chat with the staff. Nader does not remember that the people at *Krokodil* were flustered by the appearance of a footloose American; they were proud that they were among the limited number of Russians who were permitted to read *Time,* and they showed him their copies of the newsmagazine.

Nader liked the absence of automobiles in the Russian cities, and he enjoyed the food. "It was still solid, basic food rather than the sleazy processed stuff we get," he recalls with approval. He was depressed by the lack of spontaneity in Soviet life; a man who described a hunting trip to the Caucasus was the only Russian he met who seemed to have done something on a fling. With what he thought was pathetic curiosity, Russians kept asking him if he had seen Elgin Baylor or read the latest work of Truman Capote. They could hardly have found a less likely American to put their questions to; in Nader's pronunciation of the fashionable novelist's name, the final *e* is silent.

When he left the USSR, he brought with him a heavy bundle of Russian dictionaries, and an impression about the dead weight of human nature. "How bourgeois the people are," Nader says. "You got the idea that if Communism was lifted everyone would want to go into business and do exactly what we were doing in America. It hadn't changed the so-called character of the people at all."

After spending the winter on his Connecticut projects, Nader managed, in the spring of 1963, to get an assignment from *The Atlantic Monthly* to write a report on Colombia. This project, combined with an arrangement with *The Christian Science Monitor* to write short pieces for its business page, gave him the funds for a trip to Latin America. He invited Joe Page to go along and introduced him to editors at *The Atlantic Monthly*, who agreed to let Page try an article on Argentina. He had started Page on a writing career a few months before, putting him in contact with the editor of *The Nation*, who bought an article Page had done about Edward M. Kennedy, who was then seeking the Democratic nomination to the Senate from Massachusetts; Page had seen Kennedy making a blatant ethnic pitch to a group of Boston Italians. "Kennedy was kind of crude," Page says, "and I thought it was kind of funny." Page credits Nader for seeing the possibility of expanding his anecdote into a political commentary. "Ralph's chief gift," as Page believes, "is getting you excited enough to go out and do something."

Nader and Page, between June and August, 1963, touched down at Caracas, Recife, Rio de Janeiro, São Paulo, Montevideo, Buenos Aires, Santiago de Chile, Lima, Quito, and Bogotá. Nader, in serviceable college Spanish, conducted interviews that enthralled his companion. "For the first hour, nothing much would happen," Page says. "Then he'd zero in. For Ralph, an hour was just a warm-up, to set the mood. Then he'd start asking his penetrating questions. People would get insulted, or they'd get mad. But they'd say the damnedest things to him, make the most incredible admissions." Nader wrote his stories, oftentimes, on a portable typewriter on his lap in airport waiting rooms. With his passion for print, he picked up anything in writing that he could get his hands on. He staggered from country to country under a large number of shopping bags stuffed with magazines, pamphlets, and documents.

The unsigned articles Nader wrote for *The Atlantic Monthly,* including a report on Brazil coauthored with Page, and his pieces for the *Monitor* probably paid his expenses. An article on Recife brought him a modest amount of fame when it was quoted by John Gunther in his book on Latin America. His voyages, including a later one to Africa, were not commercial ventures. "I looked on our trip as half lark," Page says. "For Ralph, it was a learning experience." What Nader seems to have learned is that foreign affairs, the great interest of his early youth, did not provide a field for the offensive lawyer that he was making of himself. The whole world, for the time being, was beyond the reach of even the most passionate American citizen. In his travels, he saw what was happening in the world as a result of American enterprise, and it wasn't, he says, what one read about. "There's not much that can be done overseas," Nader said in later years. "What happens to people abroad as a result of our actions is just an aspect of the impact of policy on people at home."

Beginning with the dead sparrows at Princeton, growing with his increasing involvement in the offhand death connected with the automobile, something closer to a mood than an intellectual position came over Nader. If there is such a thing as rational panic, then this was what seized him as his youth ran out, and propelled him into his cycle of prophecy and purification.

4

Playing the Game, Living the Cause

There's an impression that I'm willing to expose my friends if necessary for the cause, and there's a loyalty issue there. . . . Some of these people are blistered by moonbeams.

RALPH NADER

In the lives of all public men, there is a certain wastage of relationships. They join in a cause, commit their reputations, loan a portion of their power, divide the credit or share the blame, succumb to envy, move on, lose interest in the issue or in each other. It is a rule of the game that there are no hard feelings, but the rule applies only if the game is played. Nader, of course, does not play the game. He lives the cause.

There are men in Washington, and elsewhere, who believe that Nader's fame somehow deprived them of credit for their accomplishments. Their reaction varies from the amused to the embittered, but they share a sense of surprise that things happened as they did. Nader was regarded, until it was too late, as nothing more than a useful craftsman. "Along comes a guy," as Robert Wager of the Ribicoff subcommittee thought, "who's got the facts and doesn't care if he's not up front. He's perfectly willing to let a senator take the credit." Beyond that simple proposition is something else: the insider's index of who is responsible for bringing credit to a public figure. Senate staffers, presidential assistants, and civil servants mix, in this category of fame, with experts and academicians whose specialized knowledge is the real source of policy. Nader confounded everybody by slipping off this index of the faceless, where he should have remained, and into the media, where only senators and Presidents are supposed to be.

Publicity, to paraphrase Marx's remark about money, has a life of its own, feeding on its own body. Publicity is also a great simplifier. The headline and the sixty-second film clip converted the issue of automobile safety from the social and political panorama that it was into a close-up of Ralph Nader. A lot of reputations were left on the cutting-room floor, including some that did not belong there.

The record of any human activity is a palimpsest, and Nader's activity with respect to auto safety is as much so as any other. Nader did not particularly seek the credit that came to him. He just happened to be a brilliant publicist, exercising his talent at the right moment. He was less than a technician and more than a politician, and he did not so much outfox the other men in the field as excel them in timing and in credibility. He was reckless where others had been cautious, rude where others had been courteous, public where others had been discreet. He turned an academic subspecialty, in which the experts could be counted on the fingers of one hand, into a cause. "All the twenty years of research which preceded Nader's book did not have its impact," says Dr. Robert Brenner, one of the pioneers in the field. "It was one of the turning points of our civilization."

The data used by Nader, and even some of his vocabulary, were developed by persons in the background of his accomplishment. In his book Nader gave most of them credit, and *Unsafe at Any Speed* remains the best short history of automobile safety research yet written. A few of his sources still believe they may be owed a footnote or two, but none has ever found serious fault with his reporting—being careful always to say that it was reporting, not research. This was, of course, long before Nader became the national interloper, so the vigor of his approach was not yet taken for granted.

This community of scientists, underfinanced and, as it turned out, underregarded, had been informing itself for two decades that cars were designed in such a way as to be inherently unsafe. In crash tests at Cornell, the University of California at Los Angeles, and a few other testing facilities, the researchers had demonstrated that instrumented dummies could be protected from many serious injuries by the installation of such rudimentary safety equipment as seat belts, collapsible steering columns, and interior padding—and by the elimination of the sharp knobs and levers on the instrument panel.

The glittering dashboard attracted buyers of automobiles only to crush their skulls or sever their arteries when the cars crashed and the bodies of its occupants, obedient to the laws of physics, went smashing into the dashboard and windshield. This impact of the passenger on the interior of the car was the "second collision," so named by an Indiana highway patrolman identified in Nader's book as Sergeant Elmer Paul. The researchers concluded that this sort of occurrence was a normal, not an exceptional, event. As their first gifted propagandist, Daniel P. Moynihan, said, "One out of every three cars manufactured in Detroit ended up with blood on it." The scientists' statistics tended to show that the situation had been getting steadily worse because manufacturers showed little initiative in eliminating the elements of unsafe design.

Although Nader cited the findings of the researchers with

approval, he was less than satisfied with the uses to which the scientists had put their knowledge. "Scientists," he wrote, "have not displayed much commitment to giving a broader significance to their work. . . . They have been in possession of information that is relevant to the elimination of millions of casualties, and the expertise to utilize that information. . . . They have shown only a slight appreciation that their special roles should require them to state forcefully in public forums the issues for discussion and resolution. . . . These scientists who do not make known to the public the importance of their work and the possibility of a vastly safer vehicle cannot, of course, enjoy public support." Cornell's automotive crash injury research was supported by grants from the federal government and the Automobile Manufacturers Association, but its findings were made available only to the manufacturers. The U.S. Public Health Service, from which the federal money came, chose not to receive the Cornell data. Nader regarded this as a device to protect the manufacturers: if the government did not have possession of information that might embarrass Detroit, it could not release it to the public. "To permit public funds to be mixed with industry money in such a project . . ." Nader wrote in one of his milder comments on this situation, "[and] to give data to manufacturers while denying it to all others is nothing short of an abdication of the public trust."

Nader made the point elsewhere in his book that the entire traffic safety establishment—the National Safety Council, the American Automobile Association, and the President's Committee for Traffic Safety, among others—was under the domination of the manufacturers. The approach of the traffic safety establishment was to prevent accidents by concentrating on the education of the driver rather than to prevent crashes and injuries through improvement of the vehicle. Nader regarded this as a gigantic cabal designed to deceive the public about the real causes of injury and death while selling it cars that were the biggest factor in the production of that injury and death. The obvious effect of his criticism of the researchers was to link them to the cabal.

This produced resentments that remain very much alive. Brenner, who worked in UCLA's Institute of Transportation and Traffic Engineering, is still annoyed that Nader said his project was operating with auto industry funds. "Industry didn't give us five cents," Brenner says. "I told him he was all wet in some of the stuff in *Unsafe at Any Speed.* . . . For example, he doesn't even acknowledge a magnificent man, our dean of engineers, L. M. K. Belcher, who was and is my patron saint. . . . Ralph really did not pick up the fact that there were competent and dedicated people who were laying a lot of groundwork."

Brenner, who became deputy head of the National Highway Safety Bureau, puts into plain words the murmur of his colleagues about Nader's book. "The advocate presents his case to win it," Brenner observes. "The scientist can't do this, and that's something that Ralph can't accept. There's a difference between scientific detachment and inertia, but Ralph seems to think that a careful approach to the facts betrays a lack of zeal. To Ralph, there is no substitute for zeal."

In Jerome Sonosky's view, it was the Senate subcommittee's "attack on the product" and not Nader's book that gave birth to reform. "In '65, what Abe Ribicoff was saying," Sonosky says, "was . . . safety is being decided privately, and that ain't right. It took a politician to make it go." The undertone of a good deal of this sort of commentary is resentment of the parvenu. "Hell," says Brenner, "I welded my own seat belt anchors in my car in *1949.* Where was Nader in 1949? In high school."

No doubt it is too late to reconstruct the episode. The press simplified the details after Nader had simplified the issue itself. He wrote a book that was read not for text but for tone. This may be hard for scientists to forgive, but it should be easy enough for politicians to understand. What perhaps the politicians did not understand right away was that Nader belonged more to the era than they did, that he summoned a combination of factors, including themselves, to make a new force in society. They misjudged him as well as the issue. There was an unperceived kinship between him and the last hero the media had helped to create. Nader was a dark Kennedy, kissing conscience back to life with results that would be deeper than those produced in the presidential campaign of 1960 and its aftermath.

Nader first heard of Daniel Patrick Moynihan in 1959, when he was at Fort Dix and someone sent him a copy of Moynihan's article, "Epidemic on the Highways," from the *Reporter* magazine. Moynihan's piece is regarded by many in the field of auto safety as the opening gun of the campaign to awaken the issue. It is possible to argue, as many do, that the ideas popularized in *Unsafe at Any Speed* were Moynihan's ideas. This view is a source of some discomfort to Nader, who likes to point out that his own article in *The Nation* came out sooner. Nader's article was published on April 11, Moynihan's on April 30. "Mine was the first on the auto," Nader says. "Pat's was broader, as I keep kidding him." Nader's piece, entitled "The Safe Car You Can't Buy," is largely confined to a discussion of the design shortcomings of American cars, which, he wrote in an early variation of the phrase that was to end as the title of his book, "are so designed as to be dangerous at any speed."

Moynihan's article has points of remarkable similarity to *Unsafe at Any Speed*. It is possible, as friends of both men will say, that the dwindling warmth in their friendship has its source in this fact. If Moynihan had any feeling, as some of these friends suggest, that Nader had encroached on his specialty, he does not now believe it was a very serious matter. "Yes, why not?" he says, when asked if he saw resemblances between Nader's book and his article. "I had that feeling, that the ideas were much the same. But those ideas weren't altogether my property. Where would I have been without my colleague in Albany, Bill Haddon?" Moynihan, with his professorial background, is committed, as he says, to "the process of people building on each other's work."

Moynihan's article, published more than six years earlier, made the same major points as did Nader's book. There are, if allowances are made for Moynihan's style being based on wit and Nader's on outrage, similarities in approach. Both works display the same willingness to assign blame to the manufacturers (and to name them in print); to draw the connections between Detroit and the auto safety establishment; to describe governmental inertia; to dissect motives, and to make the plain statement that contemporary policies were disastrous. Some things that were regarded, in Nader's book, as fresh formulations were expressed just as clearly by Moynihan—two examples being the contrast between the close federal scrutiny of aircraft safety and the virtual absence of official control over motor vehicles, and the fact that most injuries and fatalities occur in cars moving at relatively low speeds.

Both works expressed the same alarm over the hazardous nature of the interior of cars, the same disgust with advertising emphasizing speed instead of safety, the same conclusion that since the auto industry seemed unable or unwilling to deal with the safety problem, it must be regulated by the federal government. Unlike Nader, Moynihan did give some emphasis to the role of human error in accidents, as it is influenced by psychology or alcohol, but he arrived at a similar conclusion. "Significant personal characteristics seem to be so personal," Moynihan wrote, "that it is hopeless to think of doing anything about them for the limited purposes of traffic safety." In short, the vehicle, not the human operator, must adapt to the realities.

If Moynihan was, in fact, the first to perceive and publish the realities, it is still no mean thing that Nader, a few years afterward, turned them into the basis of a great cycle of reform. The role of pollinator is one Moynihan played in a good many other situations. As an assistant to Governor Averell Harriman of New York, Moynihan had been working on the auto safety issue since the mid-fifties. He thought that his *Reporter* piece "created a small stir, not a large one, but a respectable little stir." There was almost no reaction to Nader's piece. Moynihan's reflected the conclusion he had reached, in collaboration with a physician and scientific theoretician named William Haddon, Jr., that death on the highways was a public health problem that would yield, as the title suggested, to an epidemiological approach.

"In Albany," Moynihan says, "we solved the problem of traffic safety, in the sense that physicists arrive at a theoretical conclusion. It's a very different order of intellectual achievement, but when the problem is finally faced and solved it will be rather like the first nuclear chain reaction under that stadium in Chicago. I know it will work." Out of the work in Albany, Haddon emerged as an accepted expert in the field, and Moynihan became known, as Nader wrote in *Unsafe at Any Speed,* as the first political scientist to devote attention to auto safety.

When the Kennedy Administration came into office, Moynihan, who had been a Kennedy delegate at Los Angeles and later a speechwriter for the candidate, wanted to become a member of the President's Committee for Traffic Safety. During the campaign, Moynihan had written a phrase for Kennedy characterizing highway safety as the nation's most important public health problem. "Of course," Moynihan says, "John Kennedy probably never knew he had said any such thing, and it certainly created no excitement." Moynihan gave

up any idea of membership of the President's Committee
when Arthur Goldberg, Kennedy's Secretary of Labor, invited him to join his staff. Moynihan saw this as an opportunity to bring highway safety into the Labor Department,
which already had programs in occupational health and safety.
Moynihan was named a special assistant to the Secretary of
Labor, and in 1963 became Assistant Secretary of Labor for
policy planning.

In the process of setting up his policy planning staff, Moynihan discovered that no one in the government was charged
with overall responsibility for the problem of traffic safety.
The executive director of the President's Committee for
Traffic Safety hardly qualified, Moynihan thought, as a dis-
passionate spokesman. This official was paid, not with government funds, but with money raised by the automobile industry. This arrangement was the result of an exchange of
letters between President Eisenhower and Harlowe Curtice,
then the president of General Motors, suggesting the establishment of a body to promote the objectives of the White
House Conference on Traffic Safety in 1954. It was continued in the Kennedy Administration, although the secretaries of Labor, Commerce, Defense, and Health, Education,
and Welfare were added as ex-officio members of the committee. Moynihan served as Secretary of Labor Arthur Goldberg's legman to the committee, doing what he could, with
almost no discernible results, to change the focus of the
committee's work from education of drivers to a more comprehensive approach that would acknowledge the role of vehicle design in accidents.

In 1964, Moynihan invited Nader to join his policy planning staff at fifty dollars a day as a consultant on highway
safety. Nader, Moynihan remembers, accepted like a shot.
Nader says that his views and Moynihan's, when they first
met, were identical. Their personalities certainly were not,
and their relationship must have had some of the qualities of

a friendship between Puck and Kafka. Moynihan has the academic's toleration for eccentricity, and he took a certain delight in Nader's unbureaucratic methods. "His working environment," Moynihan says, "was a sea of papers and books. He kept odd hours." They saw little enough of each other because Nader preferred to work at night in the deserted building. Moynihan conceived feelings about his subordinate that were a mixture of respect and amusement. "Ralph was a very suspicious man," Moynihan recalls. "He used to warn me that the phones at the Labor Department might be tapped. I'd say, 'Fine! They'll learn that the unemployment rate for March is 5.3 percent, that's what they'll learn!' But he kept on warning me."

Nader's assignment was to write a study he subsequently titled "A Report on the Context, Condition and Recommended Direction of Federal Activity in Highway Safety." He fell on the task with his accustomed single-mindedness. David Swankin, now director of the Washington office of Consumers Union, shared an office with Nader. "When Ralph talked," Swankin says, "it was all auto safety. This was a terrible thing and something had to be done about it. Passion and zeal. He had a fantastic desk—piles of stuff, tons of stuff. It was work, work, all work." Mrs. Ellen Broderick, Moynihan's assistant at the Labor Department, recalls that a certain aroma of mystery surrounded Nader's activity. "No one except Pat," she says, "knew what Ralph was doing in that cluttered office of his."

Even Moynihan was not always sure how far Nader might think his franchise extended. "Right away," he recalls, "there developed that tremendous quality of ferreting around that he has. In a matter of days he was over at Justice, trying to find out if the auto industry might be guilty of antitrust violations. I thought, 'Jesus Christ, all I need is for Bob Kennedy to get wind of this.' The auto companies had been pretty much pro-Kennedy."

Nader finished his report, 234 double-spaced pages of text and 99 pages of notes, in the spring of 1965. His work had been delayed by the loss of all his notes for the report in a Washington taxi, so he had had to reconstruct his research before he could write. Moynihan believes he has a copy of the report somewhere among his papers; Mrs. Broderick doubts that he ever read all of it. It is possible that no one else did, either. Moynihan did not give the report wide circulation inside the government. It was a background document—and the function of a background document is to exist, not to be read. The worst way to convince the White House to do anything, Moynihan reflects, is to present it with a three-hundred-page report. Instead, the wise advocate merely mentions that he can back up his arguments, if necessary, with weighty scholarship.

Moynihan wanted to stimulate a major presidential initiative on traffic safety. He wanted legislation that would identify the vehicle as the cause of crashes and injury and death and bring the manufacture of vehicles under federal regulation. He discussed his idea with members of the Cabinet, with White House assistants, with key bureaucrats like Paul Sitton of the Bureau of the Budget. Moynihan was not without sympathizers, and he points out that there was considerable ferment inside the government on the issue of traffic safety long before Nader's adventures with General Motors gave it an emotional focus.

The victimization of Nader provided the political opportunity to regulate the auto industry. But the groundwork laid by government officials like Moynihan and Sitton made it possible for Washington to act quickly when the opportunity presented itself.

Nader's report has had, in all, an enigmatic history. All copies of it have vanished from the files of the Labor Department, and there seems, in fact, to be no copy in the possession of any government agency. Mrs. Broderick believes that it may have been bundled up with other documents after Moynihan left the Labor Department and sent for safekeeping to the Library of Congress. It does not figure in the Library's catalog, though a member of the staff believes that it may well repose in a packing box in the basement, like an unclassified fossil in the cellar of the Smithsonian Institution.

If the report did nothing else, it gave Moynihan the opportunity to say in the White House that the priorities of the federal traffic safety program were, in his words, "all wrong." As a sidelight of his research, Nader discovered the President's Committee for Traffic Safety was using the Presidential Seal on some of its material. "This was something that the White House could react to," Moynihan says. "Unauthorized use of the President's Seal! This was serious stuff." At a meeting called to discuss this problem, Moynihan seized the occasion to talk about death and injury on the highways. He does not know if his argument was heeded. "But Ralph and I left behind the initiative, at least, to do something about the problem," he says.

There is a persistent belief, expressed by Nader's friends as well as others, that the report he produced at the Labor Department is, in fact, the rough draft of *Unsafe at Any Speed*. A cousinship can be perceived in the two works. Nader deals in both, and in very similar terms, with the shortcomings of the Corvair, and the chapters in his book describing the government's activities reflect, not unnaturally, the earlier study. Apparently some of the material in *Unsafe at Any Speed* was gathered in the course of research for the government study.

Leonard J. McEnnis, Jr., now an information officer at the Federal Trade Commission, was interviewed by Nader when the latter was working for Moynihan. McEnnis was at that time the director of public relations at the Insurance Institute for Highway Safety, and Nader asked him why the insurance industry had not taken a harder line on automotive design. McEnnis, assuming that he was speaking to a government official and not for publication, replied, "They don't want us telling them how to build autos and we don't want them telling us how to sell insurance." McEnnis was astonished when his words turned up in *Unsafe at Any Speed.* "I took a lot of ribbing," McEnnis says, "but of course that was the philosophy at that time. It was very embarrassing, all the same."

As Nader told the Ribicoff subcommittee, his book had been gestating since 1960 at least, so it is doubtless true that he brought as much material into the Labor Department as he took out of it. In the sense that the arguments are the same, the government study can be viewed as a dry run for the book. The two works are quite different as to the weight of material, with the study concentrating through most of its length entirely on the government role. It is not difficult to find stylistic similarities, because Nader is Nader. But there are few, if any, duplications of phraseology.

If there was a reluctance within the bureaucracy to give the Nader study a calm reading, this is understandable enough. The report, which was supposed to be an internal document, had the scent of a tract. "As an economic phenomenon," Nader wrote, "the highway epidemic is a multi-billion dollar industry which provides income for hundreds of thousands of people and companies. . . . The close couplings between the pursuit of traffic safety and the pursuit of economic gain and administrative tenure are the sources for impediments to a more optimum performance against this mass trauma. In spite of privately recognizing this reality, federal personnel involved in highway safety programs have persistently avoided its explicit consideration in their policy deliberations or administration. . . . Under such conditions, the likelihood for a traffic safety policy of substance to emerge from federal policy making is zero."

In *Unsafe at Any Speed* this judgment was repeated in language that was more readable but no less harsh. The book omitted the term *highway epidemic*, with its echoes of Moynihan's philosophy. However justified Nader's assessment of the bureaucracy's work may have been, it was stated in the study in terms not calculated to please the bureaucracy, its supposed readers.

The bureaucracy, of course, eventually had to take notice. The reforms Nader recommended in the conclusion of his study were, in 1966, translated into unprecedented laws that brought the automobile industry under federal regulation. Other themes, lost in the legislative shuffle, have remained a part of Nader's public vocabulary. A prophetic phrase in the study regrets the absence of an "organized consumer constituency to provide a functioning counterpoise to industry-backed priorities." His principal recommendation became, with some modifications, a reality. In the language of the study, this was a call to the President to "request legislation to establish a Federal Highway Transportation Agency as a separate administrative body directly responsible to the President." This body would "a. develop safety and testing standards; b. develop a prototype safety vehicle as a basis for standard-setting; c. develop in-house staff and/or extramural scientific and engineering knowledge to promote the development of a safe, efficient, and economical highway transportation system." Nader asked also that the Treasury invest in a tax-exempt foundation on traffic safety "to determine if industry activities influence legislation," and that the Justice Department look into the possibility that industry policies had a tendency to restrain competition in product safety. The Attorney General, he wrote, ought to examine the "undesirable practice of jointly acting oligopolies from an antitrust perspective [to see if this practice might] warrant recommending stronger antitrust legislation." He recommended that the President's Committee for Traffic Safety be abolished outright.

"Both the forces of government and business," he wrote, "have promoted an explanation of the accident-injury occurrence . . . chiefly conceived as a psychological or attitudinal problem. . . . [Reforms] have been ignored whenever they clash with powerful interests profiting from, or staffing, a system whose change they want to avoid." It may have come as a surprise—arising from what Nader might call a failure of sensitivity—to government officials involved in highway safety to be told so unequivocally that they were part of a conspiracy.

After Nader completed his report, he went off to work on *Unsafe at Any Speed,* a sequence of events that doubtless had something to do with the legend that the two works are more similar than in fact they are. Moynihan learned of the existence of Nader's book when Mrs. Broderick found it advertised in *The New York Times.* "I took it to Moynihan," she says, "and said, 'Did you know we had an author celebrity here?' Pat was amazed, and Ralph was kind of embarrassed by it all. Ralph operated pretty close to the vest, and I guess he thought there was no need to mention it." Moynihan, in his equable way, points out that a number of other meritorious books, including one coauthored by Haddon, were published at about the same time. Only Nader's was struck by lightning.

Moynihan had signed a contract with a publisher to write a book on auto safety along the lines of his "Epidemic on the Highways." When Nader's book was published, he says, it seemed superfluous to continue with his own work. His protégé had covered the ground before him and opened the gates to the reformers—which is all that Moynihan had hoped to accomplish himself.

5

To Attack Is to Build

[Haddon] deserved it. I told him very clearly. . . . I
said, "Bill, we've been friends and all, but it's my job to
keep an eye on the bureau from my perspective."

RALPH NADER

President Johnson signed the Traffic and Motor Vehicle
Safety Act of 1966, in the presence of Senator Ribicoff,
Ralph Nader, William Haddon, and others, on September 9,
1966. At the White House gates, after the ceremony, Ribicoff
turned to Jerome Sonosky and said, "Jerry, do you think
we've saved any lives?" Sonosky replied that he did not know,
but that that was not the issue. "The issue," as he explained
later, "was who decides what's safe? Who decides whether
these lives should be saved?"

With the President's signature, the issue was resolved: the
automobile industry had lost its power to decide how safe its
products should be. From that point onward, the federal government would set the standards for safe vehicle design.
Nader, reflecting the hope in Ribicoff's question, and for the

moment ignoring the doubt, said that "President Johnson has launched the nation on a great life-saving program."

It would not be long before doubt rose again to the surface of Nader's public statements. In a matter of weeks, he would launch a fierce attack on some of his most important allies in the campaign to enact this historic legislation. But, for the time being, he joined in the camaraderie produced by the rout of the auto industry. The traffic safety bill passed the Senate by 76 votes to 0 and the House of Representatives by 331 votes to 0. The leonine mood of Congress never changed after the hearings before the Ribicoff subcommittee concerning the General Motors investigation of Nader. Something of the tone of the hearings on the bill itself, held before the Senate Commerce Committee, is captured in the reply Senator Maurine Neuberger of Oregon made after hearing testimony from John Bugas, a Ford vice-president. "I say," Mrs. Neuberger told him, " 'Ha ha.' "

Nader considered that the law, as adopted, was less than adequate. The two provisions he regarded as most important—criminal penalties against corporation executives and federal powers to order manufacturers to recall defective vehicles—were omitted from the final version. The law was a great deal stronger than it had started out to be. Nader had said of the original administration draft that it was a "no-law law." The bill finally sent to Capitol Hill by the White House was a product of compromise.

The President's men had wanted a bill that would *require* the Secretary of Commerce to set safety standards. The Secretary of Commerce, John Connor, argued for a formula that would *permit* him to set standards after two years if the automobile industry had not, in the meantime, corrected its designs in response to the threat of federal regulation. Connor won his point, and the weakened bill was sent to Congress. Nader thought that giving the Commerce Department, with its mission to foster commerce and industry, jurisdiction over the auto companies was a paradox; to give it discretionary powers rather than a clear order to act was, he believed, a formula for circumventing reform.

Ribicoff, on the Senate floor, said the administration bill would take too much time to effect changes. He urged that the Secretary of Commerce be required to set safety standards, and that the standards applied by the federal government's housekeeping agency, the General Services Administration, to the cars it purchased for the federal government be applied in the meantime to all automobiles. Senator Warren G. Magnuson of Washington, chairman of the Commerce Committee, said as he opened his hearings that he would sponsor amendments requiring that the GSA standards be applied to all cars by January 31, 1967, and that the Secretary of Commerce be required to set new standards one year after that. The likely success of Magnuson's amendments was foreshadowed on March 29, 1966, when the Senate passed, by a unanimous vote, Senator Gaylord Nelson's bill setting stringent standards for the manufacture of safer tires. Nelson, stimulated by Nader's arguments in private, introduced a separate bill to make GSA standards applicable to all cars.

Sonosky believes that the breaking point for the industry, and the final loss of any residual goodwill for the industry in the Senate, came not with the Nader hearings, but with an action by Ribicoff. Nader had been telling Sonosky since the first hearings of the Ribicoff subcommittee in 1965 that the auto companies had quietly been recalling cars because of safety defects. Sonosky, in the absence of hard information, did not believe the problem was as extensive as Nader suggested. After industry spokesmen refused in the Commerce Committee hearings to support the concept of any federal regulation, Ribicoff wired the auto companies, demanding details of their recall campaigns.

Their replies revealed that there had been, since 1960, a

total of 426 recall campaigns, involving eight million cars, or almost one in every five manufactured in that period. Most of the recalls had been made because of faults in brakes, steering, and suspension systems. There were no figures to show how many of the cars had actually had defects or how many had been repaired. Because notification was made to dealers, not owners, it could not be known how many customers had actually found out that their cars might be defective.

After reading the figures, Sonosky contacted the manufacturers on Ribicoff's behalf. "I told them," he says, "that they had until four o'clock that day to change their position on federal regulation. They didn't, so I said to my secretary at four sharp, 'Roll 'em!' " What the secretary rolled was a press release containing the facts about the recalls. "That's what really did it," Sonosky says. "This was an attack [by a Senate committee] on the product. That shook Detroit, Ralph's book didn't do it. The Nader hearings killed the Corvair, and *Mustang* sales soared. I bet Henry Ford laughed himself silly."

According to Paul Sitton, Nader's book had an effect all its own. During most of 1965, Sitton was working at the Commerce Department as head of a task group charged with preparing the administration's package on highway safety. The report of Sitton's group contained a recommendation for standard-setting by the federal government, and Secretary Connor delayed sending it to the White House. Sitton's chief, Under Secretary Alan S. Boyd, finally transmitted the report under his own signature. It lay dormant, Sitton says, until *Unsafe at Any Speed* was published in November. "At which time," Sitton says dryly, "a call was received from the White House saying go ahead full steam in the preparation of legislation." Moynihan has similar recollections: "I've heard Joe Califano [President Johnson's assistant for domestic affairs] say that one of the reasons for the legislation was that they knew Ralph's book was coming out." In Moynihan's view, an element of political expediency was involved as well. "We couldn't press for legislation in 1964 because all the auto companies were for President Johnson," Moynihan says. "In 1965 it was possible. It was as simple as that."

With all the evidence about the true condition of auto safety in the public domain, there was no lack of enthusiasm among politicians for a strong law, and no mercy for Detroit. After the Ribicoff hearings, Nader moved through this press of headhunters, urging his ideas on Senate staffers, making certain that newspapermen understood the issues, and, in his new role as a public figure, making speeches and giving interviews. Drew Pearson championed a strong bill in his column and was kept supplied by Nader—and by the congressional network—with leaks. Those who sought to weaken the bill by night could expect to find themselves exposed next morning in the Pearson column, the last place any public man ever wanted to find himself when he was on the unpopular side of an issue.

Nader was making his views very plain to the Commerce Committee staffers, Michael Pertschuk and Gerald Grinstein, who were drafting the Senate version of the bill. "There was a flow of one- and two-page memos from me up to the committee," Nader says, "and a lot of oral. I didn't sit down and draft the bill—they wouldn't let me. And you saw how bad it was."

He contracted a tactical alliance with Senator Vance Hartke of Indiana, who introduced nine amendments closely reflecting Nader's views. These included provisions for the publication of the technical basis for the new standards, government funding for a prototype safety car, stringent enforcement powers including investigatory powers for the new traffic safety agency to be established under the Act, and some specific provisions for standards, such as a requirement that doors, trunks, and hoods be equipped with safety devices to stop them closing on hands.

The most explosive of the Nader-Hartke amendments was a provision to provide criminal penalties against manufacturers who failed to comply with federal safety standards. It is a persistent theme of Nader's that businessmen who exploit the public safety and welfare for profit are criminals and ought to go to jail. This was not an idea that sat well in the Commerce Committee or in the Senate. Senator John O. Pastore of Rhode Island said the automobile executives were not criminals and should not be treated as criminals. Hartke's amendment, which would have confronted them with jail sentences of up to one year and fines of up to $50,000, was defeated in committee, and an attempt to revive the provision for criminal penalties lost on the floor of the Senate by 14 votes to 62. In the House, criminal penalties lost on the floor by 15 votes to 120.

Nader took the defeat hard. "The bill has been detoothed," he told *The Washington Post*. He regarded the criminal penalties amendment as an opportunity for a philosophical breakthrough, a chance to strip businessmen of the immunity he believes they enjoy from the human consequences of their actions. There is, he believes, no clearer example of the breakdown of law and order in society than the casual violence done by industry to the environment and to the health and happiness of individuals.

In the face of the tide of political sentiment that was rising against it, the automobile industry hired, as its Canute, a Washington lawyer and lobbyist named Lloyd N. Cutler. After registering in April as a lobbyist for the Automobile Manufacturers Association, Cutler began working within the Senate to modify the bill. The heads of the industry, after paying visits of state to a number of senators and congressmen, apparently came to the conclusion that they could count on almost no one who had not been elected from Michigan. Cutler, a skillful and patient man, offered a series of alternatives to the least acceptable provisions of the bill. In the end, Cutler could have had no doubt as to where the battle line was drawn, and who was on the other side. The Commerce Committee approved the bill on June 21, and the Senate majority leader, Mike Mansfield of Montana, decided that it should come to a vote on June 24, a Friday. The committee staff, therefore, was given a mere forty-eight hours in which to prepare the printed report required by Senate rules; they had the rest of their careers to deal with the sensibilities of the interested parties.

The staff coped with the situation by seating the industry's counsel, Cutler, in one anteroom and Nader, the symbolic citizen, in another. Staff members scurried between the two with pages of the draft as they came out of the typewriter. This system may, as the staff hoped, have ensured accuracy, fairness, and completeness in the report. It also marked the first time in American history that the power of the government and the power of wealth had to deal with a third force that had been dormant in human affairs since the end of the Roman Empire: Nader as it were became, and ever afterward was considered, the American tribune.

The first person to discover that the tribune's writ ran not just to conventional villains but also to the virtuous was Dr. William Haddon, Jr. Haddon, then forty years old, was appointed as the first head of the National Traffic Safety Agency, which was established as a part of the Department of Commerce, under the new law. He brought to the job impeccable credentials: a bachelor's degree from the Massachusetts Institute of Technology, an M.D. and a master's degree in public health from Harvard, and a history of scholarly devotion to the new philosophy of highway safety covering much of his working life. As a young researcher in microbiology at Harvard, Haddon won an innovator's reputation by developing a synthetic skin on which disease-bearing insects could be studied without peril to human subjects.

When he left the laboratory, he took with him the researcher's mood, a mixture of skepticism toward assumptions and optimism toward the possibility of discovery. His first public job was that of director of the driver research center of the New York State Department of Health. There, in company with Moynihan and others, he helped to formulate the theory of highway safety as an epidemiological phenomenon. Later, he was widely regarded as having popularized the work of Hugh DeHaven, father of the concept that cars could be made safe by enclosing driver and passengers in a "crashworthy" compartment designed to eliminate the hazards within it, and to exclude the hazards that penetrated it in a crash.

DeHaven, founder of Cornell automotive crash injury research, embarked on a lifelong intellectual quest into the nature of accidents in 1917 when he, alone among four persons involved, survived the midair collision of two JN-4 "Jenny" biplanes. Inspecting the wreckage of the two planes, he concluded that he had lived through the crash because the cockpit in which he had been seated remained almost intact while all the others had disintegrated.

During World War II, DeHaven's work led to the design of aircraft cockpits free of protruding knobs on which pilots might be injured, to the standard use of lap and shoulder belts, and to cockpit structures that could withstand the tremendous forces of high-speed crashes. Through his innovations, the lives of countless pilots were saved and injuries were greatly reduced. With extraordinary stamina, DeHaven pursued his ideas over five decades in the face of almost universal indifference. His ideas were so novel that when, in the course of researching the history of packaging in the New

York Public Library, he told library assistants he was interested in "packaging people," they refused to help him further. "They decided," DeHaven said, "that if I was serious, I
was away off my rocker!"

DeHaven believed in the application of aircraft safety
technology to automobiles. So did Haddon, and he had a gift
for translating scientific data into understandable programs.
"At first," Moynihan says of the early days of his campaign
on auto safety in Albany, "we just had feelings about these
things. Then Bill Haddon joined and moved us on to concepts of vehicle design. We understood that it was just a matter of transferring aircraft technology to the automobile in
the first generation of improvement."

Haddon's expertise was sufficiently appreciated for him to
be summoned to Washington early in 1965, together with
Robert Brenner, as a consultant to Alan S. Boyd, who, as
Under Secretary of Commerce for Transportation, was
charged with responsibility for preparing the administration's traffic safety legislation. For six months, Haddon
commuted to Washington from Albany and Brenner from
Los Angeles two days a week to confer with Boyd and with
Paul Sitton as the administration's bills were drafted.

Haddon had been asked, before this, to head the new federal traffic safety program when it came into existence. Haddon declined; did not want a job in Washington. He was,
he says, content to remain in Albany. But a memory of John
F. Kennedy's inaugural speech ("Ask not what your country
can do for you . . .") took hold of him, and he accepted.
After that, his neutrality was protected by a prohibition
against his testifying before the Senate committees holding
hearings on the legislation. Brenner was similarly insulated
from the hazards of public exposure; he became Haddon's
deputy in the National Highway Safety Bureau.

This discreet silence was anomalous for Haddon because it
was he, in a way, who had touched off the series of events

that led to the passage of the new law. Ribicoff, reading *The New York Times* on a Sunday in December, 1964, came upon an article referring to a book, *Accident Research: Methods and Approaches,* that Haddon had coauthored with two other men. "It was the first time I'd heard of the car as a factor in accidents," Ribicoff says. "I was intrigued by the theory of the second collision; this was a new concept to me."

With the *Times* in his hand, Ribicoff telephoned Sonosky at eight o'clock in the morning and told his aide that he wanted to schedule hearings on the role of the vehicle in crashes. Sonosky saw the implications immediately. "This means taking on Detroit," he told Ribicoff. "Can you do it?" Ribicoff asked. In a matter of days, Sonosky began the train of events that brought Nader into the back rooms of the subcommittee. Before that happened, both Ribicoff and Sonosky had read "Epidemic on the Highways." Moynihan's tour de force eliminated any doubts they may have had that they were following the spoor of a great public issue.

Haddon possesses, in addition to his credentials, a reflective mind and an impatient heart. He is a slight man who is unaware of fashions or unconcerned with them: he still wears the brush-cut hair and the narrow bow ties of the fifties. Haddon has a jumpy quality; he clambers from subject to subject, revising the precision of what he wishes to say as he goes along, only to be carried off by another thought in the middle of the one he set out to clarify. He is allergic to tobacco smoke, hostile to interruptions, slightly deaf. For all his undoubted gifts, he is not a tidy administrator.

When Haddon was appointed, Nader told a newspaper reporter that he would be "another Goddard"—an admiring reference to Haddon's friend, Dr. James L. Goddard, the chief of the Food and Drug Administration. Nader and Haddon had soldiered in the same cause for a considerable time. Haddon remembers furnishing Nader with information during the days of his obscurity. He seemed then to Haddon someone who was genuinely interested in facts. The two men had been introduced, had exchanged a letter or two, and had run into each other by accident in a Washington hotel lobby at some time before November, 1965; early in that month, Haddon went to Washington to give a five-minute speech on motor vehicle accident prevention before the White House Conference on Health.

While Haddon was going through the security check required for entrance to the conference, he was told that Ralph Nader was looking for him. Haddon went searching for Nader, but couldn't find him. No written message had been left. Haddon gave his speech on auto crashes as a public health problem, which was limited by the terms of his invitation to five minutes, and went home. In early December, he received the following letter:

Dec. 8, 1965

Dear Bill,

By now you should have received a copy of my book. I hope you enjoy the contents and would appreciate your noting it in the Department's Bulletin—or perhaps an editorial could issue forth. I wouldn't be displeased to see you review it in some medical journal as well.

Sorry to have missed you at the President's Conference last month. A main reason for my coming was to get together with you for a few minutes. Apparently you were too busy but that doesn't excuse all that steam you pre-censored out of your mild statement. Fire away, Bill, it's becoming more and more conventional you know—it wasn't much different from Ross's [McFarland, a Harvard professor] statement which was about as bold as an inverted three-toed sloth. You had a great audience and press coverage which you did not take advantage of. Remember that

grand speech you made before SAE—is it age? or all
those respectable advisory committee posts?

                                    Sincerely,
                              [signed] Ralph

Haddon thought that this was an unusual sort of letter to
receive from a man he hardly knew, but he sent off a prompt
reply, making no reference to what he supposed was a passing
fit of pique. In later years, Haddon regarded Nader's note,
with its tone of accusation and suspicion, as an early example
of "a very common posture of his over all the years I've
known him, namely, that the possibility of the invidious immediately becomes the fact of it."

Haddon's tenancy of the new traffic safety agency was
nothing if not an education in the invidious. The unpleas-
antness began, Haddon believes, even before he was
appointed, when his opponents leaked a story to *The Washington Post,* forecasting that Haddon would be appointed to
head the new agency. "They figured correctly that this would
touch off President Johnson . . ." Haddon says. "Johnson
called [Secretary of Commerce] Connor and chewed him
out, demanding that he issue a retraction." Somehow Connor's retraction was released too late for the afternoon papers,
and they ran the morning story unchanged. The President,
despite his displeasure over being upstaged twice in one day,
went ahead and appointed Haddon administrator of the
National Traffic Safety Agency on October 15, 1966. On
November 3, the name of the new entity was changed to National Highway Safety Agency, and when it became part of
the new Department of Transportation on April 1, 1967, it
was known as the National Highway Safety Bureau.

During its first two incarnations, Haddon's agency was
part of the Department of Commerce. As Nader and others
had foreseen, Commerce did not provide an atmosphere in
which new bureaucratic plants could easily flourish. The

new agency was understaffed and underfunded to accomplish the mission that Congress had assigned to it. It was expected to promote policies that would, in the language of the Traffic and Motor Vehicle Safety Act, ensure that "the public is protected against unreasonable risk of accidents occurring as a result of the design, construction or performance of motor vehicles . . . and against unreasonable risk of death or injury to persons in the event accidents do occur. . . ." It was expected to carry out this order through a combination of persuasion and standard-setting.

Haddon's agency was under statutory instruction to issue the first motor vehicle safety standards by January 31, 1967. It received its first funds on October 15, 1966, on which date its total staff consisted of Haddon. By the end of the month, strength had risen to eight, including his deputy, Robert Brenner. Only one employee was assigned to the Motor Vehicle Safety Performance Service, the section concerned with translating the congressional mandate into safety standards. By January 31, 1967, Haddon had a total of seventy-three employees, only thirteen of them in MVSPS. He had no direct control over personnel or over the legal and public relations staff, which remained a part of the existing apparatus of the Commerce Department.

Haddon believes that the old traffic safety establishment in the government, including Commerce's Bureau of Public Roads, began to sabotage his agency even before it was born through attempts to deny it personnel and to vitiate its independence. To counteract the trend, he called on Ralph Nader. In the period when the legislation was being written, Nader floated between the Senate and the administration, carrying principles and messages. Haddon and Robert Brenner, lodged in a room in the Congressional Hotel, were drawing up an administrative plan for the unborn traffic safety agency. They ran into difficulties, traceable in part to their lack of familiarity with the mysteries of the federal personnel system, in setting up an organization chart. In order to attract high-quality personnel, the new agency needed to be able to pay relatively high salaries. The civil service term for officials who are in the higher salary range is "supergrades." Haddon and Brenner believed that they needed about sixty-five supergrades, for which there was no provision in the draft of the law. High officials at Commerce, according to Haddon, thought that the new agency should be authorized no more than three officials at the supergrade level.

Nader, after a talk with Haddon, attempted to have an authorization for supergrades written into the legislation, but there were problems of jurisdiction in the Senate, and he did not succeed. Later, he was tapped again by Haddon in an effort to have the new agency designated as a statutory, or quasi-independent, body within the Department of Transportation, which was then being legislated into existence and under whose authority it was being placed. Alan Boyd, who was to become the first Secretary of Transportation, was already faced with the prospect of dealing with a number of existing satrapies, such as the Federal Aviation Administration and the Bureau of Public Roads, and was not anxious to create another. Haddon was fearful that his infant would be gobbled up by one of the satraps. "It seemed to me," as Haddon says, "that the risk to [our] program more than justified this sort of subversion on our part, and that was why we tipped Ralph off to what was going on."

The subversion did not entirely succeed. The Transportation Act provided some safeguards for Haddon's bureau, but it did not specify where in the bureaucracy it was to be, with the result that it was tucked away in the Federal Highway Administration (FHWA). The bureaucratic effect of this was to place the head of the FHWA between Haddon and the Secretary of Transportation in the line of official communication and to make Haddon's agency dependent for legal and publicity services, among other things, upon the FHWA.

These may seem to be petty matters; in fact they placed serious limitations on Haddon's freedom of action. The extra layer of bureaucratic insulation meant, in effect, that he had to get prior approval, within the bureaucracy, for the reforms that Congress had mandated. This turned out, in some cases, to be a slow process. Nader, as he soon made plain, believed that it was too slow.

Soon after he took office, Haddon began to feel that Ralph Nader did not appreciate the difficulties under which he had to work. "The bureau was hardly organized," as Paul Sitton says, "when Ralph began the drumfire. I guess some of it was justified, at least from Ralph's point of view, but it sure didn't make Haddon blush with pleasure." On January 24, a week before the deadline for issuance of the first standards, Nader warned in the newspapers of "imminent concessions" by the bureau on the standards because of industry pressure. Nader, establishing a pattern of telling the world what Haddon was going to do before he did it, predicted that the standards would omit requirements for headrests, for tire and wheel rim performance, for safer steering assemblies, and a number of other matters.

Drew Pearson, on the same day, devoted a column to the situation; he named, as one of the industry "pressure boys," Roy Haeusler of Chrysler, identified as "an old friend and fellow MIT alumnus of Haddon's." Haddon, who had graduated from MIT sixteen years after Haeusler and, he says, knew him only slightly, discerned the hand of Nader in the Pearson column. He had already begun to believe Nader was engaged in a campaign "to dominate the safety program—either shoot it down or run it."

Haddon regarded the publication of the standards on the deadline as a minor administrative miracle. In the press of organizing the new bureau, Haddon says, he had delegated responsibility for drafting the initial standards to one of his subordinates, a man with a high reputation in safety engineering. It was a tricky job; under the law, the new standards had to be based on existing standards, such as those of the General Services Administration, and could only be stated in terms of performance. The government could tell the auto makers what safety results they must achieve, but not how to achieve them. If, for example, it was decided that a car must stop in a specified distance, and it was known that only, say, disc brakes could achieve the result, the standard could not require that cars must be equipped with disc brakes: it could merely specify that the car must stop in x number of feet after the brakes were applied. Moreover, the preliminary standards had to be published in the *Federal Register* on November 30, with an invitation to interested persons to submit comments within thirty-one days.

In mid-November, Haddon called in the man in charge of drafting the standards and asked for a report. Haddon was dissatisfied with the standards as drafted by his subordinate, and he decided, at the eleventh hour, to begin the job anew. He and his deputy, Robert Brenner, retired to a back room and drafted the standards themselves in a series of all-night sessions. In one three-month period early in the bureau's existence, Haddon's wife calculated that he was home for a total of four days, and four times for dinner, counting Sundays and holidays. Nader's criticism of the bureau's slow start, which took place almost entirely in the newspapers, did not have a soothing effect on Haddon and his staff. "When you're up all night writing a regulation," as Brenner says, "it's a little irritating to pick up *The Washington Post* with the morning coffee and read that you're dragging your feet."

Haddon and his staff had slightly more than three weeks in which to evaluate the thousands of pages of comments and objections to the proposed standards that had been filed on December 31 by "interested parties," mostly the auto companies. The twenty standards that were finally issued, with the force of federal regulations applying to all passenger vehicles covered under the Act, were largely based on the GSA standards for federally purchased motor vehicles. Haddon believed this was a result faithful to the intention of the Congress.

Nader had another point of view. "Dr. Haddon and his superiors did not compromise with the industry," he said. "They surrendered to it." He added that the standards were "a fraud on the American people." Senator Magnuson, partly in response to a request by Haddon, called a hearing before the Senate Commerce Committee to examine Haddon's action. Nader, as a witness before the committee, said that Haddon's agency had "a protective attitude" toward the automobile industry and "an agonizing timidity" over fulfilling its mission to protect the public. He said Haddon was "petrified" by the possibility that the standards might be challenged in court by the auto industry. Haddon and his superior, Lowell K. Bridwell, head of the Federal Highway Administration, replied that Nader was overstating the extent of industry pressure. "What do they think [Lloyd] Cutler does during his working hours?" Nader asked. "Survey the Washington Monument?"

Although the initial standards omitted some of the reforms Nader regarded as indispensable, they were a considerable improvement over no standards at all. They included requirements for energy-absorbing steering columns, laminated windshields, seat belts for all occupants, standard windshield washing, wiping, defogging, and defrosting systems, safeguards so that cars with automatic transmissions could not be started when the car was in gear, double braking systems with warning light in case of brake failure, interior padding of the passenger compartment, and improved locking systems. The auto makers were given until January 1, 1968, to incorporate the standards into their products.

Haddon believed the standards went as far as the state of the art permitted. Where, as in the case of the omission of standards on tires and headrests, some regulations had been deferred until the next year, he argued that there were insufficient data to make a rational decision. To Nader, nothing was less rational than the loss of life that he said delay would cause. Haddon was caught by Nader's onslaught, and not for the last time, in a position that was scientifically defensible but politically vulnerable. He had tried to apply and, as he thought, succeeded in applying the standards of the laboratory to the public arena. "We were," Brenner says, "operating in a climate of pressures that cannot be described as conducive to leisurely thought. To regulate the world's largest industry in a matter of three or four months was a formidable task. But we did it."

Nader, of course, was telling the public that they had done no such thing. Brenner drew a wry lesson from the experience of watching his reality and Haddon's collide on the front pages with Nader's reality. "What does it matter," he asks, "if you are right technically and wrong politically? This guy [Nader] has a terrific sense of timing—he knows how to touch the right nerve at the right time."

Nader's knack for playing upon Haddon's nerves achieved a high level of virtuosity. Through a combination of scolding letters, public denunciation, and what some regarded as the techniques of espionage, he kept Haddon and his bureau in a state of unease. Not the least maddening of Nader's methods was his habit of giving his letters to Haddon to the newspapers before Haddon had received them in the mail. A. B. Kelley, director of public affairs for the Federal Highway Administration, addressed himself to this problem in a letter to Nader on October 2, 1968. Nader had written Kelley on September 13 as follows, in part:

This is to request that the next time you prepare a release dealing with a matter raised in a letter of mine . . . and the release makes mention of my inquiry, then a copy of my letter should be available for any inquiring reporter or citizen. . . . The Bureau's release on the Mustang strut problem brought forth an inquiry by one reporter for a copy of my letter and he was told it was not available. . . .

In reply, Kelley wrote:

This office has no policy of withholding your letters. . . . Such a policy would be neither justified in terms of sound information policies, nor realistic in view of the fact that your letters are normally made available to the press by you at or prior to the time they are received by the addressee.

There was little Haddon could do about Nader's letter writing, except to reply to the flood of denunciation that he received from Nader on the work of the bureau and what Nader regarded as its shortcomings. On September 27, 1968, Nader wrote to Haddon about what he regarded as the bureau's laxity in enforcing compliance with the new auto safety standards:

Without the Department's own testing facilities, difficulties were bound to arise concerning the necessary arrangements for testing compliance. However, the absence of a top priority enforcement concern is all too prevalent and cannot be excused. Judging by the laxness in replying to responsible inquiries . . . the Bureau is in need of being reminded that, however nominal the existing standards are, the law requires that the companies meet them.

In this letter, among other matters, Nader raised the question of Volkswagen gas caps, which, Nader said, "loosen or disengage during collisions thereby permitting a flow of gasoline—in some cases entering the front passenger compartment." Nader's letter was received after the bureau had decided to require Volkswagen to correct its gas caps; the publicity with which Nader surrounded the issue did not make that clear.

A number of experiences of this kind shook Haddon's faith in Nader's good intentions. In an internal memorandum on January 25, 1968, Haddon attempted to dissuade his superiors from writing letters in reply to Nader's that might provide further ammunition. "Nader consistently tries to set up exactly this sort of interminable exchange on details he interprets in his own terms," Haddon wrote, "and, it is our experience, frequently without any attempt at common accuracy, interpretation and substance, and I do not think it is in the public interest to engage in this game any more than necessary."

This recommendation may have had some effect. On the following March 29, an irate Nader wrote as follows to Secretary of Transportation Boyd:

> I can no longer condone the dilatory response or the non-response to letters of inquiry made to Departmental Bureau [*sic*] on the basis of a new Department getting organized. . . . I have always thought that one month should be the maximum delay in replying to letters from citizens. . . . Would you kindly inform me what the Department's policy on time spans for answering letters are to (a) the White House, (b) other Executive Departments, (c) the Congress, (d) state officials, and (e) citizens? . . . Are you planning at present to reassess the workings of any such rules and their violation?

Nader's letters were not always addressed to matters of procedure, although they can be read as early reflections of his belief that procedure and structure may be the disease, rather than the symptom, of what he regards as the malaise of government. On May 6, 1968, he wrote to Haddon to urge him to issue a public warning on the dangers of power windows in automobiles:

> These power windows were callously designed to thrust upward with cruel force and have strangled and injured thousands of children and infants. The most elementary engineering remedy could have avoided such vicious window speeds if auto company management cared more for human life and less for the aggressive and powerful performance of these upward-bound glass guillotines. . . . I look forward to positive action by the Bureau no later than May 20th which is more than ample time to issue such an advisory. . . .

On May 16, Haddon replied that the bureau was issuing an advisory warning on power windows to the press and public. A dispatch from United Press International noted that the question had been raised by Nader. Nader added a whole series of other points, often buttressed by letters from the victims of auto crashes or the victims' surviving relatives, about design features he believed to be taking lives and causing injury.

Sometimes Haddon was working, in his methodical fashion, toward a solution, and on more than one occasion he was made to appear, by the timing of a Nader complaint, to be responding to the complaint. He found the situation maddening. Mrs. Broderick, who had moved over from the Labor Department to the highway safety bureau, did not understand Haddon's reaction. "Dr. Haddon," she says, "would have had a perfect setup to get things done. Ralph could have identified public issues, created interest, and the bureau could have acted. I could never understand why Dr. Haddon was so upset when Ralph attacked the bureau—it was all for the cause, after all."

If Nader's public statements were addressed to matters of principle, his private arguments often took the form of a direct personal attack on Haddon. Paul Sitton, who by this time was Secretary Boyd's deputy, remembers that Haddon was much in the focus of Nader's concern. "Ralph would call me up at Commerce and later at Transportation," Sitton says, "and say Bill is not doing this and not doing that. . . . I didn't have time to sit down with Haddon and hash over with him everything he was doing or not doing. . . . It was Haddon's job to handle as best he could. Bill's best was not good enough for Ralph, of course, and I doubt that many people can meet that standard."

"There is," Brenner observes, "one massive weakness in Ralph's approach to the problem—he's addressed himself to the vehicle to the virtual exclusion of the driver and the highway. There's a hell of a lot more to 50,000 yearly dead than just the vehicle. . . . Half our highway deaths occur when the driver is blind drunk." Haddon was among the pioneers of objective research into the drunken driver. His study, made when he was working in Albany, of single-vehicle fatal accidents over an eight-year period in Westchester County, New York, showed that 70 percent of the drivers were either drunk or near drunk at the time of the crash. Nader does not normally deal with phenomena, like drinking, that shift the focus on the auto safety problem away from the vehicle.

Nader sometimes attempted to put pressure on the bureau in ways that Haddon regarded as bordering on the unethical. In 1968, Haddon says, Nader saw on Haddon's desk the schedule for release of a report he had written on the effect of alcohol in highway crashes. Haddon believed that Nader then asked Professor Robert F. Borkenstein of the University of Indiana, an expert in forensic studies, to make a public attack on the report. As Borkenstein recalls it, Nader merely asked him to join in his objection to a draft press release that connected drunkenness and accidents in what both Nader and Borkenstein believed was a dogmatic way.

Nader's third technique, apart from letter writing and publicity, was a penetration of what little secrecy Haddon's bureau tried to maintain. Nader, with eerie frequency, had advance notice of matters that were being considered by the bureau, and many of his letters seemed to be based on an intimate knowledge of the inner workings of Haddon's office. "There were almost witch-hunts," Mrs. Broderick says, "as to who was giving Ralph information. Plenty of stuff was going to him, and of course Ralph was using it in the papers." There is a question as to how much of this purloined material came to Nader as a result of his own initiative, and how much was spontaneously furnished to him by true believers within the bureau. It is a timeworn Washington technique to tip the balance toward one viewpoint in an official deliberation by leaking facts to the press. Mrs. Broderick does not recall that Nader was ever even faintly improper. "He'd ask you a question and if you said, 'I can't answer that,' he would accept that," she says.

Nader had, nevertheless, very reliable sources, and at least one of them, according to a veteran of the bureau, was within Haddon's immediate entourage. "Had Haddon known the extent to which this assistant was dealing with Ralph," says the source, "he would have fired the person on the spot. He could not have understood that this person was never a traitor to the bureau or to the cause of highway safety." Haddon was, in fact, using this same assistant to leak material to outside sources; what seemed treason to some was, to Haddon, judicious use of a willing double agent.

Haddon himself refrained from giving Nader information that might have cleared up what Haddon still regards as grievous public misunderstandings. One case in point is Nader's continuing attack on the 1960–1963 Corvairs; Nader believed that the government had authority to issue public warnings about what he regarded as the car's defects. "It is dismaying," he wrote in a letter to Bridwell on April 24, 1968, "to see the NHSB proceed month after month without making a start in this direction. . . . The question which is beginning to emerge with increasing insistency is whether or not the Bureau is shortly to become an institutionalized delusion whose formal approvals of declared industry preferences and whose widespread inaction in other areas constitute a betrayal of the public trust. Candidly, Mr. Bridwell, would Henry Ford II do it any differently?"

Haddon, on May 14, asked the chief counsel of the Federal Highway Administration for an opinion as to whether the bureau could legally require manufacturers to notify customers of defects in vehicles produced before the passage of the 1966 legislation. Howard A. Heffron, the chief counsel, replied on May 17 that "a respectable legal argument could be made to support Nader's position that the defect notification requirements of the Act reach vehicles manufactured prior to the effective date of the Act. . . ." On June 4, Haddon sent a memorandum to Bridwell, proposing that "we take this to the National Academy of Engineering and request them . . . to appoint a blue ribbon *ad hoc* group which would undertake to answer just as thoroughly and as objectively as possible the questions which have been raised with respect to the early Corvairs." Haddon says that he never received a reply, oral or written, to his memorandum.

On December 1, 1968, Nader, releasing information to *The Washington Post* concerning the failure of brand-name tires to pass government safety standards, was quoted as saying that "Haddon himself does not take the law seriously

enough." Haddon had already preempted nearly all the tire-
testing facilities in the United States, including some of the
Army's at the Detroit Arsenal. He had put pressure on a
number of manufacturers and had given the makers of
Mohawk tires twenty-four hours to announce a recall campaign on tires failing to meet standards, or face public disclosure. Mohawk complied.

Haddon was having his problems, within the Department
of Transportation, in finding approval for a policy of public disclosure. "The minimum level of acceptance," he wrote
in a memorandum on February 5, 1969, "is *no* failures on
the test. . . ." Haddon had evidence, based on the tests, that
the tires of "many companies, including many of the most
prominent in the business," had failed the performance tests.
He argued forcefully for the release to the public of all test
data. On January 30, 1969, in a memorandum to John R.
Jamieson, deputy federal highway administrator, he wrote:

> . . . The Department should permit us to make . . .
> full public disclosure of all supportable data. . . . I
> regard it as clearly contrary to the public interest for
> the data to be withheld from the public. I regard it as
> politically indefensible for the Department to con-
> tinue to withhold the data, as repeated inquiries from
> members of the Congress and press . . . clearly indi-
> cate.

Haddon says that he spent his last day in office in February,
1969, trying, unsuccessfully, to convince the Under Secretary
of Transportation "to favor the public with the specific information as to the extent to which various brands of automobile tires were failing the federal standard." (After resign-
ing, and being replaced by a Nixon appointee at the
beginning of the new administration in 1969, Haddon became president of the Insurance Institute for Highway Safety

in Washington. Under his leadership the Institute, denounced by Nader in 1965 as a handmaiden of the auto industry, has become a fount of scientific data on auto safety. It was Haddon who commissioned the North Carolina study on the Corvair, Haddon who provided Congress with hard information on the fragility of automobile bumpers.)

Haddon's feeling about his experiences with Nader seems to be that he was having enough knives plunged into him from expected directions without being impaled, as he walked by the windows, by the shafts of an archer inside the battlements. Haddon never managed to recruit as many competent people as he wanted, and eventually some of his hard-won supergrade positions were taken away from him by the Civil Service Commission. "I don't blame Bill for not hiring the kind of people Ralph was recommending," Sitton says. "You can't have a bunch of freewheelers—they have to be responsive to the organization."

Haddon thought that Nader misunderstood the bureaucracy; Nader believed that Haddon showed too little of the fire of idealism in his dealings with it. Haddon estimates that for four-fifths of the time he was at the head of the bureau he was subjected to freezes in spending or staff. In 1968, the bureau's budget request was cut 69 percent by Congress. Nader said that Haddon accepted the reduction "without a fight." "Ralph must have known the sources of the problems with which we were faced," Haddon says, "but he nonetheless attacked on those very issues." Haddon's chief problem lay in establishing the authority of his bureau in the face of industry resistance and obstruction from within the government. Nader's attacks upon the bureau's credibility resulted in what Haddon came to regard as a perverse alliance between Nader and the automobile lobby. "Every time Ralph attacked us," Haddon says, "he gave the industry an opportunity to say, 'Look, even *Nader* says the bureau is no good.' " Robert Brenner believes that Nader thought of himself as the bureau's foster parent. Haddon wonders "why Ralph was so intent on smothering the baby in its crib."

In the summer of 1968, Haddon invited Nader to his office to discuss their differences. Haddon told Nader that he believed they were on the same side in 70 percent of the issues. "I asked him," Haddon says, "if it wouldn't be possible to get his help and support for appropriations and personnel and the many other things the lack of which was hurting us badly. Ralph replied, and I quote verbatim, 'The best way to build government is to attack government.' " This explained a lot, Haddon says, but helped nothing.

Nader has no retrospective regret over the approach he took to Haddon and the infant bureau. He thinks he was right on specific issues and on the general proposition that nothing justified any delay whatever in applying the maximum safety standards to automobiles. The realities of bureaucratic inertia and of political timidity on the part of Haddon's superiors did not seem to Nader to be realities. The dead and the injured were his reality, and the unpunished arrogance of the corporations.

They were Haddon's, too; to the extent that an impression was created that this was not so, Haddon will be afflicted for a long time to come with a result that is very like an injury to a crash victim. The political vehicle in which he was riding simply was not designed to withstand the force Nader applied to it. Haddon might say that the collision threatened to destroy the vehicle; Nader wanted it to perform according to standards it could not meet.

However that may be, Nader maintains that Haddon was given fair warning. "He deserved it," Nader says. "I told him very clearly when he went on the job. I said, 'Bill, we've been friends and all, but it's my job to keep an eye on the bureau from my perspective.' That's not his idea of friendship."

6

Information Is Power

I'm an activist. If you're an activist you orchestrate, you
do things that play back to strengthen one another.

RALPH NADER

It is a happy prophet who is chosen by the moment in which
the world is ready to listen to him. Serendipity was missing a
long while from Ralph Nader's life; for years, as Ted Jacobs
says, Nader was regarded as a kook. Neither Nader's message
nor Nader himself changed when he was transformed into a
seer. He just stopped running into the cynics who had
plagued his earlier life. The odds against the transformation
were astronomical. "This town is full of guys," James
Bishop, Jr., of *Newsweek*'s Washington bureau says, "who
wander around with stacks of paper under their arms trying
to see senators or bust into magazine offices. Ralph is one
who got through the guards."

The guards, of course, had been strangled by Abraham Ribicoff and Robert F. Kennedy. Nader was invested, as a re-

sult of the hearings on the General Motors investigation, with what might be called credibility-by-contrast. Those who had tried, as he thought, to destroy him had failed so publicly, and had had their motives so enthusiastically impugned, that all the virtue that they lacked became Nader's. His wolf was shown to be a wolf. The afterimage of that original truth has, with a kind of sorcery, stayed by his side ever since as he has driven new wolves, subspecies after subspecies, out of the vast hiding places of American enterprise and government. He was right the first time, and for the most part he has been assumed to be right since.

Nader does not forget that he was right for a long time before anyone realized it—or, if anyone did realize it, before his information was given any importance. In the threadbare days of his idealism, he made the rounds as much as he ever did afterward, trying to expose his facts to the light. A reporter for *The New York Times*, after Nader had walked in off the street to make an earnest plea for safer cars, told him, "So what else is new? We've known that automobiles were unsafe since about 1900." In Nader's eyes, this man's problem was that he had become jaded. If Nader's career has done nothing else, it has scourged a good many reporters of this quality.

Morton Mintz of *The Washington Post* is an irascible, studious, graying man who is, as a colleague remarks, in a perpetual state of outrage about the injustices of society. According to Mintz, this was not always so. During the early years of his career he was, he says, a conventional reporter. Something in the newspaperman's trade alerts its practitioners to facts while desensitizing them to truth. A police reporter will get the name and age and address of the victim; it is not his job, as it is Nader's vocation, to see apparitions of cruelty and greed hovering over the wreckage of the victim's car. "Public knowledge of accidents and their real causes were not advanced one bit by Morton Mintz," says Mintz.

"When I read Ralph's book I began to understand. I was intrigued by the whole subject of protruding knobs, radio knobs going into kids' skulls."

Long before the publication of his book, Nader began to make friends with a small group of Washington newspapermen who were able to respond to his sort of imagery. These men were not the swashbucklers of the press corps, but the skillful and honest men who wrote the inside pages of their newspapers. Nader had, always, a gift for putting a finger into the wound of discontent. That wound, among reporters in general, is the way their idealism is lacerated by publishers. Every small-town newspaper has its sacred cows—a judge who is a friend of the owner of the paper, an organization that gets more coverage than it deserves because the editor's wife is a member. On big papers and magazines similar considerations apply, depending on the interests of the publisher: liberal papers like *The Washington Post* do not come down very hard on people like Senator Fulbright, whatever his civil rights record may be; conservative ones like *The Chicago Tribune* do not send investigative reporters on the trail of the FBI.

Reporters don't like to dismember the truth in this way, but by and large they accommodate to the practice. For example, very little of the private disgust that a majority of political reporters felt toward President Eisenhower leaked into their copy. This had something to do with the sensibilities of their readers. Eisenhower was unassailable because of his popularity, which extended even to the subscribers of the more liberal newspapers. Richard Nixon, when he attempted to succeed Eisenhower in 1960, was not unassailable, and a case could be made that some of the visceral hostility he aroused in the working press stemmed from its self-disgust over the way it had pandered to Eisenhower. Mixed up in the reaction to Nixon, of course, were other matters, such as memories of the Alger Hiss case and his Senate campaign against Helen Gahagan Douglas—and, of course, Nixon's manner and vocabulary as preserved in the amber of the Checkers speech.

Working reporters have always practiced a kind of ideological retaliation against their publishers. They create sacred cows of their own, and while it would not be fair to say they alter facts to protect their heroes, they are more understanding of the shortcomings of these figures than they are of those less attractive to them. It is interesting to speculate what the coverage of Richard Nixon would have been if he had run for the presidency in 1960 partly on the basis of a "missile gap" that did not exist, and if, after his election, he had permitted himself to be insulted by Khrushchev at Vienna, sanctioned the invasion of Cuba by mercenaries, countenanced the construction of the Berlin Wall, begun the American commitment for combat in Vietnam, and failed to gain passage of any significant legislation through a Congress dominated by Republicans. It is a safe assumption that he would have passed through this series of events with more scars on his image than were inflicted by the press on John F. Kennedy.

From the instant of his birth as a public figure, Ralph Nader enjoyed a great measure of tolerance from the press. No Kennedy was ever held in higher regard or quoted more freely. Nader was perceived by reporters to be what in fact he was, the enemy of their enemies. He was, moreover, untainted by politics or even by any of the more understandable forms of political ambition. Nader has described himself as a noninstitutional source, meaning that the information he provides to the press is uncontaminated by the interest of any group except the public. He was virtually the first such source in our history, so in addition to his accuracy and his idealism, he had novelty going for him. The Ribicoff hearings made his motives so plain, and his honesty so palpable, that reporters were largely freed from the necessity of viewing him, as they train themselves to view traditional sources, with suspicion.

Mintz, who has written more newspaper copy about Nader than has any other reporter, speaks very plainly about the satisfactions of covering his activities. "This kind of news—and it is news," Mintz says, "is not pamphleteering, not crusading or advocacy. It's reporting matters of importance. Ralph's campaigns let you feel that there is some relationship between doing your job and the benefits flowing therefrom. Most reporters should be proud to do this. Ralph feels it's important and I feel he's right." Mintz probably would have become the tough investigative reporter that he is even in the absence of a Ralph Nader. For others, Nader's gift for the exposé filled a gap; reporting him became a sort of muckraking by proxy.

In Nader's handling of the press there was an element that in a more frivolous man might have been called flattery. This did not take the form it takes with certain politicians, who solemnize newspapermen by asking their private advice on national policy. Rather, Nader chose, in a subtle way, to include reporters in the secrecy, the strategy, and even the hardship of his cause. He made participants of them. Journalism is a passive, not to say a parasitic trade, but many reporters are frustrated activists. Nader made insiders of them by taking them into his confidence, not so much about his purposes as by giving them access to his person.

The press, through accurate reporting, pictured him as elusive, private, inaccessible. His address and his phone number were known to be secret. To chosen reporters, Nader gave both; they guarded them as zealously as members of an underground movement protect their passwords. Where the normal source would call a reporter during working hours for a quick conversation, Nader would call at midnight, or after, for a long talk that would convey his mood toward an issue as clearly as it communicated the information he wanted to deliver. A telephone that rings in a bedroom late at night assumes an importance the same instrument, ringing at noon on a desk in a babbling city room, does not have. The hour at which Nader called gave weight to his message; he may not have planned it that way, because he has always lived at night, but the effect was present.

As Nader has been transformed, partly by his publicity, from a lone operator into what Mintz calls a conglomerate, his midnight calls to reporters have dwindled. Newsmen who used to hear from him several times a week may now wait months without a call. This has produced surprisingly little resentment in the reporters, and even a kind of relief in some of them. In at least one household, the absence of telephone calls has ended the husband's unavailing efforts to convince his wife that Nader's lack of manners is unimportant. "I don't hate him, really," says Caroline Bishop, wife of the *Newsweek* correspondent. "It's just that telephone manner of his. Never saying who's calling. The middle of the night! And always, 'Is this the house of Jim Bishop?' As if I don't know who that voice belongs to."

None of these psychological factors would have meant much, of course, if Nader had not had something newsworthy to say. Nader's natural fascination with information for its own sake is akin to a reporter's insatiable curiosity. His ability to judge which information will arouse curiosity in others is a higher form of the talent that is called in reporters a nose for news. Nader was a reporter's dream because he not only had accurate, and sometimes sensational, information, but he knew how to present it to a newsman in a way that often saved the reporter from having to do much work. The facts were straight, the quotes were vivid, and the substance was a declaration of conscience. "Here was this incredible man," as Mintz recalls, "generating all these stories and contributing to the desperately needed education of the newspapers. . . . These stories provide light. I wish that editors could understand how important this stuff is, compared to the columns and columns of page one shit we run on what the Secretary of State says when he gets off an airplane."

In the early years of his public career, Nader formed something resembling friendship with a number of reporters. These relationships were based on the reporter's respect for Nader and his work, but the reporter got an echo: Nader has a genuine sympathy for journalists, so long as they stick to the issues. It has been an unspoken but clearly understood part of his relations with reporters that his privacy could never be violated; there were no intimate little pieces in the Sunday papers about his favorite recipes, no flash of his restless humor to lighten a news story.

And, considering the way Nader ripped the skin off his targets, there was very little adverse comment about him in the form of commentary from people who did not like or agree with him. The hundreds of clippings in the morgues of the Washington newspapers leave an impression that no one has ever been blessed with more temperate enemies than Ralph Nader. Either the objects of his attacks could not be reached for comment, or they were remarkably undisturbed by the charges leveled at them. In a town where the public quarrels of noted figures are spiced with a sense of sly gamesmanship, Nader's opponents may have realized, almost as soon the reporters did, that he was dead serious.

A reporter who has had a close relationship with Nader throughout his Washington career still vividly remembers their first lunch together. Before the soup was cool, Nader simply blew away his companion's professional cynicism. "Ralph and I, I discovered very soon, agreed on many things," the reporter says. "I was the only reporter who stayed with the Roberts hearings [on auto safety in 1956], and Ralph was the only person I'd met who had read the hearings and, I felt, really understood the issues. . . . It was natural to think that there should be someone or something to represent the public." The reporter had no doubt that Ralph Nader would soon be filling that role. When Nader explained that he could not afford to buy an extra copy of the reporter's publication, for clipping purposes, or to pay three dollars for the government reports that came to the reporter free, his companion offered to save these things for him. There is still, in the reporter's office, a straight chair piled high with press releases, documents, and clippings; it is known as "Ralph's chair." Every few days Nader, no longer poor but still thrifty, sends someone around to pick up the material.

Any expectation that Nader would be a one-issue evangelist vanished very soon after he gained the public platform. Just before Christmas, 1966, in a speech before the National Press Club, Nader stated a theme that was to run through much of what he subsequently said and did. "Unless the challenge of corporate reform is undertaken," he said, "this country will be headed toward a choice between a corporate state or a socialist state. Present indications are that the winner will be a corporate state."

Through most of 1966 and 1967, Nader remained primarily a critic of the automobile and its makers. Despite Haddon's belief that he did not help the Highway Safety Bureau as much as he might have done, Nader did deliver a tart attack on the House Appropriations Committee when it cut the bureau's budget for 1967. "Something is basically wrong with the committee's sense of proportion," he said, "when it can appropriate $197 million for a dubious SST project and then slash by 69 percent, down to forty-one million dollars, the requested budget to do something about the millions of Americans killed or injured on the highways." [1] A few weeks later, he criticized the Federal Highway Administration for

1. Quotations are from *The Washington Post* unless otherwise identified.

accepting the budget cut without a fight and pointed out that Haddon's bureau had failed to supply Congress with over-due reports on alcoholism, used-car safety, safety research, and the cost of safety; the bureau, he said, had shirked its responsibilities for the development of an experimental safety car, among other matters.

In 1967, Nader began publicly to turn his attention to sub-jects other than the automobile, showing the first signs of becoming the universal critic of society he is now acknowl-edged to be. He fired the opening guns of campaigns that would lead to legislation regulating the dangers of radiation, gas pipelines, and the meat industry. He attacked the textile industry for conditions that, he said, led to a high incidence of byssinosis, or brown lung, among workers. In a speech at the Shoreham Hotel on November 2, President Johnson in-dicated his sympathy for Nader's sense of the national priori-ties. On the following January 7, Nader accused the auto industry of maneuvering the President into a tacit endorsement of an "outrageous" increase in new car prices. On New Year's Day, Drew Pearson and Jack Anderson sin-gled out Nader as one who had "worked hard to make de-mocracy live . . . all the while paying his own way and living in a spartan, twenty-dollar-a-week room."

On January 29, 1968, at an informal lunch for government information officers, he said that neither the press nor the government had worked hard enough to make the new free-dom of information law work. (The freedom of information law, which went into effect on July 4, 1967, requires govern-ment agencies to release most information in their files un-less it bears on national security.) Some publications, he added, apparently did not want to alienate certain agencies from which they got preferential treatment. In March, he called on Secretary of the Interior Stewart L. Udall to "end the cruel depletion of human beings in the coal mines." The Bureau of Mines, he said, "displayed little more than lassitude toward the demands of mine health and safety conditions," despite the fact that "roughly 20 percent of all coal miners have coal pneumoconiosis, which begins with breathlessness and ends with death." Udall conceded, in a letter to Nader, that the Bureau of Mines had been lax in protecting the health of coal miners, but said he was seeking stronger legislation.

In April, he attacked the processing and packing methods of the fish industry. In May, he said that Negroes were given a higher dose of radiation in hospital X rays out of a folkloric belief that the bones and skins of black people are harder to penetrate. A spokesman for the American College of Radiologists accused Nader of sensationalism and "a completely distorted approach." A couple of days later, Mintz wrote a story confirming that higher X-ray dosages for Negroes had been recommended by a leading textbook on radiology and by the General Electric Company, the largest manufacturer of X-ray equipment; neither subscribed to the theory any longer.

Testifying before the Senate Small Business Subcommittee, Nader said there were solid legal and economic reasons for breaking up General Motors: "The only obstacle is political. . . . [With 51 percent of the market] GM passes the test of unreasonable market power." He added that the "Byzantine-like secrecy" of corporations produced by a lack of genuine competition concealed such facts as that "the direct and indirect labor costs of a medium-price car do not exceed three hundred dollars." Styling changes, he charged, cost the consumer at least four hundred dollars.

He attacked the Rolls-Royce for having unsafe door catches and was treated with dignified silence from England. He told the Senate Public Works Committee that "I think it is hard to find a more dangerous car than the Volkswagen"; the German car, he said, had a defective fuel tank, weak latches, and a dangerous steering column, combined with fading brakes, poor visibility, and poor resistance to the force of collisions. "We don't have any evidence that the Volkswagen gets into any more accidents than any other car," replied Arthur R. Railton, public relations vice-president for Volkswagen of America, Inc. Nader, who refuses to ride in Volkswagens, did not believe this answer went to the substance of his charge. Small cars in general, he said elsewhere, have a crash resistance "reminiscent of Japanese lanterns."

The number of hospital patients electrocuted annually by faulty hospital equipment, Nader charged in early 1969, averaged twelve hundred, or "five times the death toll from riots in all our cities in the last three years." Dr. Carl W. Walter of the Harvard Medical School, identified a few days later as the source of Nader's precise figures, said that he believed that many electrocutions were caused by inexperienced hospital personnel trying to hook up incompatible equipment, causing surges of current. "Who's to prove," Dr. Walter asked, "that electricity did not cause the heart stoppages?"

On December 9, 1969, Nader petitioned the Federal Aviation Agency to ban smoking on all flights. On December 21, he denounced the railroads for their "repulsive corporate practice" of dumping, according to Nader's estimate, "two hundred million pounds of human excrement" on the tracks every year. Public health officials, he said, had been "intimidated by the Association of American Railroads, which is intent on perpetuating the freedom of enterprise to defecate on open land and in crowded stations." The FAA never banned smoking on airplanes, but on June 12, 1971, the Food and Drug Administration ruled that passenger trains must stop discharging sewage on the tracks by July 1, 1972; all other trains will fall under the same ban on January 1, 1975.

The newspaper files reveal relatively little in the way of response to Nader's attacks. Henry Ford II, speaking at the opening of a stamping plant in Woodhaven, Michigan, on April 7, 1966, departed from his prepared text to deal with

Nader. "Frankly, I don't think he knows much about automobiles," Ford was quoted as saying in *The Wall Street
Journal*. "He can read statistics . . . and he can write books,
but I don't think he knows anything about engineering
safety in automobiles. . . . You will agree that we are being
attacked on all sides and we feel these attacks are unwar-
ranted. Naturally, when fifty thousand people are killed on
the roads of the United States this is a bad situation. On the
other hand, to blame it solely on the automobile is unfair."
George M. Romney, then governor of Michigan, said after
Ford's speech that the death rate would be higher if it were
not for Detroit's "leadership in all areas of auto safety."
Charles G. Mortimer, chairman of the executive committee
of the General Foods Corporation, speaking before a meeting of the Business Council in Hot Springs, Virginia, said the
"auto safety flap" was an example of unnecessary undermin-
ing of consumer confidence. He blamed Nader for a drop in
auto sales and speculated that he had made "a personal gain
from the flap [that] will undoubtedly be appreciable."

In the best of circumstances it would have been difficult to
answer Nader's barrage of charges, for the reason that they
were mostly true. An occasional voice was raised in Detroit
or elsewhere to protest that they might not always be the
whole truth, but it does little good to protest that a car is a
complex machine, with fifteen thousand separate parts, when
Nader is saying that the parts that fail cause death. The Association of American Railroads could hardly call a press conference to protest that trains dumped only *one* hundred million pounds of human excrement on the tracks each year.

One corporation executive has the sort of admiration for
Nader, he says, that might be expected in a smart infantry
general whose headquarters have been hit by the Vietcong.
"I just admire the audacity of the son of a bitch," he says.
"Nader can turn on a dime. At Senate hearings he's drinking
it all in when we testify. As soon as it's over—over to the

press table! I can't do that because I haven't got the authority and I haven't got all the facts. He doesn't need all the
facts. So he ends up with the headlines, and four days later
we get three inches on page fifty-eight." Aled P. Davies, vice-
president of the American Meat Institute, who represented
his industry in the battle that led to passage of the Wholesome Meat Act of 1967, describes the general problem: "I used
to get calls—can't you do something about this SOB? No.
He's as clean as a hound's tooth. There's no point in taking him on when he's right. What's fair and not fair? There
was enough truth in what he said to make a damn good
case."

To the natural verisimilitude of his information, Nader
added some singular techniques for dealing with the press.
The first of these involved timing. Nader almost always gives
his material to reporters on a Friday night or a Saturday; he
has been known to hold a press conference on Sunday. Mintz
explains why such events are uniformly well attended. "I
didn't know why I was going down to the Dupont Plaza on
a Sunday morning," he said after one such press conference.
"But if Ralph says something is a good story you have to believe him on the basis of his track record. Not many public
figures apart from the President can command this kind of
response." It is very difficult, on a weekend, to find government officials, much less corporation executives. The result
often is that Nader's story will liven up a Saturday or Sunday
edition, in which there is usually a scarcity of breaking news,
without comment or contradiction from the other side of the
controversy.

John D. Morris, of *The New York Times,* remembers an
occasion in February, 1969, on which Nader dropped off a
story in the middle of a housewarming party in the new
offices of the *Times*'s Washington Bureau. In a letter to Senator Warren G. Magnuson, Nader charged the Federal Trade
Commission with slipshod investigation of the market in

used Volkswagens, which were being reconditioned in Germany and sold here as new cars. Because of the lateness of the hour, Morris was unable to reach officials of the FTC for comment, and Nader's version ran in the *Times*'s first edition. Subsequent checking with FTC officials disclosed that they had abandoned the investigation of a dealer in the South because the man had gone out of business, and that there was a plausible explanation for the delay in other action. "Ralph's story made it sound like it was a national scandal," says Morris, "and the truth of the matter was that it really involved just one or two cases." Morris adds, "I've never known Nader deliberately to say anything that isn't true, but he gets a little careless with his facts sometimes and he should be checked out. . . . He's liable to float something just to see if it's true."

In the case of the FTC action on reconditioned Volkswagens, Nader made no retreat when his charge turned out to be exaggerated. Michael J. Vitale, an FTC lawyer who was named by Nader as having abandoned the investigation, still thinks that he is owed an apology. Vitale says he had tracked one dealer through Virginia, North Carolina, and California in an effort to prosecute him before his superiors decided there was insufficient evidence to proceed: when the man closed his business, the evidence vanished. Vitale maintains that Nader's charges, all the more embarrassing because they were made in a letter to Senator Magnuson, were "inaccurate and untrue." Nader, he says, never attempted to speak to him or to the other lawyer involved in the case in order to get their version of the facts. "You pick up *The New York Times*," Vitale says, "and it makes you look like you're involved in some kind of a swindle. People write in and say I should be fired. How am I supposed to defend myself against that? One of his young people came in here recently and I related the incident to her. I said Nader owed me an apology and if he had any class or character he'd make it. I haven't heard from him yet." The charge that Vitale had closed the investigation was repeated in the report on the FTC by the first group of Nader's Raiders later in 1969.

Nader's second technique is the key to his extraordinary success as a propagandist. He takes care always to link his accusations to a call for corrective action. He does not simply declare that the railroads are fouling the tracks; he says so in a letter to the Secretary of Health, Education, and Welfare, who is put on notice that the government had better forbid the practice. He does not merely point out that a gas pipeline may explode beneath a housing development; he demands, in testimony before a Senate committee, that legislation be enacted to forestall the disaster. The National Highway Safety Bureau and William Haddon might not have been frog-marched through the media if Nader had merely issued his condemnations into free air; instead, his charges were made in official letters to Haddon and in prepared testimony before congressional committees. These communications were, however, almost superfluous. Nader's signals are directed upon his targets primarily because they bounce off and show up on the radar screens that are the media. By combining an exposé with a demand for reform within the system, Nader invests his objectives with moral authority. The method is a subtle mime of the traditional techniques of Presidents and powerful congressmen, who are always calling upon each other to repair omissions in the public weal. Nader's demands take on an added force because it is understood that he, unlike Presidents or representatives, who depend for their power upon votes, will not settle for less than he says he wants.

In his methods, Nader displays a shrewd understanding of how the press works. Information is power, but scandal is news. Newspapers do not report pure information. They report the actions of men and consistently report the actions of colorful men. The intense personalization of Nader's issues

did not, for a long time, involve the invasion of privacy that
most public figures more or less gladly accept. The Nader
who stalks through the proscenium of events was, until recently, the only Nader whom the press described. The fact
that little was known of him as a private person contributed
to the legend of the public figure. The lonely scholar in the
spartan room remained offstage when the fearless witness approached the microphones on Capitol Hill.

Even now, when Nader appears in public in a role that he
might call nonfunctional—attending the annual dinner of
the White House correspondents or appearing at a retirement party for Chalmers M. Roberts of *The Washington
Post*—the act has the flavor of transubstantiation. When, in
1969, Nader was given *The New Republic*'s first Public Defender of the Year Award, uncertainty as to whether he
would be on hand to accept it somehow added to the conviction that he deserved the honor. "He's the only guy I know
in whose honor you can hold a banquet and you don't know
whether or not he'll be there," *The New Republic* publisher, Robert J. Myers, said happily. Ted Jacobs remarked
to a passing reporter that Nader was not at all happy about
being praised in public. As Nader accepted the silver trophy
bowl, he said, "I'm only doing what I should be doing, and I
shouldn't get an award for it." Few would doubt that these
were Nader's real sentiments, but being able to deliver a line
like that to a room full of experienced Washingtonians requires a reckless purity of ego for which almost no one else
would have been rewarded with sympathetic applause.

Nader's long association with a group of reporters and
other admirers who feel so strongly the resonances of his
character did not prepare him for the writers from national
magazines who have begun to describe him and his work.
The magazine article, a factual narrative that uses some of
the techniques of fiction, attempts to depict its subject as a
rounded character, moving through events. It is standard

practice to seek out the enemies as well as the friends of the subject of a profile, and to quote them. The result can be something like a preview of Judgment Day in which the subject sees revealed in print the sort of things that allies as well as adversaries say about him, though not necessarily to him. This, for Nader, has been an uncomfortable development. He has always been sensitive to criticism. Having loaned his person to the issues, he feels that an attack upon him is an attack upon the cause. Others feel the same. "I don't want to be associated with any negative stuff about Ralph Nader," Morris says. A staffer for one of the newsmagazines, after reading an article containing a few lines critical of Nader, remarked with an air of worry, "We have to watch that kind of stuff—it sets back the cause."

"Ralph is a worrier," Ted Jacobs observes. "I don't think he expects everyone to have wholehearted approval of him and what he does, but I'm sure he'd like it. I think he worries unduly about trivial criticisms. I used to tell him, when he'd dwell on something trivial, to forget it—that's yesterday and it's the price you pay for being a public figure." Paul Sitton has another view. "Ralph has really become something of a matinee idol," he says. "He's being taken in by the blandishments of the public at large while he lambastes Establishment figures for being taken in by the blandishments of the special-interest groups. Ralph is more human than he thinks."

Nader says that he is sensitive only to certain kinds of criticism. "I hope I always am," he adds. "I don't get so mad over ideological things. What I do get angry about is people imputing very sensitive things that I was never asked about, putting words in my mouth. . . . To say that all I'm interested in is power, that's really outrageous. You don't say that to anybody who has no economic base and no political base. . . . [If] he becomes powerful or persuasive it's a pretty good bet that it's because of his case, because he's up against all those odds, the system. The same sensitivity to that kind of criticism makes me never jaded when I see what I think are abuses. . . ."

Nader does not seem to mind rough treatment in television interviews. In Cleveland, after a series of peppery questions ("How much are you getting out of this?") from a local TV interviewer named Ann Medina, Nader leaned back when the cameras were switched off and gave her a warm smile. "You're very good," he said. "You have just the right sting." Nader has understandable confidence that he can defend himself in any face-to-face confrontation. "It's a facet of his nature," as Joe Page says, "always to have a comeback and to have the last word." The magazine, which is not instantaneous like television and not even daily like the newspaper, deprives him of the last word.

After the fact, Nader is likely to let his displeasure be known. When a profile in *Fortune* devoted space to the counterarguments of business figures, Nader called the magazine and offered to write a rebuttal. *Fortune*'s editors agreed, but Nader never delivered the copy. Nader was outraged by a line in the *Fortune* piece, which was written by Richard Armstrong, suggesting that "at the time [of the Gillen investigation] Nader was convinced that G.M. planned to have him bumped off." Nader says he never believed any such thing, and he thought that Armstrong had agreed to remove the material. "He knew it was wrong," Nader says. "That's journalistic dishonesty. It's vicious. . . . He knew what purpose it would serve." Armstrong was astonished by Nader's anger over what he, Armstrong, regarded as a favorable article. He believes that the statement of Nader's fears, which was derived from an interview with a close friend, is accurate, and he has no recollection of agreeing to remove it from his article. If Nader is shown an advance copy of an article about him, he will sometimes contact the people who are quoted to determine if they meant what they said—or if they said it at all. One man, quoted by the author in a magazine profile, was told by one of Nader's associates that he had been "misquoted" and was urged to call to correct the mistake. When the statement was read back to him he said, "That's what I said."

This sort of activity can have an inhibiting effect on those who value Nader's goodwill. A Senate aide, interviewed by a magazine writer, called the writer in some anxiety to ask whether he was the anonymous Senate aide to whom a mildly unflattering remark was attributed. He was relieved to learn that he was not, so that he might reassure Nader. Anonymous quotations, a traditional device to protect the identity of sources who might embarrass their employers by frank talk, are anathema to Nader. He goes to some lengths to penetrate such disguises, though he defends the right of the men behind them to free speech. "There are a lot of quotes that come from these people in *Fortune*-type magazines," Nader says, "where the whole series of quotes are 'a Senate aide,' 'a legislative expert,' 'a Labor Department researcher.' I've got a pretty good idea where some of that comes from. I don't have any right to retort. Why the hell shouldn't they say what they think?" Nader, in his own view, is merely reserving the right to tell his critics when they are wrong. Whether they are sinister as well is a matter for their own conscience, and for the judgment of the public.

7

Without Sleep or Pleasure

Ralph is a star to every wandering bark.
                                  RICHARD FALKNOR

"I think the reason Ralph and I have remained friends for such a long time," one man says, "is that I have never tried to approach any part of him which he considers private." As an adolescent, Nader's reading ran to historical novels about Alexander the Great, Genghis Khan, and the silent woodsmen of Zane Grey—all of them bearers of secrets, all of them alone at the center of nature. As a man, he has driven the mystical out of his life; had he been born with anything in his fist he would have chosen, not Genghis's clot of blood like a ruby, but a spool of computer tape. He dislikes any descent below the surface of behavior, his own or anyone else's. Men are what they do. There is nothing about himself that cannot be explained by what he does in full view of the world. The rest is unimportant.

To his friends, Nader is a parlor game, pieced together out of anecdotes. Their recollections of him, and their speculations, are lit by baffled laughter. He has a unity of personality seldom found except in children or in historical figures. "I keep thinking," one of his associates says, "there must be something else. Part of the fascination of the man is that he reveals nothing while convincing you that he is confiding everything." What little is known of him even by his friends is derived from a sort of archaeology. They are alert, in the dust of his public life, for fragments; the shape of his personality is construed from the enigma of a marble limb or the puzzle of a worn inscription.

Nader's clandestine methods do not make comprehension easier. He is the chief of intelligence for the dumb multitude, and he uses most of the methods of a real spy. His network of operatives—senators and congressmen, editors and reporters, bureaucrats and legislative aides, students and corporate executives—is very like the sort of apparatus a CIA station chief would try to establish in an adversary nation. He keeps his movements secret and his sources ignorant of one another. He communicates with his apparat through a system of cutouts (e.g., a suburban housewife who receives some of his sensitive calls on her home telephone) and deaddrops (e.g., the newsstand of the National Press Building). On the telephone, and even in his own rooms, he speaks in ellipses, to defeat hidden microphones. "I've picked it up from Ralph," says one of his young lawyers, Mark Green. "He'll say, 'That memorandum, the one yesterday—you know.' And I'll reply, 'Yeah, that memorandum.' Our eyes will sort of pass the secret across the table . . . it's like ESP, in case there are bugs. Sometimes I think of myself as a detective, the FBI or the CIA, moving around like a secret agent. That's Ralph, of course."

"I always have the feeling," a Senate ally says, "that there are ninety-nine Ralph Naders, and which one do I know?"

Another friend, a middle-aged matron who is regarded as one of his few confidants, can say, "I don't know whether Ralph trusts me." Ted Jacobs, less mystified, thinks that Nader's reaction in a given situation is absolutely predictable. "The best way to explain his actions is to think about what is the most rational path to take," Jacobs says. "That's usually it."

For a man who can become, as Jacobs says, emotionally and physically shaken over an injustice, Nader goes about his life in a curiously bloodless way. He thinks of catastrophes in terms of their prevention. When the earthquake struck Los Angeles, he called Jacobs to read him the newspaper account of the disaster. What moved him, on the surface, was the stupidity, not the suffering. "It doesn't need to happen," he cried. "They know how to predict these things. *Why don't the fools use their knowledge?*" He does not mention victims except as a product of the phenomena that engage his interest. His view of the world is a well-lighted, black and white photograph. "There is," he says, "a technological solution to everything."

Nader explains, "I've always looked at challenge as an endless engineering science. It can be systematized. The way a scientist or an engineer looks at his work, that's the way I look at mine." Others insist on misunderstanding him, and some of the irritation he feels over the published comments of his acquaintances must stem from his frustration over not being able to make himself plain by being straightforward. Because he does not seek opinions in private, he is assailed by them in public. He is annoyed by the very idea that the reactions of his associates should be thought important. "You're probably hearing things that I absolutely never hear," he told the author. "Not only do they never tell me, I never give the occasion. . . . I say, What do we do next? If they have thoughts about me, fine, they're going to express them one way or another, or stay or leave." Unlike Alexan-

der, he is not going to humor his army by permitting it to
make him a god.

It is ironic that one who believes so profoundly in technique should be assigned qualities that are spiritual. He is a
terminologist who is persistently mistaken for a poet. A
congressional aide named Richard Falknor says, "Ralph's
great strength is his spiritual quality. He moves around town
like some fifteenth-century Franciscan, compelling men to
act for the good." For Paul Sitton, he evokes Savonarola.

This image of Nader as a monk is natural enough when
applied to a man who has so much to say about vocation and
so little to do with women. No aspect of his character is so
mystifying to others. Friends of his mother worry for her that
her son has presented her with no grandchildren. "All this
energy of Ralph's," says one of his close associates, "is based
on sublimated sexual energy." A female friend says, "When
I first knew Ralph I thought he was comfortable with me because I was a perfectly safe married woman with small children. I think he feels threatened by young girls." Nader is a
handsome man, and one with an aura. No one can watch the
faces of young women in an audience while he is speaking
and be unaware that some of them are moved by instinct. If
Nader notices, he is careful to give no sign, and if girls approach him at the end of his speech he indicates his distance
in a manner that can only be described as arctic.

Nader's coldness to strange women undoubtedly has something to do with his belief, going back to the General Motors
investigation in 1966, that he has reason to be wary. It is not
his usual attitude toward girls. In the company of women he
knows, or with whom he deals professionally, he has a very
different air. There is about him no trace of the male chau-
vinist. He treats women, even beautiful women, exactly as
he treats men—without condescension, and in language
directed exclusively to the mind. Their gender, to Nader, is
not another country. Nothing in his manner draws attention

to the fact of sexual difference. "He'd never call you 'dear' or 'honey' or even 'miss,'" says one young woman. "I always think that he is silently calling me 'Citizen.' It's refreshing but a little uncanny." (Nader is not unaware of the plight of women in society, and he doesn't think that the Women's Liberation movement is likely to relieve it. "There's a tiny militant majority, about ten people in the East, that controls the grapevine for everyone," he says. "I could have turned this around. I'm just waiting for the time. [My] basic message is: Who are you to tell the oppressors that they have no right unilaterally to liberate their victims? *Who are you?* The presumption, the arrogance, of these so-called militants, looking over the scene of desolation and alienation that they call women, and then to say only we—all ten of us—only we are going to do something about it!")

A friend has noticed that Nader sometimes transfers his own sexual reactions to him. "If we're walking down the street," he says, "and a great girl goes by, Ralph really looks— but then he says, 'I caught *you* looking at that.'" His speech to outsiders is remarkably free of obscenity, but he is a secret swearer. "Off the record," says the same friend, "he says 'fuck' in private *all the time*." Of a lovely dark girl who worked on one of his summer projects, Nader once said with admiration, "She's really pretty." A friend says he replied, "'Ralph, she looks just like you.' And he almost blushed— I'd caught him unawares."

To Nader, there is nothing puzzling about his celibacy. It is a matter of priorities, a rational choice. "Mostly it's realism," he says of his unmarried state. "What wife wants never to see her husband? It's natural to want the man around to help, to share emotions. I couldn't do that and go on with what I'm doing." A close friend, merrier than most about Nader's eccentricities, believes that a room in the future has been reserved for connubial activity. "I think," he says, "that one day—probably already marked on Ralph's mental calendar—he will select some nice Lebanese girl and procreate. When he does, he'll devote the same zeal and attention to detail to being a husband and father as he did to General Motors. It should be quite an experience for the wife and kids."

To go on with what he is doing, Nader works twenty hours a day. This leaves him four hours for sleep, beginning just before dawn. Occasionally he will sleep the clock around to restore himself. "He was working on this," says a friend, "when he was in basic training, developing these tremendous powers of concentration, the ability to go without sleep or pleasure. No doubt he was equipped in childhood with his absolute dedication and his absolute incorruptibility." In this schedule, and in the devotional style of his work, there is a whiff of sackcloth and ashes. "He is always," a woman friend observes, "wearing a hair shirt." Perhaps he does achieve, in the speed-reading of documents, something similar to what the devout derive from prayer.

Nader has no time for such fanciful formulations. "They simply don't understand," he says. "Americans understand the concept of challenge in athletics, on the battlefield, in economic competition. You wouldn't ask an Olympic swimmer or a chess player why he works twenty hours a day. They don't understand why I do it because we haven't a tradition which explains me. Someday I think we will have."

Nader knows what the alternatives are. Riding through the Virginia countryside with one of his young associates, he looked back for an instant on the options that fame opened to him. "I could have gone to Hollywood," Nader told his companion, "and married a starlet and gotten fat and talked about what I used to do." It was never a temptation. Nader says that if he had accepted all the honorary degrees which universities and colleges have offered him, he would now have more than eighty—several more than the current world record holder. He has declined all but five. Unearned doctorates are nonfunctional.

The world of celebrities is very remote to Nader. In Los Angeles, he was introduced to Jack Lemmon, the actor, who identified himself as one of Nader's admirers. Nader did not know who he was. He returns from trips with fragments of experience that astonish him. "Ralph got off a plane and told me, 'Hey, these guys got on the plane *and everyone knew who they were!*'" recalls Donald Ross, one of the young lawyers associated with Nader. "I said, 'Who were they, Ralph?' . . . 'The Philadelphia 76ers!' My God, these ten seven-foot black guys get on an airplane—who else would they be? But Ralph was astonished. . . . He said, 'Pro basketball is a big sport now—did you know that? I sat next to Jumping Jim Washington and talked to him about consumer exploitation and environmental factors in the ghetto, and he was really excited and wants to do something.'" Afterward, Nader began to scan the sports pages. "I see Jumping Jim pumped in twenty-four points last night," he'd tell Ross. The point of the story, in Ross's view, is that Nader immediately translated his chance meeting with the athlete into an opportunity to work on the problems of the ghetto.

The tendency to turn Nader into a celebrity seems to him not merely distasteful but illogical. It interferes with what he is trying to do and corrupts the cause. He is not certain that this is accidental. "The government points to Lone Ranger efforts," he says, "and solaces the people with rhetoric: 'Look what Ralph Nader has done all alone! What do you mean this isn't a free country?'" He believes that appeals to his vanity cannot succeed. "I have none," he explains. "I want the focus to be on the issue, not the person. The Hollywood syndrome is not going to solve the problems of this society. . . . People come up to me and ask for *autographs*. It's come to that. I say, 'What is this asking for an autograph? You should be asking what you can do.' "

Nader has difficulty understanding how any activity apart from work can have meaning. When Jacobs and his wife took a summer house at the beach, Nader asked with genuine curiosity what they did when they went there. "Oh, we lie on the beach, we read the papers, we go for walks, we have lunch on the porch," Jacobs replied. Nader said, "That takes *all weekend*?" His feelings about some of his student volunteers are mixed. "Many of them have a low tolerance for sacrifice, for economic and time discomfort," he observes. "Now we've got the gentlemen reformers. They want heart-warming bull sessions and the two-day weekend. I remember one guy involved in a merger fight who went to the beach for two days right in the middle of it. I said, 'Do you think your adversary, the president of the corporation, is taking two days off to swim? He's up all night, and you should be, too.' " Nader's attitudes are felt by those who work with him. "You get the feeling around here," one former Nader's Raider says, "that if you go to a movie you're a sellout." David Zwick, a former Raider who has become a permanent Nader associate, remembers an occasion when the heating system broke down in a building in which he and some other students were working on a report. It was a cold autumn night, and the youngsters gathered in one room for warmth. They were sitting on the floor, silently working over their documents, when Nader dropped in at three o'clock in the morning. "As Ralph looked over this scene of dedication and discomfort," Zwick says, "you could just see the glow come over him."

Until 1961, Nader smoked fifteen cigarettes a day. Now he uses no tobacco at all. He has never drunk anything stronger than an occasional glass of wine, or an even rarer aperitif. He drinks no coffee or soda pop, eats no sugar except in pastry.

He has a sweet tooth, and retains the enormous appetite he had in college. In a restaurant, he will stop a companion who declines the baked potato, and eat it himself. He is always happy to have an extra dessert if he is accompanied by someone who does not eat it. "I hate waste," Nader says. He loses few opportunities to agitate against American eating habits. Last spring, in a Holiday Inn on the outskirts of Minneapolis, he brandished a sugar bowl at a hapless waitress. "Sugar has absolutely no food value, let me tell you something," he told her. "Do you eat sugar?" The waitress confessed that she did, and fled. Nader ordered a steak, using its full flowery name as printed on the menu. He sent it back because it was too rare. "The grand old tradition in restaurants of sending the meal back needs to be resurrected," he has declared elsewhere.

When he visited Japan in 1971, Nader ate nothing at a banquet organized by his hosts. The menu featured many variations of Japan's national delicacy, raw fish. Ted Jacobs, who accompanied him, assured the puzzled Japanese that Nader didn't eat fish. "I could hardly say," Jacobs explains, "'Your tuna is full of mercury.'" Probably the absence of mercury would not have persuaded Nader to try raw fish. "Ever since a guy described amoebic dysentery to me when I was nineteen, there is no way I'll eat strange stuff," he says. "I'll throw it by my ear."

Nader has little hope that this idea will catch on; America's collective taste buds, he thinks, have been debauched by the food industry. "Almost any food can be sold so long as it's palatable, easy to chew, and visibly pleasing," he says— and those features have little to do, in his view, with the quality of the food but a great deal to do with chemicals and additives. "Here is my picture of you," he told a college audience in Oklahoma. "In one hand you have a Coca-Cola, in the other a hot dog, and in your mouth a cigarette—or worse. What do you think the cumulative effect is going to

be on your body?" In Cleveland, he asked a gymnasium full
of teen-agers, "How many of you look at a glass of water in
the morning and say, 'Ah yes, cadmium and arsenic levels are
up today!' " "If you could see how hot dogs are made, you'd
never eat another one unless you're a self-confessed maso-
chist," he tells audiences. He cites statistics: 20 percent of supermarket sausages contain "rodent remains." (The Department of Agriculture and the meat industry maintain that
this sort of material enters the product with spices, which
may be contaminated before harvesting. "The picture of big
fat rats shitting in the sausage machine is pretty far-fetched,"
says Aled Davies of the American Meat Institute.)

In Nader's public speeches, as in his private conversations,
he is not sanguine about the motivation of the American
people. "As long as this country is populated by people who
fritter away their citizenship," he told an audience in New
Jersey, "fritter it away watching TV or playing cards or
Mah-Jongg, or just generally being slobs, it will never be the
country we should want it to be." When he utters such sentences, which is fairly often, there is a glimpse of the fire. Although he practices no religion, and is careful never to use
any of God's names in public, he has a quality that in the religious was called holy disgust. If Nader is a Mahdi, raving
out of the desert, he has gathered his followers not because
he is in the grip of a mania, but because they believe he is so
utterly sane. "To me," said a woman who heard him in New
Jersey, "he is just like Jesus."

There is, of course, something comical about a man who
applies his convictions so assiduously to his private life. People like to lure him into cars to see what he will do. Dr. Michael Halberstam, a whimsical man, remembers driving
Nader to a party after he had made a speech before a
Washington medical group. "I like big, noisy cars," Halberstam says. "I'm a reckless driver, and having Ralph Nader in
the car would bring out the viciousness in anyone. I went

like hell, and old Ralph was clutching at the seat belts like a drunkard with the D.T.s." Paul Sitton and his wife scored something like the ultimate ploy when they enticed Nader into a pre-1964 Corvair convertible in the dark and drove him from Georgetown to Dupont Circle. "Ralph was very nervous," Sitton says, "and kept telling us all the way about the lethal danger of that car. I told my wife she could keep it anyway, and she still drives it." Nader's usual defense against cars of all kinds is to buckle his seat belt tightly and fall promptly asleep on any drive of more than thirty minutes' duration.

The occasions on which Nader can be driven home from a dinner party are increasingly rare. He has never socialized much, and as his life has become more and more crowded, he sees less and less of old friends. "Ralph used to call me every Sunday night," says one. "Now months go by and I don't hear from him. If I invite him to dinner, I figure the chances are 90 percent that he won't come." In the old days, he sometimes turned up as a lonely bachelor at the homes of friends. The evidence that Nader does not like dogs, but loves children, is very strong. He is a compulsive newspaper clipper, and he frequently stuffs an envelope full of articles on child care and health and sends it to his sister Laura, his only married sibling, who has small children. Nader speaks to children in the same terms as adults: it is never too soon to become interested in the issues. "He likes children and is comfortable with them," says Michael Pertschuk. "Most zealots don't know they exist." On one occasion, as Nader proselytized her long-haired twelve-year-old son, Mrs. Pertschuk said to the boy, "Listen. You may grow up to be a Raider." Nader said, "You'll have to cut your hair. It may get in your eyes when you're trailing someone." Nader is not a proponent of the pageboy bob for people who are associated with him; he makes it plain to the Raiders that there is nothing wrong with short hair and suits and neckties.

Richard Falknor believes that Nader's social aloofness is part of his general technique. "Ralph didn't get co-opted by the country houses," Falknor says. "When we meet him, it's always in some little place on Pennsylvania Avenue, usually on a Sunday afternoon. He won't go to a congressman's house. It sounds like a little thing, but it's terribly important." Not even Nader was able to resist the allure of Hickory Hill, apparently. He was known to turn up for dinner at the Robert Kennedys' on at least one occasion and, a friend said, "broke precedent by getting there before the dessert was served." Averell Harriman gave him a ride home in his limousine.

Nader admires very few political figures, and almost none of the recent generations. He liked Robert Kennedy. "Well, you know, he had a spirit to him that wasn't programmed," Nader says. "Although he was a politician, he had the ability to become spontaneously concerned or indignant . . . which is more than you can say about the others." Nick Kotz, a newspaperman and sometime Nader collaborator, encountered him on the night of Kennedy's funeral. The crowd was still clustered around the grave. "There was Ralph, all alone in that ridiculous scarecrow raincoat of his," Kotz says. "I said, 'Ralph, do you have a ride?' Ralph never has a ride. In the car, he kept saying, 'What are we going to do now? What will we do now?' " Nader does not remember this incident; he thinks he took a bus back from Arlington.

8

Meat, and Other Insults

I learned pretty early that you don't travel very far
alone in this town.

NICK KOTZ

All the legislation in which Ralph Nader has interested himself, and very nearly everything else that he has discussed in
public, has to do with the protection of the human body. He
believes that men are biologically obsolete, that their senses
can no longer preserve them from harm, that almost everything Americans eat or drink or breathe has been corrupted
by a shadowy order of corporate poisoners. Nader is very
careful about what he eats; he will not ingest anything that is
ground, stuffed, processed, or touched by additives. He will
cross the street or walk to the next block rather than pass by
a construction site where, perhaps, deadly asbestos is being
used. It seems sometimes that his body is to him a map of the
world, with continents of lungs, heart, liver, and brain
bounded by a sea of apprehensions.

Nader's onslaught against the automobile manufacturers sprang from his emotional conviction that unsafe cars were an insult to the person. What he is trying to do for Americans, above everything else, is to reawaken them to a sense of ownership over their own bodies. He finds it an uphill struggle; even his best friends go on eating hot dogs, drinking Coca-Cola, driving Volkswagens. He suspects that almost everyone else is semicomatose before the television set. "My impression of people is that their attention span is about two minutes," Nader says. "A two-inch nose is the most important thing to an American individual, regardless of the fact that the world is collapsing around him."

He is alert to small cracks in the edifice as well as to the largest fissures. When Michael Pertschuk mentioned that his daughter was keeping pet turtles, Nader called the child on the telephone to warn her that the little reptiles were known to transmit salmonella. One of his less celebrated campaigns was an attempt to forestall what he called "Rock 'n' Roll Deafness." "This country may be producing a new generation . . . with impaired hearing," he warned Senator Philip Hart and Senator Magnuson, suggesting that musicians and band-hall workers be required to wear ear protectors—if the places where loud music was played could not be declared public nuisances.

"People are being victimized at high levels of abstraction, so they don't feel it," he says. "Going back three or four hundred years, you saw the person who was victimizing you." To Nader, the king's men are everywhere visible, swinging the knout. Possibly it has become more important to him that the exploiters be seen than that action be taken against them. He has lost his faith in the sort of action that the system is able to take. The law itself—even law he has helped to pass—is in many cases a deception. Laws are adopted but not enforced. Abuses are not so much corrected as forced into new channels. His ingenuity struggles against conspiracy and con-

sistently loses. Nader had an early faith in the efficacy of the
government; he thought the encroachments of the corporations could be controlled through federal regulation—a law
to make cars safe or meat clean, a bureaucracy to stop the
cheating of consumers. After passing through that philosophical stage, he appears now to believe that the impersonal
forces of government cannot improve, and that in most cases
they even compound, the impersonal activities of the corporations, which, as he thinks, ravage modern life.

"What happens in this kind of society," Nader says, "is
that . . . decisions are made and then seven or eight tiers
below, the impact is felt. That's why Marx has had such a
terrific impact. He developed an analysis which clearly focused on the victims, whom he called the oppressed, and the
perpetrators, whom he called the ruling class, the capitalists.
I've always been convinced that his principal appeal was that
he took the first stage of abstract perpetration in the early
stage of the industrial revolution and made it personal."

In 1967, Nader still had some public faith in the idea that
legislation could correct abstract perpetrations. He moved
from the auto safety legislation, with which he was disappointed but not yet enraged, to an issue hardly less dangerous to the body: unclean meat. Like the automobile, meat
enjoyed a reputation Nader believed it did not deserve. If
Americans took anything for granted, it was the purity of
beef and pork and veal, stamped with the purple of the government. Within six months after Nader fixed his attention
on the packing houses—and the complex of politicians, civil
servants, and merchants who supported them—public optimism had been badly shaken.

The federal meat inspection system had its origins, of
course, in Upton Sinclair's novel *The Jungle,* published in
1906. Sinclair's descriptions of tubercular spittle and dead
rats being ground up with the sausage produced a national
outcry that culminated a year later when Theodore

Roosevelt signed the Federal Meat Inspection Act of 1907. The act set up what was assumed to be, and to a remarkable degree has been, an incorruptible system for the inspection of meat by federal employees. For sixty years the law remained largely unchanged; public confidence in the cleanliness of retailed meat was shaken only by an occasional scandal, exposed almost always after the malefactor had been detected and punished.

The weakness of the 1907 Act was that it brought under federal inspection only those packing plants that shipped meat in interstate commerce. Packers who sold meat within the borders of states in which their plants were located were exempt from federal inspection. It was assumed, in harmony with contemporary convictions about the limitations of federal authority, that the states should regulate their own internal commerce.

In 1967, when the Wholesome Meat Act was passed by Congress, 85 percent of slaughter and 75 percent of meat processing was under federal inspection. The 25 percent that fell under state jurisdiction amounted, according to Nader's calculations, to almost 8 billion pounds annually, or enough to supply the needs of 50 million people. "In some states, there was a considerable disparity with federal standards," according to Aled P. Davies of the American Meat Institute. "Some were very good, but in some standards were nonexistent." In testimony before the House Agriculture Committee in 1967, Davies observed that the state meat inspection programs "have provided the kind of consumer protection . . . that the people living in those states have thought necessary and have been willing to pay for."

By 1967, Congressman Neal Smith, a Democrat from the Fifth District of Iowa, had been trying for more than five years to amend the Federal Meat Inspection Act to bring intrastate meat packing under more adequate inspection. He was not a member of the Agriculture Committee, and he enjoyed little success. In *Sowing the Wind,* a report on agriculture published in 1971 under Nader's auspices, Smith is described as "dedicated," but "shackled by his preference for working within the 'system' of the House." Smith's proposal for applying federal inspection to intrastate meat packing and processing companies whose activities were deemed to affect interstate commerce was not brought before a House subcommittee for hearings until June, 1967. The hearings, and Smith's proposal, attracted virtually no publicity. Since Smith had begun working on this issue in 1961, a lack of tenacity cannot be listed among his shortcomings.

The chain of circumstances that brought the meat issue to the attention of the public began in May, 1967, with Neal Smith's legislative assistant, Edward Mezvinsky, and a young Washington correspondent for the *Des Moines Register* and *Minneapolis Tribune* named Nathan ("Nick") Kotz. Mezvinsky and Kotz played handball together on weekends, and between games they talked about Smith's concern that diseased and dirty meat was being sold across the counter. "Mezvinsky kept telling me that I should look into dirty meat," Kotz says. "I thought it was dull until he told me that the Department of Agriculture had horrifying reports and wouldn't show them to Smith or [Senator] Magnuson." The "horrifying reports" were the result of a survey conducted five years earlier by the Agriculture Department into conditions in intrastate plants in forty-eight states. The department took the view that the reports were confidential, internal documents.

"That kind of raised my competitive reportorial juices," says Kotz. He went to the Department of Agriculture and asked to see the reports. Officials refused to show them to him. "At first I was told they were hand-written reports, hidden away in packing cases or burned," he says. Kotz spent the next three weeks pushing and prodding officials of Agriculture's Consumer and Marketing Services. "Finally, on

July 14 [1967]," he says, "someone gave them to me." The reports (neatly typed and tidily filed) revealed conditions in intrastate meat plants that recalled some of the most scarifying chapters in *The Jungle*. Scenes in which rodents and insects infested meat, in which the meat of dead animals and diseased animals was processed into sausage, in which animal hair, pus, fecal matter, and the unwashed hands of workers contaminated meat, were described in the matter-of-fact language of the professional inspectors. These practices were, if not universal, then so widespread as to suggest that at least some meat processed under these methods had passed through the body of almost every American.

Kotz published his first story in the *Register* and the *Tribune* on July 16, a Sunday. The first pieces were based on Agriculture's reports for about ten states; Kotz concentrated, in the beginning, on the farm states within the circulation area of his papers—Iowa, Minnesota, Nebraska, the Dakotas, Wisconsin. On the Monday following the appearance of his first article, Kotz had lunch at the Capitol Hill Democratic Club with Nader, Congressman Thomas S. Foley of Washington, Foley's assistant, Richard Falknor, and Mezvinsky. Congressman Foley was a member of the House Committee on Agriculture.

During lunch, Nader began to play the role—subtler than Kotz's exposure of the facts and more intimate than any that can be played by a reporter who identifies self-respect with objectivity—that was essential to the success of the issue. "Ralph," according to Falknor, "supplied the consecrated oil for Foley." Through a combination of horrific facts (supplied by Kotz) and the force of his idealism, Nader persuaded Foley that he should support Smith's efforts for a stronger bill. "It was the key time for Foley," Falknor says. "Ralph and Nick, on that day, got him turned on to meat as a consumer issue. . . . Foley was certainly concerned before that, but it may be that he never would have done anything about it if Ralph hadn't given him the inspiration. Nick Kotz gave him the means." Soon afterward, Foley joined with Smith in introducing his amendment, which would have subjected all meat packing and processing plants, except those doing less than a quarter of a million dollars in business a year, to mandatory federal inspection.

Kotz told his companions that he was going back to the Agriculture Department after lunch to get the remaining reports. "It was a lark," Kotz says. "Ralph decided to come along." On this visit to the offices of the Consumer and Marketing Services, Nader had his first glimpse of the secret reports. He spent the next seventy-two hours virtually without sleep, reading the Xerox copies of the reports he and Kotz had obtained from a sympathetic official.

On July 20, Nader wrote a strong letter to Congressman Graham Purcell, chairman of the House Subcommittee on Livestock and Grains. Nader appended a summary of the Agriculture Department reports and released the whole package to the press. His letter articulated his belief that the Purcell subcommittee, which had been holding hearings—up to this point, all but unpublicized—on meat inspection reform, was being misled by the testimony of the meat lobby. "Misleading the subcommittee," Nader wrote, "amounts to misleading the public."

Nader's involvement in the issue predated Kotz's stories, although it was Kotz's investigation that produced the reports on which the entire campaign for a stronger law revolved. As Nader now recalls it, "I know we went down there and broke down the big door together. Nick was down there [previously] and checked out the Iowa and Minnesota ones."

Kotz and Nader had had, for some time, a professional friendship based on mutual usefulness. Kotz knew that a bill introduced by Congressman Purcell was gathering support in the House Agriculture Committee. The Purcell bill was weaker, in many significant respects, than Smith's proposal.

Kotz believed that Nader's prestige and his ability to focus national attention on an issue, combined with the information produced by his own investigative reporting, might move the balance of power toward stronger reform.

"I learned pretty early that you don't travel very far alone in this town," Kotz says. "It seemed important to me that as many people as possible read the reports. In most cases I dug up the stuff and Ralph publicized it. We were trading information. He wasn't my publicist, but he has a genius for the dynamics of making news."

This was a reversal of the usual relationship between Nader and a reporter. It was Kotz who had discovered a scandal and provided its details to Nader. Partly because Kotz's writings were published in Minneapolis and Des Moines, and partly because of the Eastern media's custom of treating Nader as the key figure in any muckraking situation in which he is involved, the impression grew that it was Nader who had first exposed conditions in the packing plants. On July 21 *The Washington Post* said Nader had "shaken loose . . . from Agriculture Department files" the reports on which his letter to the House subcommittee was based. Harrison Wellford, the author of *Sowing the Wind,* states in his book that "Ralph Nader provided the opening shot for the meat fight with an article in *The New Republic* entitled 'We are Still in the Jungle.' "

This is technically correct. Nader's article was published on July 15, shortly before Kotz's first pieces appeared in the *Register.* The first Nader article, however, contained no details from the suppressed Agriculture Department reports; these, Nader wrote, "remain inaccessible in the Department's files." It was not until August 19, in a *New Republic* article called "Watch that Hamburger," that Nader wrote under his by-line on specific conditions in the plants. In the earlier *New Republic* piece he expressed accurate suspicions about those conditions. "[Compared to] conditions prevailing at the turn of the century . . ." he wrote, "the likelihood is that the current situation is worse! The foul spectacle of packing houses in that earlier period has given way to more tolerable working conditions, but the callous misuse of new technology and processes has enabled today's meat handlers to achieve marketing levels beyond the dreams of their predecessors' avarice."

Nader believes it was his first *New Republic* article that energized Kotz. "Like a lot of newspapermen, it's always mañana, he's got more important things to do," Nader says. "What really got him in there was the *New Republic* piece. Then he really got on his horse. . . . I knew [the information] was down there before I wrote the *New Republic* piece and I was trying to get a handle on it." Nick Kotz provided the handle.

Before Kotz broke his story—which was to win the Pulitzer prize for 1967—the bill sponsored by Graham Purcell had been introduced with the support of the Johnson Administration. The Purcell bill proposed paying the states 50 percent of the cost of upgrading their meat inspection services to parity with federal standards, but it did not make improvement mandatory; the states could decide for themselves if they wished to improve their meat inspection programs so as to bring them up to federal standards. At the time, twenty-four states had laws for the mandatory inspection of meat processing, and twenty-six for the mandatory inspection of slaughter. Thirteen states had voluntary meat inspection, and nine had no meat inspection statute at all. One of these, Alaska, was worried that mandatory meat inspection would destroy its efforts to revive the reindeer industry, and others had more sophisticated objections, which were expressed in testimony before the Purcell subcommittee by spokesmen for the National Association of State Departments of Agriculture.

The American Meat Institute and the other meat lobbies at first opposed the enactment of any legislation. After Kotz's

story broke, AMI, together with Secretary of Agriculture Or-
ville Freeman, and the National Association of State Departments of Agriculture, shifted ground to support the Purcell
bill. It passed the House on October 31 by a teller vote of
403 to 1. On the same day, the Smith-Foley amendment was
defeated, 98 to 140.

When the Purcell bill moved to the Senate, it was invaded
by amendments offered by Senator Walter Mondale of Minnesota, who cited Kotz's stories on the floor, and by Senator
Joseph M. Montoya of New Mexico. The Mondale amendment would have extended federal inspection to all plants in
the nation unless the states could demonstrate that their
standards were already equal. Montoya's amendment would
have given federal funds to the states to improve their inspection under the threat that federal inspection would be imposed if the states failed to act. An attempt by the White
House to bring the Purcell bill, unamended, to a vote on the
Senate floor without holding hearings before the Senate
Committee on Agriculture and Forestry was frustrated by
Mondale, who threatened a filibuster.

The meat lobby, led by Aled Davies of the American Meat
Institute, would have preferred to have lived with the Purcell bill, for which Davies had lobbied hard and skillfully in
the House. Nader had lobbied just as hard for Smith-Foley.
It was a confrontation between the visible political power of
the meat business, with its thousands of employers in congressional districts, and the interests of the consumer, which
Nader had made visible to Foley but to few other congressmen. Nader had made the tactical mistake of coming rather
late into the fight. "I wouldn't say that Nader was a johnny-
come-lately," Davies says, "but he came in when the forces
were already in full flower."

Nader's last-minute attempt to scythe the special interests
included a tour of ten cities where, armed with copies of the
secret Agriculture Department reports, he contacted local

newspapers. Some of them sent reporters to nearby meat plants and published exposés of their own. The Public Broadcasting network did a three-part series on meat inspection. Kotz's stories were picked up by the wire services and some of the Eastern newspapers. The story, competing with the early escalation of the Vietnam War and a flurry of other developments, never spilled over as a major issue into the national media. In the absence of an uproar in the press, the effect of Nader's fervor was not as strongly felt by Congress as was Davies's pragmatism, based on the old-style honor system of favors done and favors returned.

When the Purcell bill moved to the Senate, the climate changed dramatically, largely due to fresh embarrassments uncovered by Kotz. "Nick Kotz," says Falknor, "was the real hero at this stage." Kotz obtained a copy of the confidential membership list of the American Meat Institute and published the fact that some of the organization's adherents—including Armour, Swift, and Wilson—operated uninspected intrastate plants. According to Davies, only Oscar Mayer among the big producers had all its plants under federal inspection in 1967. "A hell of a lot of them had uninspected intrastate plants," Davies says. "They were phasing out, but it's damn expensive and no one does things till they have to." Swift refused to tell Kotz and refused to tell Smith and Foley how many intrastate facilities it operated, on grounds that these plants did not sell meat across state lines.

For the hearings before the Senate Agriculture Committee, at which Nader was the star witness, Mondale summoned three federal inspectors from the field. "They were," as Kotz says, "typical Nader resources—the good civil servant." Their testimony confirmed the state of affairs described in the secret reports. Afterward, in the corridor outside the hearing room, Kotz chatted with the inspectors. One of them said, "Whatever happened to the samples we collected from the supermarkets? They were all analyzed in the lab." Kotz dug up the laboratory reports and wrote stories showing that uninspected meat, slaughtered and packed and processed in what Nader had called "revolting" conditions, was being routinely sold to housewives.

Kotz's final blow to the meat lobby fell on the eve of the vote in the House on the strengthened bill. He discovered that I. Blaine Liljenquist, president of the Western Meat Packers Association, had written a circular letter to meat-packing firms soliciting funds (up to a maximum of $99) for congressmen who were "working to preserve our free enterprise system." Kotz, and his readers, saw Liljenquist's letter as an effort to give money to members of Congress who stood fast for the weaker meat inspection bill. Congressman W. R. Poage of Texas, chairman of the House Agriculture Committee, lost no time in denouncing Liljenquist's action. "To say that I was shocked . . . is indeed an understatement . . ." Poage wrote to Liljenquist. "No matter how innocent this solicitation may have been intended, it is absolutely impossible to disassociate it from the pending meat inspection legislation. It could prove deeply embarrassing. . . ." He asked that Liljenquist withdraw his letter and refund any money he had received from donors. Aled Davies called Liljenquist's letter "a most unfortunate, ill-timed, and utterly stupid activity initiated by an official of a regional trade association in the meat packing industry."

Davies, whom Kotz describes as "an attractive scoundrel," is a jolly, white-haired man with a tinge of the Celtic inflection that he brought with him from Wales when he emigrated as a boy of nineteen. He is an amateur of sailing and a professional judge of the Potomac winds. "This was a political turmoil and we had to trim our sheets," Davies says. "There's nothing wrong with tacking to make progress." Robert Gray of Hormel was, at the time, chairman of the board of the American Meat Institute. He and Davies set out to persuade the industry that they had better accept what was being called the Mondale-Montoya bill before they were saddled with something even worse.

"I don't care to get too far ahead of my troops," Davies says, "but I'd felt for some time that the status quo could not be defended. To put it mildly, I saw public relations problems. . . . We cannot be insensitive to public opinion, and that's where Nader and Kotz came in. We were very fearful it would have an effect on meat consumption, but it didn't. Nevertheless, the public was aroused. . . . Some of the charges were exaggerated, but there was enough truth in them."

In what was probably his most important public gesture of the whole affair, Nader took Betty Furness to task in the newspapers for her silence on the legislation. Miss Furness had recently been appointed as President Johnson's adviser on consumer affairs, and her credibility in the liberal community, which recalled her chiefly as a person who opened the doors of Westinghouse refrigerators in television commercials, was not strong. On October 12, Nader noted to a *Washington Post* reporter that Miss Furness had not replied to a letter he had written to her on July 20, in which he asked for her comment on the pending legislation. Miss Furness responded, in line with the administration position, that she favored the weaker bill. But she added that she wished that state inspection were mandatory. As the pressure and publicity mounted, the White House broke ranks with the Secretary of Agriculture and sent Miss Furness to the Senate to testify in favor of the Mondale-Montoya bill. Kotz regards his revelations, combined with Nader's public challenges, as an example of reforming the system by describing how it works.

Davies, who had prepared a collection of press clippings to show to recalcitrant meat packers, persuaded his membership to accept the stronger measure. "Public opinion was focused by Nader," he says. "When you're a monolithic thing like

the industry you're not used to being pushed around. . . .
We're not shellbacked, but we don't panic easily." There was
still reluctance to accept a measure that was going to cost the
industry $16 million in 1970 in overtime charges for federal
inspectors, a cost that is charged directly to the owner of the
inspected plant. Eventually most of the 365 members of AMI
decided that this was the least expensive course open to
them.

"They're hard-headed businessmen, and I never would
have changed them if they hadn't realized the situation
themselves," Davies says. "I was positive the only way we
could get sanity in this thing was to go along with the bill
and get it amended. The federal inspection system is basically good—otherwise we would have fought like screaming
hounds." Davies did not stop defending the interests of the
industry. In the House-Senate conference on the Mondale-
Montoya bill, pressures to weaken the legislation became so
intense that Mondale and Foley asked Kotz to find out from
Nader what position he would take on the compromises they
believed they would have to accept. "I called Nader," Kotz
says, "and he said, 'You tell them to do what they think
best.' " In English, that meant that Nader expected they
would perceive political realism as a defense of the bill's
strengths. "It was consistent," Kotz says, "with Nader's policy
of forming no permanent entangling alliances with anyone."
It also left the way open for compromise.

The Wholesome Meat Act, amended so as to pay 50 percent of the states' costs while giving them two years' time to
bring their inspection systems up to federal standards, passed
the Senate with only two dissenting votes on December 6 and
was approved on the same day by the House by 336 votes to
28. President Johnson signed the bill on December 15, in the
presence of its congressional sponsors, Nader, Miss Furness—
and Upton Sinclair, who was eighty-nine years old and
confined to a wheelchair.

Mondale, who had shepherded the bill through a Senate Agriculture and Forestry Committee of which he was the only member really in favor of it, took the floor to praise Nader's contribution—and to note Kotz's articles in a single sentence. "I commend those selfless private citizens," Mondale told his colleagues, "who wrote courageously and creatively in this field. I would name Ralph Nader as one of these. I am proud, as a lawyer, that we have some people's lawyers, who seek no profit, but who, guided only by the motive of public service, are digging out the facts, and leading such blameless lives that they can stand up as examples of the finest of our profession." Nader reminded him, he said, of Louis Brandeis, who, when he appeared without a visible client in the New York-New Haven case, had announced, "Your Honor, I am the lawyer for the people." Nader was silent about his promotion to the gallery of the icons he had despised at Harvard Law School.

The difference between the Purcell bill, which was denounced as a sellout to the interests, and the Wholesome Meat Act, which was hailed as a grass-roots consumer victory, has not in practice been very great. Purcell would have paid half the costs of a voluntary reform of state inspection services. The Wholesome Meat Act paid half the costs but gave the states two years to reform—and empowered the Secretary of Agriculture to extend the deadline by another year if he found that honest progress was being made. Nader's goal— uniform inspection of all meat—was not achieved. At the end of two years, only three states (California, Florida, and Maryland) were found to have equaled federal inspection standards, and one, North Dakota, was placed under the federal inspection system. By May 1, 1971, forty-four states were deemed equal, with six others and Puerto Rico being placed under federal inspection. There are no penalties against the states for noncompliance other than federal takeover—which means as a practical matter that Washington pays all instead of half the state's costs. Criminal violations in individual plants can be turned over to the Department of Justice for prosecution, and twenty-three court cases were initiated by May, 1971.

In determining whether state systems are equal, the Department of Agriculture, according to one of its officials, depended primarily not upon inspection of all plants but upon an examination of the state's laws and regulations and its budget. In addition, all plants in a random sample of those within a given state must be judged equal before the state can be certified as having matched federal standards. A plant is deemed equal to federally inspected plants if it scores 70 percent in compliance with a range of requirements— standard in the federal system—from clean water and adequate sanitation to control of vermin.

Wellford, in *Sowing the Wind,* suggests that the system of flexible deadlines in the act became a disguise for inaction, and worse. He notes the "ironic" possibility that "consumer legislation which was made necessary by the failures of state government provides a pretext for turning the whole inspection system over to state government." This is likely to happen, he argues, because "enforcement of the Wholesome Meat Act is ideologically out of tune with the Nixon Administration," which is committed to a lessening of federal controls over state programs. The Department of Agriculture, Wellford charges, is under orders from the administration to turn the federal program over to the states. This extraordinary step, which the administration denies is being contemplated (it says it wishes to decentralize, not dismantle, the federal inspection system), would mean the end of the federal inspection system created under the legislation of 1907, and its replacement by fifty separate state systems, a prospect no more pleasing to the meat industry than to Nader. "Once you open an act," Aled Davies observes, "God knows what will happen."

Wellford argues that the inspection of meat by fifty separate state systems—operated by inspectors who are inadequately trained and controlled by state officials who, in Wellford's view, are more likely to be corrupt than their federal colleagues—would turn the Wholesome Meat Act on its head. This is likely to happen, Wellford contends, because the U.S. Department of Agriculture has deliberately frustrated the will of Congress in a series of acts that amount to "bureaucratic lawlessness." He quotes a remark by "one observer" to the effect that "lawlessness in the government occurs when statutes (what Congress says it wants to do) fail to correspond to realities (what the bureaucracy *does not* want to do)." He concludes that "the consumer coalition which passed the Wholesome Meat Act was aware that USDA did not fully endorse its goals, but it lacked the resources and persistence to follow it through to enforcement."

In retrospect, this does not surprise Ralph Nader. He now talks about the futility of passing reformist legislation unless the reformers can compel its implementation. He speaks of recruiting the federal meat inspectors, whose esprit has been damaged by the decline in standards, as a consumers' fifth column. He dreams of finding dedicated citizens to act as watchdogs over the Department of Agriculture and the rest of the federal bureaucracy. This seems to him the only possible way of assuring the honest operation of the government; he regards the Nixon Administration and the civil service as being joined in an alliance with the vested interests that is by its nature fatal to reform of almost any kind. His obsession with the special interests and their assault on the public interest seems extreme even to friends who share his anxiety and admire his goals. "Ralph defines a sort of Manichean heresy," says the urbane Paul Sitton, "with the forces of good and the forces of evil always in conflict. They aren't always." Even if they aren't, Nader sees formidable obstacles in the nature of the civil service. "These people have been turned into complete moral neuters and professional neuters," he says. "They're not working, they're not producing, they're not creating."

Nader works, produces, creates with indefatigable energy. But if he were to be judged as harshly as he judges those who frustrate him, it might be said that he does not understand the system he is trying to change. If all that Wellford says about the enforcement of the Wholesome Meat Act is true, then Nader ought to have foreseen that the act—weakened by compromise, forced on a bureaucracy that did not want it and that lacked the machinery to administer it—did not represent genuine reform. If the Wholesome Meat Act achieves the opposite purpose from the one intended, that will be, as Wellford says, a terrible irony; but perhaps such ironies are the inevitable lot of a man who looks upon politics not as the art of the possible, but as a system of imperatives.

The bills with which Nader has been associated have, all in all, suffered an unhappy fate. The Natural Gas Pipeline Safety Act of 1968 resulted in the employment of one engineer to deal with five hundred thousand miles of pipeline; the Wholesome Poultry Act of 1968 has shortcomings analogous to those of the Wholesome Meat Act; the provisions of the Coal Mine Health and Safety Act of 1969 were so far from being enforced that some of its congressional sponsors brought a court action against the administration to compel its implementation (and lost); the Radiation Control for Health and Safety Act of 1968 has resulted in reforms more limited than Nader envisioned.

Looking back upon these battlefields, Nader has something of the air of a general who won brilliant victories in a lost war. He still loves the cause. He did not see through the euphoria of the battle to the result that has disillusioned him. He wants no more spoiled victories. "There's one thing that people really don't understand about me," Nader says. "I have no pride of authorship. Those bills have been associated with me. Associated with five bills! They are frauds, and if they're frauds, I'll call them frauds. They are frauds! They don't have to be—they're written much better than they're enforced or administered."

As the decade turned, Nader went off, all but unnoticed, to his own Colombey-les-Deux-Eglises. Unlike that other general who was, in the French saying, late for the last war, Nader did not wait for events to summon him back. He set out to change the way in which events are shaped.

9

Marriage, Capitol-Hill Style

I've never known anyone like Ralph Nader—one man
who believes he's a majority.

ABRAHAM RIBICOFF

On the afternoon of May 10, 1971, Ralph Nader stopped in
on an old friend in the National Press Building. A few hours
before, Nader had publicly insulted the Senate Commerce
Committee, which might have been described as his last institutional friend. "It was the first time Ralph had been in
the office for ages," says the friend. "He was like a little boy,
on the defensive and protesting too much. 'How'd I do?' he
wanted to know. I said, 'Ralph, you're always angry. If you
do this in public, people are not going to understand. You
can't lose your cool all the time without losing something
else, too.'"

What Nader lost, or discarded, was the sympathy he had always displayed toward the Senate. He did not say in public
what he was prepared soon afterward to say in private—that

he no longer wished to be a part of a lawmaking process that was, by his stern standards, a device for deceiving the people. He was already making plans to expose the Congress, and its individual members, as unresponsive, and even insensitive, to the wants of the nation. Nader had nursed his disillusion in secret, for the most part, and the Congress did not read the trend placing Nader in opposition to it. Many senators and their assistants still do not believe that the Ralph Nader whom the Senate created—and who, in return, did so much to bring the Senate into his new knighthood of reformers—can have turned against this most serene of American institutions. It was its very serenity that displeased him. At lunch with a congressman after his testimony, Nader explained why he had gone on the attack. "Congress is not doing its job," he said. "They shouldn't be polite. They should be at each other's throats."

Nader, in his testimony before the Commerce Committee, which has jurisdiction over most consumer issues, put flesh on that maxim. The committee, he said in front of the television cameras, was "groveling" before the Appropriations Committee because it had not requested a specific sum of money to administer a bill designed to control the cost of repairing automobiles. The bill's language, requesting "such sums as may be necessary to carry out the provisions of this Act," was, in Nader's view, a formula for inadequate funding—and hence inadequate enforcement of the law. The bill itself, Nader said, was too weak to correct "massive thievery" and "fraud" by the automobile industry. It was just such timidity and lack of adequate funds, Nader said, that had already led to the "utter failure" of the Natural Gas Pipeline Safety Act and the Radiation Control for Health and Safety Act. It was startling language from a man who was regarded as responsible for the enactment of those two laws.

Senator Theodore F. Stevens, a Republican from Alaska, was reduced to astonished anger by Nader's charge that the

auto industry is engaged in "criminal fraud" because it manufactures cars that are easily damaged and can only be repaired with parts made by the industry itself. Pounding on
his desk, Stevens shouted, "You look for the worst in people
and not at what's good that's happening in this country."
Nader shouted back, "Do you give credit to a burglar because he doesn't commit burglaries 90 percent of the time?
What kind of nonsense is that?" "Get the indictment! If you
can, take it to a grand jury," Stevens cried. "You find a district attorney with the guts to do that," Nader suggested. Stevens said that Nader himself was committing fraud by making charges before a Senate committee that he was unable to
bring in court.

The bill Nader attacked was introduced by one of his Senate favorites, Philip A. Hart of Michigan, who estimated that
it would cut at least $15 billion from the $25 billion that
Americans are believed to spend each year on automobile repair and maintenance. The bill's sponsors estimated that
consumers would be saved about $1 billion annually by a
provision requiring that after January 1, 1975, all cars would
have to be fitted with front and rear bumpers that would
protect the vehicle from any damage at all in a crash into a
fixed barrier at five miles per hour. This standard, Nader
charged, was "virtually obsolete," and he demanded a provision requiring bumpers able to withstand a ten-mile-
per-hour crash. (Dr. William Haddon, Jr., in his new capacity as president of the Insurance Institute for Highway
Safety, had told the committee that five-mile-per-hour crashes
of 1971 models produced front-end damage amounting to
$202.25 for the Plymouth Fury; $341.20 for the Ford Gal-
axie; $367.90 for the Chevrolet Impala, and $415.40 for the
American Motors Ambassador. At ten miles per hour, the
cost of repairs more than doubled. At fifteen miles per hour,
described by Haddon as "the speed at which football players
regularly collide," repair costs rose to $870.65 for the Plym-

outh; $1,170.50 for the Chevrolet; $1,206.98 for the Ambassador, and $1,207.45 for the Ford.)

"If, after being exposed to details about the auto industry's massive thievery, its massive contempt for both the consumer and the Congress for the past five years," Nader testified, "if this is the best legislation your political antennae permit you to come up with, then it is respectfully suggested that some of you who are most concerned take some time out and begin to ponder, like Lucretius, on the nature of things . . . relating to the corporate state of our times. . . .

"How many examples of deceptive packaging must this committee send to the Senate floor before it ceases groveling before the Senate Committee on Appropriations? When is this committee going to fight for adequate funding support for its consumer protection bills? . . . When is this committee going to stand up to Lloyd Cutler and his industry cohorts and say that if there are criminal penalties for the poor and deprived . . . then there must be criminal penalties for the automobile industry?" What Nader wanted corrected on this occasion was, in his words, "the yearly toll of billions of dollars and unnecessary hazards imposed on motorists by the calculated design" of the American automobile, "which, from bumper to taillight to engine, supports a parasitic aftermarket, a many-billion-dollar-a-year market, marked by enormous and monopolistic company markups on replacement parts."

He could hardly have made it plainer that he thought the bill proposed by Senator Hart would not achieve this objective. It is one thing to disagree with a Senate committee; it is another to question the motives of its members and to link them to the perpetuation of a fraud. As Nader said afterward, "It was another of those 'it just isn't done.'" The language he used—speaking of the "stylistic pornography" of tail fins and implying that the auto industry was indifferent to the human damage resulting from a "leering sharp fin structure"—was not new. But it was a new experience for senators and a shocking lapse of manners on Nader's part to group them with the makers of the tail fins as the passive portion of a conspiracy to cheat, maim, and kill the public. Always before, Nader had taken pains to make the Senate feel that it was on the side of the angels. In return, senators had with few exceptions permitted Nader to punish his adversaries in committee hearings and be rewarded with the compliments of senators. Nader's pungent testimony, it was predicted, had ended this arrangement; there was special resentment that of all the Senate committees he might have attacked, he chose the Commerce Committee, which had been the most complaisant of his partners. "Ralph is a fanatic and a fanatic always has to have his own way," one Democratic senator said on the day after the hearing. "After a while he outlives his usefulness. You begin to question his judgment."

It is significant that this senator, who has worked closely with Nader over the years, declined to have his name attached to such a bitter judgment. A powerful Senate staff member, reflecting on the episode a week or two later, explained why. "There was an initial reaction that Nader had gone too far," says the aide. "But then public reaction to the TV was favorable to Nader, and that's the lasting effect. As long as Ralph has access to the media and is a hero to the public, senators are not going to cross him."

The evening news, which carried an entertaining film clip of Nader's shouting match with Stevens, reassured Nader that he had scored a coup with the public by revealing the depths of his disgust. "I wouldn't have done it differently," he said a few days later, "except that I'd have more words. . . . Tactically it was very effective—oh, very effective. From a viewer's, a citizen's point of view, it reduced it to its simple issue: Let's cut out the pretense—who are you representing, Senator? As far as alienating some of the Senate goes, how can you alienate Stevens? He's alienated to begin with; he's always going to vote wrong. Furthermore, I'm really tired of getting bills that are deceptive practices passed through Congress. I don't want to be part of that deception. What good is it? Who cares whether the bills go through? I don't care for that kind of legislation. We've reached a point where forget it! Don't defraud the public."

Nader's rhetoric describes abuses and demands their abolition. He leaves out, and has always left out, any discussion of the political means for accomplishing his objectives. His political sympathies may be clear enough, but his political beliefs are not known. Democrats may assume that he is on their side, but Republicans cannot think that he is one of them. President Nixon had hardly taken office in 1969 when Nader said that consumers looking for a protector in Washington should write off the administration, "composed of leading presidential advisers from advertising agencies, ex-lobbyists from industry, and multimillionaire construction and manufacturing magnates." The Nixonian key phrase could not have been better designed to provoke Nader, whose purpose it is to shock the generations out of their silence. "This country was not founded by a silent majority and it is not going to be saved by a silent majority," he repeats in his speeches. Some of his disenchantment with Daniel Patrick Moynihan stems from the latter's connection with the Republican President. "When I first worked for Pat," Nader mused late one evening, "he and I had identical views. Now I can hardly talk to him. That adulation of Nixon!"

Nader's allies in the Senate have tended to be liberal Democrats, or at least Democrats who will support consumer issues as a matter of practical politics. Some of them—Mag-

nuson, Hartke, Hart—are members of the Commerce
Committee. Others, such as Ribicoff and Gaylord Nelson,
have committee assignments dealing with problems of the
government bureaucracy or the regulation of business.
Nader's list of the political figures he admires is a very short
one—Norris, La Follette, and, with reservations, Borah and
Kefauver. It includes no contemporary officeholders, and no
Kennedys. He thought the Kennedy Administration injected
some spirit into the country but accomplished almost nothing of substance. (He thinks that Congressman Paul J.
McCloskey, the California Republican who has recently
been trying to organize a rebellion against Nixon, has a future. "He may well be President someday," Nader says. "He's
got everything the Kennedys had—and guts to go against the
powerful, which they didn't have.")

In a speech on April 19, 1971, before an audience of students at Cuyahoga Community College in Cleveland, Nader
expressed a sentiment to make the blood of a party worker
run cold. "We can no longer say," he said, " 'All we need is a
few good men in government.' We're beyond that. Even
good men in government can't make these institutions
work." His plea to that audience, and to his larger audience,
the whole American people, is for what he calls *"ad hoc
power,"* or "noninstitutional sources of power." What he is
calling for, in truth, is a citizen uprising—and not necessarily one that works within the system. In his view, the citizenry is locked out of the system. "You have an allegiance to
your fellow man," he told the Cleveland audience, "which
goes far beyond that to any organization." A few weeks later,
in private, Nader said, "I think people are being lulled and
duped into thinking that all it needs is for a leader to come
along and it'll be okay. It's not that simple. Even if we do get
a new leader and a new party he won't be able to do anything because he'll be surrounded by the forces that we're
criticizing as being insufficiently responsive. . . . Would

this country be any different if 6o percent of it thought like, say, Senator [George] McGovern? You know, [Congress] really can't behave much more in conditioned response. . . . Congress is a buoy on the sea. It's almost irrelevant."

Nader's mood of disillusion had not taken hold, to outward appearances, as recently as 1970, the last year in which he took a strong hand in the shaping of a law. In the early stages of his career, when he was new to the realities of institutions, he gave no sign that he felt as he does now. In those days there was a dewiness about him that amused some of the people in the Senate. "I remember thinking," says a high-ranking Commerce Committee aide, "that he was a visionary. He was talking about the sort of things that this committee was never likely to do. I was close to dismissing him as a nut—and this shows a lack of insight on my part." Nader had a gift for taking literally the purposes of the government, and the force of his naïveté was such that for a time he succeeded in persuading some politicians, bitten by this unusual experience, to behave according to his vision of their duty. "When Ralph was around," a congressional aide says, "some of these guys were like daddies, driving at the speed limit because the kids were in the car."

Sometimes he seemed to old hands in the government to be exceptionally innocent about the way power flows beneath the surface of institutions. John Walsh, speechwriter to President Johnson's first consumer adviser, Mrs. Esther Peterson, recalls Nader's efforts to get Mrs. Peterson to back his campaign against unsafe cars. This was in the period before the publication of *Unsafe at Any Speed,* and of course before the passage of the traffic safety act. "Nader wanted Esther to take on the auto companies," Walsh says. "Esther was a very womanly person. She'd flutter around Nader's head and cry, 'I'd *love* to!' After he'd left, we'd say, 'You'll get hit on the head by the President again.' If Esther had done anything, Henry Ford would have called up Johnson and LBJ would have said, 'What's that goddamn Esther doing now? Tell her to shut her goddamn mouth!' So she never did anything." The Nader of 1971 would have known what the hungry Nader of 1965 apparently did not perceive: that Mrs. Peterson had no personal influence with the President, and that the very idea of setting up a consumer advocate in the White House, at the center of all political gales, was a virtual guarantee that the advocate would be neutralized. Nader has since given up any effort even to maintain a liaison with Mrs. Peterson's successor, Mrs. Virginia Knauer.

Nader was welcomed into the congressional process, particularly in the Senate, the more theatrical of the two houses, with enthusiasm. Nader, in his early days, was rather like a young actor cast as a juvenile foil to the stars of the show. By the time the leading men noticed that the audience's eyes were always on the younger actor, it was too late to remove him from the cast, because it was he whom the public had paid to see. This is, of course, sometimes an indication that the whole style of acting has altered while established players, too settled in their technique to change, go on with the gestures and the intonations that thrilled an earlier generation but mean little to a newer public.

The extent to which the political situation has changed is implied in two statements by a powerful Senate staff member. In June, 1970, he said, "We try to keep Nader at arm's length. We're accused of being vassals to Nader." Eleven months later, when Nader had already retreated into the wings, the same man said, "We always try to make sure that someone from Ralph's shop is involved [in consumer legislation]. These are enormous resources and we seek them out." When he was reminded of his earlier remark, he could not believe that he had made it. "When I first came here," he mused, "much of this legislation was not thought of as practical. Ralph's not as significant a day-to-day figure as he was, but the legislation goes forward because of the attitudes he

set in motion. . . . We did whatever we did partly because
Ralph energized us."

"All my life in politics," says Senator Nelson, "I've heard
that there ought to be someone to represent the general interest of the public. Ralph is the first to come along and show
us the impact that a single informed voice can have. His contribution has been greater than that of anyone else in contemporary times." In a good short explanation of Nader's influence, Senator Hartke observes, "Ralph is interested in
truth. As a result, when you say 'Nader,' people say, 'This is
good, this is wholesome.' He has a following which extends
beyond any single group. He's become a watchword." It does
no harm, as a Senate aide remarks, to have a watchword on
your side when you're running for public office. "With
young people, as we all know, Nader is great to have on
your side," he says. "When he goes to Indiana and speaks
about what Hartke has done, he helps Vance. Hartke has a
checkered record in many ways, but he's great from Nader's
point of view." Nader refuses to endorse candidates, but he
speaks well of his allies when an occasion arises in their
home states—and, in extreme cases, he will bend his neutrality a little. "In my 1970 campaign for reelection," Hartke
says, "Ralph said he would not endorse me. But he gave me a
TV clip saying that I was the most consistent and persistent
voice on behalf of consumers in America. I was honored."
Hartke was reelected by one of the smallest majorities in the
history of Indiana politics, so Nader's assistance was, as
Hartke acknowledges, most welcome.

Nader, in his secretive way, has done a great deal in private to change the complexion of congressional activity. His
points of leverage have been those of a technician: the staffs
of congressmen and senators, and of the committees. Congressional staffs hunger for information and search for issues.
Nader, as in the traffic safety bill, has often provided them
with both. In former times, he would identify an issue, work

up the data to support legislation, suggest the outlines of the law, and then work late into the night going over the drafts of a bill.

This sequence occurred with the Natural Gas Pipeline Safety Act of 1968. "He conceived it," Michael Pertschuk says. "There was an explosion in Louisiana. Ralph came to staff members and began to talk about it. It took a year and a half to get the bill passed." Nader first drew attention to the hazards of gas pipelines on June 29, 1966, in a speech before the Washington chapter of the American Society of Safety Engineers, describing the devastation caused in Natchitoches, Louisiana, when a buried pipeline exploded near a housing development in 1965. Seventeen persons died. He took the case to Capitol Hill in testimony before a subcommittee of the Commerce Committee. The resulting law was designed to correct the hazards of half a million miles of pipeline, which included pipes that were old or too thin, or badly welded, or even, in some cases, made of wood.

Nader was dissatisfied with the law for his usual reason: it contained no criminal penalties against the executives of companies violating its provisions. He soon had reason to be dissatisfied for other reasons—the inadequate budget and staff, and the fact, as he pointed out in testimony before the Subcommittee on Intergovernmental Relations, that the advisory committee established to assist in enforcement of the act was dominated by representatives of the industry. "It was an understatement when you said domination," Senator Lee Metcalf of Montana told him. "It is complete. . . . There is just absolute control."

Nader grew to believe that administrative arrangements of this kind throttle the intent of the law. It was a small step from there to the conclusion that Congress does not have the courage of its intentions—and from there to the conclusion that certain laws are doomed from the start to be cosmetic. His victories merely legitimized the conditions he had set out to correct. He stopped coming around. "I've worked with him in the old way only once in the past year," says a committee staff director.

Some staff members still contend that Nader, better than anyone else, can motivate and move their congressmen. The legislative assistant to a member of the House of Representatives says Nader can achieve a level of advocacy that is foreclosed to him. "I have a good relationship with my congressman," he says. "I'm expected to argue with him and be a hired conscience. But there's a point beyond which I don't feel I should go. If there's an issue I feel very strongly he should get involved in, and it's a Naderesque issue, then I wouldn't push it myself. I'd have Ralph do it. I'd only do it once every two or three years, of course, but that's the way I'd do it. My congressman has the usual problems. It takes guts to vote, not so much against the economic interests of his constituents as against their cultural traditions. My congressman needs some sort of psychic support, and the best kind he can get is Ralph stopping in to say 'hi.' " Nader's idea of psychic support may not always be identical to that of the elected official he is attempting to shore up against the weight of temptation. He is as likely to blast an ally in the newspapers as to stop in for a quiet chat.

Gary Sellers, a volatile young lawyer who is in the unique position of being at the same time a member of the staff of California Congressman Phillip Burton and a paid associate of Nader, believes that Nader is a force because of his freedom from restraint. "Because Ralph is self-sustaining," Sellers says, "he is responsible only to his own conscience. The others aren't—they're in the middle of a web of interests, and they have to compromise their ideals to protect present income or future sources." Others believe Nader is a little too free. "Nader is assuming the role of an Ajax white knight with no reins on the horse," says a member of the staff of the Senate Public Works Committee. "My instinct is to distrust anyone who doesn't have to answer to a constituency. His love fest with the press scares the hell out of me. The press should be his constituency."

Nader's private contact with senators and representatives has been more limited than the surface of events suggests, and the hearty friendship expressed to him on public occasions has a synthetic quality. Senators and members of the House assume a vague manner when asked when they last saw Nader alone. They are not usually part of the midnight telephone network, and he refuses to socialize with them. The cocktail party and the long evening in shirt sleeves over a bottle of bourbon, classic tools of the lobbyist, are alien forms to the abstemious Nader. His style involves working through the staff, and the development of situations through publicity—the angry letter mailed to a senator and hand-delivered, faster than the mails can get to the senator, to the newspapers. A Senate staffer who is undazzled by Nader describes this technique as implied menace, openly arrived at: if the senator doesn't do something about Nader's complaint, he is in danger of being depicted as part of the outrage.

From his earliest days as a public figure, Nader has not hesitated to chastise even those who have done the most for him. No member of the Senate has suffered more from his goodwill toward Nader than Abraham Ribicoff. It is, to Ribicoff, a puzzle. "If there wasn't an Abe Ribicoff," he says with justice, "there'd be no Ralph Nader." To Nader, even if he acknowledged its truth, this proposition is irrelevant. What he requires in his allies is stamina, the willingness to stay with an issue until, in Nader's view, it is resolved. It is in the nature of issues, of course, that they are never resolved, and senators have a tendency to be waterbugs on their surface. What Nader regards as a moral Lake Superior may seem to a man faced with reelection merely a puddle after a heavy rain of publicity. "You can't get a United States senator to stay on a single issue for the rest of his life," as Je-

rome Sonosky observes. In the devil's dictionary that is
Nader's oratorical style, no word is more vibrant with bad
connotations than *dilettante,* unless it is *compromise.* "The
whole attitude here toward legislation has been one of compromise," says a Senate aide. "Ralph, of course, does not
believe in that process."

Nader detected compromise—and something worse—in
the hearings before the Ribicoff subcommittee that delivered
him into nursery of his power in 1966. On the day of the
hearing, after James M. Roche had apologized to him and
the subcommittee had, in effect, beatified him, Nader told
Sonosky that he was not satisfied with the result. His discontent was twofold: Nader had wanted, from the beginning, to
use the hearings as a means of compelling the recall of all
Corvairs manufactured between 1960 and 1963; and, sec-
ondly, he believed that the cross-examination of the General
Motors witnesses on the facts and the motives of their investigation of him did not go nearly far enough.

"You've got to distinguish between being satisfied emotionally, which in a way I was," Nader explains, "and being
satisfied substantively in terms of the issues involved, which
I was not. . . . Because this giant went down humble to the
Senate, everyone said, 'Oh, how great!' I was vindicated, but
. . . far more [was involved] than being cleared. They had
such a solicitous approach toward me because I'd been
smeared. My real interest was [to] drive it through to a conclusion and get some changes in management and get that
car recalled. Those were the issues."

Sonosky describes himself as an old-fashioned liberal who
believes that congressional hearings should have a legislative
purpose. Throughout the 1966 hearings he took the position
that testimony about the performance of the Corvair was off
limits: it was not germane to the bill, and General Motors
was engaged in litigation as a result of accidents involving
the car. Sonosky changed his tactics when GM's investigation

of Nader was revealed. "I called Ralph and said the wraps are off," he says. "That's how he came in loaded for bear on the Corvair." In his testimony on March 22, 1966, Nader presented what was at that time his complete case against the Corvair. His spoken testimony and the supporting documents he presented for the record fill about 90 pages of a printed transcript of 213 pages. The subcommittee reached no official conclusion about the safety of the Corvair; in its final report, it noted that it "lacks the technical competence to do so."

Nader's barrage of data, published by the subcommittee, no doubt contributed to the vanishing demand for the Corvair that led General Motors to take the car out of production. That was not enough for Nader; he wanted then, and still wants, all Corvairs called in for correction of the rear suspension system in the 1960–1963 models, and rectification of faults, such as the leakage of exhaust fumes into the passenger compartment, which he maintains are typical of other model years. "Holding hearings on traffic safety and holding hearings on auto hazards are two different things," Nader says. "And while Ribicoff certainly gave the initiative on traffic safety, it was very far from his mind to hold hearings on GM and Corvairs."

On this point there seems to be no disagreement, just a profound difference in the interpretation of motives. On August 30, 1969, Nader made his first public assault on Ribicoff for his reluctance to continue the Corvair hunt. "[Ribicoff]," he was quoted as saying in *The Washington Post,* "has literally closed shop on auto safety." These were harsh words to direct against a man who had humbled GM and who, as governor of Connecticut from 1955 to 1961, had been called "Mr. Auto Safety." During his term in Hartford, Ribicoff had festooned Connecticut with signs warning against speeding and introduced one of the toughest campaigns against reckless driving ever witnessed. The cam-

paign had no great effect in terms meaningful to Nader;
although the suspension of Connecticut drivers' licenses rose
from 372 in Ribicoff's first year in office to 10,055 in his second, the number of accidents and injuries increased. The
highway death rate in Connecticut declined slightly but not
as much as in the nation as a whole. This experience doubtless contributed to Ribicoff's belief that the design of the vehicle, rather than the punishment of the driver, might be the
key to traffic safety.

Nader has continued to bombard Ribicoff with letters demanding the reopening of the Corvair question. Nader's request is based on his belief that at the 1966 hearings General
Motors suppressed evidence with regard to the characteristics
of the Corvair. Ribicoff has responded to Nader's demands
by instructing his subcommittee staff to continue its investigation of the Corvair, but he has not scheduled new hearings. "When Ralph Nader doesn't get his own way," Ribicoff
says, "he strikes out. Ralph Nader wants it one hundred percent Ralph Nader. That doesn't mean he's always right."

Nader has no doubt that he is right. "I can see Ribicoff's
point of view," he says. "He's saying, 'Oh, this again!' What
he doesn't realize is that there aren't many cases that mature
to this depth. This case, if it's rounded out, will do more to
deter corporate behavior than a lot of things that seem much
bigger. . . . I mean there are a lot of shenanigans involved
here. There's perjury, there's suppression, there's distortion
of the judicial process."

That is Nader's view of the matter. But on two separate
occasions the U.S. Department of Justice, after investigating
Nader's allegations, found no grounds to prosecute any witness in the 1966 hearings. Nader has continued to pursue the
issue remorselessly. On May 20, 1971, five years after the
hearings, he attacked again. In a sixteen-page letter addressed
to Ribicoff, and released to the press, Nader said that he had
"newly obtained materials, including some heretofore non-

public documents, from which your Committee should be able to prove beyond any reasonable doubt the falsity of much of General Motors' 1966 testimony to your Committee." According to Sellers, who was charged by Nader with responsibility for the case, the purpose of this tactic, apart from a presumptive search for objective truth, was to bring pressure on Ribicoff to reopen hearings on the Corvair question. Sellers, who believes that the subcommittee has protected its own reputation and that of General Motors at the expense of the public, is a hard-liner on Ribicoff and the Corvair. "Ribicoff is worrying about his pride," Sellers says, "while people are dying in the streets because of his inaction. I'm sorry—I'm not moved."

Nader's letter to Ribicoff, drafted by Sellers, alleged that the record of the hearing, which was conducted under oath, had been "secretly altered" by members of the subcommittee staff. Certain phrases had been expunged from the printed record. The most significant of these, in Nader's view, was James M. Roche's emphatic statement that General Motors, during its investigation of Nader, "did *not* employ girls as sex lures." Sellers, in private, suggested that the erasure of this phrase could only mean that sex lures *had* been used, and that the record had been tampered with in an effort to forestall a perjury indictment. The subcommittee staff explained that the phrase was omitted from the final transcript as a result of a printing error. This was not an explanation that seemed plausible to either Sellers or Nader. The alleged use of girls to entice him during the Gillen investigation has always loomed large to Nader. It was one of the few elements in his account of GM's alleged harassment that was never confirmed. There were no witnesses to those incidents, widely reported in the press, in which Nader claimed that attractive young women had solicited him in a Washington drugstore and supermarket.

Nader maintained that other changes in the transcript included deletions of parts of questions asked by Senator Robert F. Kennedy and Senator Fred Harris and an alteration in the statement of Louis G. Bridenstine of General Motors. These changes are either trivial or pregnant with intrigue, depending on the point of view. Nader's letter states that when Bridenstine's statement that General Motors had paid $120 for its investigation "up there" was changed to read "in Connecticut" and when the words "and agents" were deleted from a question by Senator Harris about the responsibility of General Motors for its "employees and agents," the "clear pattern" was to "reduce or remove the liability of GM witnesses."

The changes, he wrote, removed "clear grounds for prosecution." Nader's charges were based on a tape recording of the proceedings and what Sellers implied was a copy of the stenographic transcript of the hearings. Nader presented, also, documents that he said proved James Roche misled the subcommittee when he "denied under oath the use of investigative procedures on 'expert witnesses,' 'critics' of the corporation, or on other parties." Nader claimed to have evidence that such investigations had been carried out in the case of others.

In January, 1967, Vincent Gillen had filed papers in connection with Nader's lawsuit against General Motors that suggested some of the testimony given before the subcommittee was false and that documents submitted to the subcommittee had been altered. Ribicoff immediately asked the Department of Justice to investigate. After inquiries were made by the Federal Bureau of Investigation, the Justice Department informed Ribicoff that it had concluded that "the evidence is insufficient to support a prosecution under the criminal laws. . . ." Nader believed that no prosecution resulted because the Justice Department looked for violations of the perjury statutes; he suggested in his 1971 letter that indictments would be easier to get under the broader law against making false statements. In his letter to Ribicoff, Nader wrote: "Now it is clear that the FBI investigation was defective from the beginning because it was based on the secretly altered hearing record rather than on the untouched original transcript. . . ."

General Motors, in a press release on May 20, 1971, replied, "In response to the written request of Senator Ribicoff, General Motors reviewed the original transcript of the 1966 hearings and marked the suggested changes which it felt were required to correct errors and omissions in the transcript. . . . This further public attack on General Motors by Ralph Nader is a continuation of his effort to injure General Motors through adverse publicity without regard to the truth or accuracy of his statements. Ralph Nader's attack on the members of the subcommittee staff and the manner in which their investigation is being conducted is an obvious effort on his part to intimidate the staff and influence their report."

Nader wrote in his letter that "the major deletions and additions to the testimony of GM witnesses . . . came at a time when the record was in the custody of the subcommittee staff—and apparently were made without your knowledge or that of any other senator. They raise, therefore, questions regarding the responsibility of certain Senate employees. . . ." One of the Senate employees Nader had in mind was Jerome Sonosky, who had left the subcommittee to enter private law practice in Washington.

Nader was annoyed at Sonosky in 1966, and has remained so ever since, because the full text of a memorandum written by Eileen Murphy of the General Motors legal staff was not entered in the record of the subcommittee hearings. Nader believes that the Murphy memorandum, which is supposed to have outlined the scope of the investigation of Nader, would show that General Motors' intention was to discredit his moral character, rather than merely discover—as GM maintained—whether he had any connection with lawyers who were suing the corporation over the Corvair. Sonosky entered only the final page of the memorandum, after the hearings were over. This page contains two innocuous typewritten paragraphs about Nader's employment at the Labor Department, followed by half a page of handwritten phrases. Of these, only one makes any reference to Nader's personal habits; the notation reads, "Does he drink?"

"Sonosky's first error, to use a charitable phrase," Nader explains, "was that he didn't bring [the memorandum] to my attention until after the hearings. . . . And he brought it to my attention in a very astute way, first indicating that he didn't know whether it was really that significant, and wouldn't it be a good idea to put the first page [*sic*] in? This way he can never be accused of suppressing it entirely. So he got the best of most possible uses out of it. He did not apply it to the hearing. . . . This was a fantastic performance, if you know what I mean." Almost as soon as Nader learned of the existence of the memorandum, he began to apply pressure to be given a copy of it. Sonosky vividly remembers the incident. "I didn't release the document," he says, "because it was the property of GM. It had not been subpoenaed. GM wanted it back. Ralph wanted a copy. Ted Sorensen in New York and Ralph Nader in Washington, and me on the phone day and night. How would you like to be in the middle between Sorensen and Nader, one asserting a property right and the other a moral right?"

Sonosky solved his dilemma by sending the document, together with other pieces of evidence, including Vincent Gillen's report to General Motors on his investigation of Nader, to the National Archives under an obscure Senate rule. The sequestered documents cannot be retrieved by anyone except Ribicoff, and by him only so long as he is chairman of the subcommittee. "It ain't classified," Sonosky says. "It's buried." Nader has never accepted the interment. In February, 1967, a story describing the situation appeared in *The Washington Post,* under Morton Mintz's by-line. "Ralph got on to Mort Mintz," Sonosky recalls, "and Mort comes in in that endearing way of his and says, 'Where is it, Sonosky?' He does a story in the *Post* about how I'm hiding it. After I sent it to the Archives, Sorensen said dirty pool and Ralph said dirty pool. I figured if they both think I'm wrong, I must be right."

Sonosky maintains that whatever changes were made in the transcript of the hearing were nothing out of the ordinary. "These are normal deletions and additions," Sonosky says. "I know guys who take out whole paragraphs. . . . I was much more careful in this hearing than in any other I was ever mixed up in." Nader says it is not normal to change transcripts of a hearing conducted under oath. Sonosky's memory is vague regarding what is obviously, to Nader, the most serious of the alleged alterations. "About the sex lures," Sonosky says, "that's where I have trouble. I don't remember. I couldn't without the original transcript." Robert Wager, who was a member of the staff under Sonosky and is still a subcommittee counsel, recalls that the phrase about sex lures did appear in the original transcript. Some of the other omissions—the words dropped from Senator Harris's question, for example—were, he believes, missed by the stenographer.

Wager has no recollection of the phrase about sex lures being deleted deliberately, and he says General Motors did not request its deletion. He believes that the phrase may have been inadvertently omitted by the printer. For its part, General Motors has never denied that Roche told the Ribicoff subcommittee that the corporation "did *not* employ girls as sex lures." The corporation's public relations office printed and distributed several hundred copies of Roche's testimony, which includes the disputed phrase. Copies are still available to any reporter who requests them.

As to the Murphy memorandum, Sonosky defends his intentions. "Why does [Nader] think Sonosky insisted on putting that one page in the record?" Sonosky asks. "So there would *be* a record of the kinds of things they were directed to find out."

The import of Nader's letter to Ribicoff is that "certain employees of the Senate" and "a Senate aide"—whose identity is clearly indicated by a description of his activities—permitted the falsification of the transcript and the suppression of evidence. These acts are, as Nader points out, an offense under the federal criminal code. Sonosky naturally does not like this implication. "It's a normal thing for witnesses to clean up their language," he says. "That happens all the time. . . . The inference that I made the changes for some sinister reason is just laughable. . . . It's a new status symbol in Washington to be attacked by these guys. I think Ralph is altered. I hate to say that, I admire him so much. But look around at this kind of stuff, and what can you think?"

The Justice Department found that there was no basis, in the evidence that Nader sent to Ribicoff, to seek indictments. In a letter to Ribicoff on July 21, 1971, Will Wilson, an assistant attorney general, said that "the information furnished to us does not foreclose the occurrence of an inadvertent printing error nor does it suggest any misconduct relating to this change."

Nader said the Justice Department's response was "disgraceful." Wilson pointed out that five years had elapsed since the hearings had taken place, and that the printing of the record would have taken place five years before as of July 25, 1971. "If there were any violations," Wilson wrote, "the statute of limitations would bar prosecutions after five years." Gary Sellers interprets the statute of limitations differently. "It is a continuing conspiracy," he insists, "which did not end when the record of the hearing was printed."

Sellers developed a system of lively theories about this en-

tire incident in the course of his investigation of it for
Nader. "I really began to doubt my understanding of people
when we got inexplicable refusals from the Ribicoff staff to
pursue the [Corvair] issue. I knew there must be a hidden
reason. . . . I told them I was going after Sonosky. By then I
wanted him—he'd lied to me on small matters so many
times." [1] Sellers' suspicions did not exclude Robert Wager.
Sellers believes that he gave Ribicoff's staff fair warning. "At
a very early stage of my investigation," Sellers asserts, "Bob
Wager said to me, for no apparent reason, 'You guys have got
a knife in my back.' " Wager has no recollection of making
such a statement. Sellers says he went to John Koskinen
(Ribicoff's administrative assistant) and said, "I think from
the way Wager is acting that you guys have got a skeleton in
your closet about the 1966 hearings. Clear it up yourself or
the shit'll hit the fan. I won't put up with it anymore."

Sellers, in addition to this sort of conversation in private,
put pressure on the Ribicoff staff in other ways. In June,
1971, he leaked to the Jack Anderson column a story about
subcommittee staffers being met by General Motors "limousines" when they flew to Detroit to continue their investigation of the Corvair. The item was not appreciated by
Ribicoff or by General Motors. "He said my people were
stooges for General Motors. What the hell kind of a way is
that to do things?" Ribicoff wanted to know. "I won't be a
stooge for General Motors and I won't be a stooge for Ralph
Nader." A General Motors executive said it was standard procedure to give the corporation's guests a ride in from the airport. "It was a gesture of courtesy," he says. "Jesus! Everything is shiny limousines."

There is no way to respond to this sort of an onslaught
with decorum. Ribicoff managed as best he could, out of his

1. Sellers, in reviewing the transcript of the author's interview notes, asked
that this sentence be changed to read ". . . he'd lied to Ralph and
others . . ." Sonosky says he has never met Sellers or talked to him on the
telephone.

combination of political poise and rabbinical calm, by sending Nader's charges to the Justice Department for a decision. Almost all of the people involved—Nader, Sellers, Ribicoff, Sonosky, Wager—were lawyers, so it undoubtedly had occurred to all of them that the statute of limitations had run out and no prosecution was possible, even if Nader's "new evidence" was supportable in court. Wilson, noting that the voice tapes and the reporter's transcript were available only from nongovernmental sources, thought they would be subject to challenge in a trial.

Ribicoff, on the day that Nader's letter was delivered to him, sat on a leather sofa in a Senate anteroom and reflected on his experiences with Nader. "I give Ralph high marks for all the good he's done," Ribicoff said. "I forgive him his childishness. . . . But he's becoming the national scold. I think Ralph's mistake is that he's begun to think he's God. If you don't agree with him he'll turn on you."

Ribicoff said he doubted that others would be able to continue to work with Nader as knowledge of that trait spread. That may not matter to Nader, so far as the Congress is concerned. As Ribicoff spoke, Nader, working in his accustomed secrecy, had already decided to conduct a searching investigation of the Congress. "The objectives," Nader explains, "are to develop the kind of information that people can use about each [congressional] district and congressman—who they are beholden to, who are the big influences in their lives, who supports them, how they behave in Congress, to what extent do they even put a day's work in." The study, begun in the summer of 1971, will cover two years and be directed by one of the original Raiders, a Harvard Law School graduate named Robert Fellmeth.

What does Nader think the reaction of Congress will be? He chuckles. "That's going to be like nothing before, I tell you," he says.

10

The Raiders

What arrogance!

PAUL RAND DIXON

There is in much that Ralph Nader does, despite the uproarious results of his activities, a quality that is almost offhand. He will send a team of zealots off to civilize a chemical manufacturer on the basis of ten or twelve lines about its dirty emissions in a book on air pollution, or decide to set up a nationwide network of activists in the universities after talking to a bright student on an airplane. "Ralph's one weakness," a young associate believes, "is for a guy who is enthusiastic. He'd buy a truckload of Fuller brushes from somebody who believed with all his heart in Fuller brushes."

Nader's whims arise always from his convictions, so they are in that sense logical. No one with his view of the condition of American civilization could ever have imagined that he might reform it single-handed. He was, of course, always

willing to try. Ted Jacobs believes that Nader would have
lived out his beliefs in exactly the same way even if no one
had ever heard of him. Obscurity was certainly a likelier fate
for Nader than the fame that overtook him. If he has many
of the attributes of genius, he has also all the marks of a
crank. Nader is aware that ridicule attends the passionate citizen. "It used to be that in the average American town you'd
have the town drunk, the town wife-beater, and the town
citizen," he tells audiences. "I think we are changing that
image of the citizen as an eccentric and an outcast."

Nader's means of changing the image are many, and not
all of them have yet unfolded from his mind. Because he
often doesn't know what he is going to do next, his adversaries cannot possibly anticipate his actions. If his mind is
fertile, his heart is promiscuous. He likes to say of himself
that he has the gift of outrage. Any detail of American life
may, on any given day, sting his conscience. Once stung, he
attacks at once, and with no particular forethought. If this
method sometimes cheats him of results, it gives him the element of surprise, and he is usually over the breastworks and
out the other side of the fort before his enemies realize that
there is no army behind him. Nader's tactics are derived
from the lesson he learned in his encounter with General
Motors. The lesson was that powerful institutions are extremely vulnerable. Communication—which includes the
concept of corporate image and of political programs—is the
flywheel of American society; bend it, and you cause the entire machine to shudder and belch.

"Nader's Raiders," those summertime apparats of young
people thirsting after the tired blood of the bureaucracy and
corporations and banks, are certainly the most inspired device Nader has conceived in his search for ways to apply the
powers of citizenship to institutions. The Raiders, who are
not yet old enough to be anything but *engagé,* are important
to his larger vision of an awakened citizenry. Nader wishes to

shame a society into reforming itself through immersion in his version of truth; the Raiders believe in his principles almost as a matter of instinct.

Unlike the ideologues of revolutionary history, Nader does not seem to have worked out a detailed political scenario to give life to his dogma. Like all conceptions, that of the Raiders is but dimly remembered by their parent. Like so much else Nader has done, the Raiders seem to have come into existence, and afterward burgeoned into a far-reaching phenomenon, almost by accident. By the summer of 1968, when he recruited the first team of Raiders, Nader had already begun to resent the David and Goliath image. "I'm not interested in the Lone Ranger effect," as he says. "The function of leadership is to produce more leaders."

Once Nader began to think of himself as a leader, the natural place for him to look for followers (or, as he would have it, apprentice leaders) was among the young. Youth, in the sixties, certainly believed that its potential was not only ignored, but actively frustrated. A large section of it was, like Nader, in revulsion against material things and what it regarded as the injustices of society. In another of the miracles of timing that have marked his career, Nader emerged as a heroic reformer at precisely the right moment. White middle-class youth in 1968 had been driven out of the civil rights movement by blacks who wished to control their own fate. As for traditional politics, the youthful idealists who had followed Eugene McCarthy were about to see their best efforts result in the election of Richard M. Nixon to the presidency. If young people could feel an emotional kinship with anyone who was not openly a revolutionary, that person was Nader. A good many youngsters made this plain to him when he spoke on campus; they would approach him with offers to work for his cause, and many sent him letters and résumés.

As the seed group of his new generation of leaders, Nader chose seven young people who must be the most unlikely revolutionary cadre in modern times. One was a great-grandson of William Howard Taft, the twenty-seventh President and tenth Chief Justice of the United States. Another was a Goldwater supporter from Hawaii. A third, less than three years later, would marry the daughter of Richard M. Nixon. Another was a master at Groton. All were attending Harvard or Yale after having completed undergraduate studies at those institutions, or at Princeton, MIT, Stanford, or Cornell.

Cynics suggest that Nader chose the group partly for its protective bourgeois coloration. It is more likely that he did not know the background of its members in much detail and merely liked the look of them, and of their credentials. William Howard Taft IV, a slender young man who has been bleached and stretched by his genes into the caricature of an aristocrat, is not quite sure how he was chosen. "I don't know what Nader's criteria were," Taft says. "If you wrote to him, he'd ignore you. If you wrote twice, he'd call you up at one o'clock in the morning." With the original Raiders, Nader established the pattern he still follows in hiring associates. The technique includes the reading of a résumé, almost always a telephone conversation, and sometimes but not always a brief personal interview. He makes up his mind almost instantly. Nader says the method works very well. It is based, apparently, almost entirely on his instinctive reaction to the applicant.

Nader does not believe in giving young reformers money, or much guidance. "We came down to Washington," Taft recalls, "and Ralph said we were going to investigate the FTC and he hoped we had a place to live and enough money to get along on." As leader of the project, Nader named a 1968 graduate of Yale Law School named John E. Schulz. Like Edward F. Cox, who was even then the favorite beau of Tricia Nixon, Schulz was a graduate of Princeton. These two, with an antic Hawaiian named Robert C. Fellmeth whom Nader regards as the quintessential Raider, coauthored the study of the Federal Trade Commission, which has been the proto-type for the avalanche of muckraking studies that have since issued from the Nader organization. The other members of the group were Judy Areen, a Cornell graduate who was at-tending Yale Law School; Peter Bradford, who went to Yale College and Yale Law School, and Andrew Egendorf, an alumnus of MIT who was then in his first year at Harvard Law School.

Nader worked with the group in the writing of an outline that identified flaws in the FTC, and turned them loose on the organization. The FTC was, for a muckraker, an ideal target. (It should be understood that, in Nader's lexicon, "muckraker" is a term of praise.) Founded in 1914 as the watchdog of the buyer's interest, the FTC had, in Nader's view but all unawares to most of the rest of the nation, settled into moral and bureaucratic sloth. Franklin Roose-velt, after failing to gain control over the FTC, turned it into a "patronage dumping ground," in the phrase of a contempo-rary member of the Commission, and subsequent Presidents generally followed FDR's practice. The Raiders, in their re-port, portrayed the agency as a whore:

> Like an aged courtesan ravaged by the pox, the FTC paints heavily the face it presents to the public. Be-cause the failures go deep the paint has to be laid on thick—thick as a mask. Keeping the mask painted is perhaps the one activity the Commission dedicates it-self to with energy. Its working materials are public relations, secrecy, and collusion.

The Raiders, who had no credentials other than their citi-zenship and Nader's sponsorship, were not welcomed by Paul Rand Dixon, then chairman of the FTC. They were, Nader believes, the first citizens many of the bureaucrats had ever seen in their offices. Accustomed to deal with the representa-tives of industry and trade associations, or with the agents of consumer organizations, they were understandably confused by a group of persistent youths who demanded to know the most intimate details of the commission's work. On many campuses at the time, the Raiders' contemporaries were defenestrating deans, rifling the files of professors, and otherwise, as a federal official notes, "behaving like a bunch of goddamn Venezuelans," so perhaps a certain amount of apprehension was inevitable.

The commission had little reason to trust Nader's motives. In recent months he had made public a report of the FTC on automobile warranties with the implication that the commission was suppressing it for reasons that had to do with the auto industry's campaign contributions to the campaign of Hubert H. Humphrey,[1] and he had embarrassed the FTC in other ways, as in his attack on their investigation of the gray market in reconditioned Volkswagens.

The Raiders' technique, in brief, was to demand access to the commission's files and budget and to request interviews with leading officials. There was great reluctance on the part of Chairman Dixon to accede to either request. The Raiders, in the end, secured a good deal of data by threatening to sue under the Freedom of Information Act, and by less conventional means. After commencing on June 17 with their interviews with upper officials of the commission, the Raiders were foreclosed from further interrogation by Dixon's ruling that they had "had ample opportunity to complete their interviews with our personnel, and . . . after August 23 they would no longer have unlimited access to staff members." The Raiders regarded this action, coming after more than two months of interviewing, as "an illegal lockout."

In their report the Raiders speak of "a tacit yet institutionalized fear—radiating outwards from the Chairman's office," which hampered their search for facts. They interviewed some officials of the commission in secret, and a good

1. Paul Rand Dixon called this "a false charge and a blatant lie."

deal of the book was derived from the information developed in these clandestine meetings. According to Fellmeth, Dixon eventually became so incensed by the content—and, presumably, the tone—of the Raiders' questions that he ejected John Schulz "bodily" from his office; what appears to have happened is that Dixon took the young man's arm and propelled him out the door in the middle of an acrimonious interview. Schulz, who has a reputation as a wit, drew a measure of revenge at a later hearing before the commission. Dixon, in his Tennessee accent, told Schulz that if he were an FTC career employee, he, Dixon, would "help you on out of this building." Schulz asked, "Like you he'ped me out of your office, Mr. Chairman?"

The Raiders' report, which was published in 1969, is not a scholarly work or even an assay into journalism; it is, as it was intended to be, an activist's tract. Like many of its successors in the Nader Report series, it abounds with unattributed quotations and assertions that are not always supported in their context by facts. The authors say, for example, that "it is highly appropriate to mention that alcoholism, spectacular lassitude, and office absenteeism, incompetence by the most modest standards, and a lack of commitment to the regulatory mission are rampant. . . . They are well known to the Chairman, who somehow has found that they add to the congenial environment and unquestioned loyalties that surround his office." The reader, given this opportunity to read Paul Rand Dixon's mind, is free to regard the judgment as perceptive or speculative.

The Raiders found what they regarded as ample evidence of lassitude and incompetence. They surprised one high-ranking official asleep in his office with the sports page draped over his face. They encountered many officials who declined to discuss their work with them or discussed it in an evasive way. They interpreted Dixon's attitude, as excerpted from his public utterances, that the FTC was a "friend of

business," as a lack of commitment to the regulatory process.
They excoriated the commission, and Dixon personally, for
what they saw as political cronyism, an insensitivity to the
need to hire more Negroes and more Republicans (Dixon is
a Southerner and a Democrat), and even a prejudice against
the employment of young lawyers from the Ivy League. Fellmeth says that the Raiders declined to mention a good many
peccadillos that were described to them by FTC gossips.
Their essential goal, he explains, was not an exposé of the
private lives of employees, but an explication of the commission's failure to fulfill its mission.

The Raiders did describe enough cases of bureaucratic inertia to give force to their central conclusion that the FTC
was meant to be, and ought to be, a stronger protector of the
consumer. They recommended a number of changes that
many within the FTC thought were rational suggestions,
which, if adopted, would improve the agency. Dixon thought
they had left out virtually all of the commission's accomplishments. "How any group could profess or claim to have
made an empirical study of the activities of the [FTC] and
make no mention of at least a single accomplishment is
beyond me," he wrote in a rebuttal of the report.

Where the Raiders did mention accomplishments, they
tended to isolate them as untypical of the work of the
commission. In the view of Philip Elman, a Kennedy appointee to the commission who was sympathetic to the Raiders, this may have been justified. "We're supposed to exercise
moral courage behind this wall of protection," Elman says.
"Sometimes we've tried, as in 1964, when we attempted to
issue a regulation that would have required . . . that all cigarette ads carry a warning that death can result from cigarette
smoking. Lyndon Johnson thought we were crazy." Congress
finally passed a law requiring a much milder warning on
cigarette packages. It was the FTC, following the Surgeon
General's report on cigarettes and cancer, that provided the

initiative for this action, which, in the context of its time, was adventurous. The Raiders' report mentions this incident but does not describe just how strong the FTC's contemplated action was—or what political forces frustrated it. A stronger warning, very much like the one originally proposed by the FTC, has since been required.

The Raiders had an opportunity to confront Dixon at an FTC hearing in November, 1968, before their report was issued; Fellmeth believes that the chairman's purpose was "to take the wind out of our sails." If that was his intention, his tactic almost succeeded. "We were testifying against the agency, against the chairman, against the commission we were testifying before," Fellmeth says. "That hearing room is incredibly intimidating—worse than the Supreme Court. They have giant nameplates, the backs of their chairs go up to the ceiling, they have giant microphones to project the voice of God. You testify at a little lectern, way down below them, like a new soul before Saint Peter." Schulz—whom Dixon kept calling "Mr. Shootz"—acted as spokesman for the Naderites. According to Fellmeth, Dixon could be heard "swearing under his breath into his giant microphone" during Schulz's testimony. Andrew Egendorf tape-recorded it all, choosing a place out of Dixon's line of vision to set up his portable machine. "A man walked up to me afterwards," Fellmeth says, "and said, 'That's just the most impressive testimony I've ever heard.' He gave me his card, which showed his name and 'Special Investigator, General Motors.' " The day after the hearing, *The Washington Post* gave the Raiders their name. "That," says Fellmeth, "was everyone's Walter Mitty dream come true."

Fellmeth catches himself looking back on the FTC raid as a lark, and then reality intrudes. "Things that are humorous in retrospect," he says, "were horrible at the time. It was hard, boring work. What made it bearable was the outrage. I can see a hundred cases of corruption and still cry, 'God

damn those bastards!' " He was surprised at the impact of the
report. "It made headlines all over the country," he recalls.
"I thought, Are these people crazy? We're just a bunch of
students. It was Nader's press agentry and the fact that we
just *said* it."

"There has . . . certainly been some awareness even
among hostile elements here that the report was largely accurate, in emphasis if not always in details . . .," says Philip
Elman. "It was remarkable that they got as much information as they did. Of course, it was much worse in some ways
than they said." Elman believes, however, that the Raiders
may have been led astray in some of their methods and
conclusions. "They were looking for bad guys, for evil men,"
he says. "Evil is not the word. These are men who had lost
their motivation, banal men. Whatever corruption was here
was moral." Elman, on completing his term as a commissioner in 1970, retired into private life.

In contrast to many of Nader's activities, his work with the
FTC has contributed to a reform of its outlook and activities.
Ironically enough, the instrument of change has been the
Nixon Administration. In the wake of the Raiders' report,
which was released on January 2, 1969, a separate report was
commissioned by the President and carried out by the American Bar Association. Its recommendations for reform of the
FTC did not differ markedly from those made by the Raiders. President Nixon replaced Dixon as chairman with a
younger man, Caspar W. Weinberger, who turned out to be
an activist. He carried out a sweeping reorganization of the
commission before he moved to the White House in August,
1970, to become deputy director of the Office of Management
and Budget. His attorney adviser, William Howard Taft IV,
went with him. Miles W. Kirkpatrick, a Princetonian and
Philadelphia lawyer who was appointed by Nixon to replace
Weinberger, has been, if anything, more aggressive than his

predecessor. Kirkpatrick was chairman of the American Bar Association Commission that studied the FTC.

From July, 1970, to May, 1971, the FTC took the following actions, among others: began an investigation of the franchise business; sponsored the formation of consumer protection committees throughout the nation; issued complaints against major magazines for "using deceptive means to get long-term subscription contracts and harassing deceived subscribers"; exposed "McDonald's $500,000 Sweepstakes," charging that only $13,000 in prizes was actually awarded; issued a complaint against Firestone Tire & Rubber Co., on grounds that it misrepresented that "all its tires are defect-free and safe and that its 'Safety Champion' tires are safer than others"; sought to require that a health warning be prominently displayed in all cigarette advertising; warned the public about the dangers of high blood pressure and other ailments in sauna and steam baths; criticized the lack of price competition in petroleum products; issued complaints against manufacturers of enzyme detergents, on grounds that they had misrepresented that enzymes remove all types of stains from fabrics; charged Coca-Cola with making false nutritional claims for its Hi-C fruit drinks and Standard Oil with falsely advertising that its Chevron F-310 additive reduces air pollution; proposed a rule giving customers of door-to-door salesmen three days to change their minds and cancel the order; told businessmen that consumers are "getting fed up with planned obsolescence"; seized job lots of flammable fabrics; released its findings on tests of tar and nicotine content on 120 varieties of American cigarettes; issued complaints against Mattel, Inc., and Topper Corporation for "using deceptive advertising which unfairly exploits children"; published a detailed staff report of complaints by low-income consumers on what they regarded as widespread deceptive pricing and credit and service practices in Cleveland's inner city; issued a complaint against Wonder Bread, which claimed to help build strong bodies twelve ways but "in reality . . . has the same amount and kind of nutrients as most other enriched breads"; began an investigation of auto parts market practices, and sought large money penalties against a number of corporations in violation of FTC rules.

The accumulated weight of these decisions is considerable; scattered through a year's newspapers, their effect may not be fully appreciated. It is, predictably, not enough for Nader. He believes, with Fellmeth, that "the powers [the FTC] needs—preliminary injunction power, criminal sanctions— still do not exist." Nader has nevertheless continued to herd the FTC toward the limits of its authority, and perhaps the most newsworthy and important action it has taken in recent years came as a result of a petition filed by Nader and one of his part-time associates, Aileen Adams Cowan.

The FTC action, expressed in its own dry language, was contained in a resolution it issued on June 10, 1971, "requiring all advertisers to submit to it on demand documentation to support claims regarding the safety, performance, efficacy, quality, or comparative price of the product advertised. . . . The material obtained . . . will be made available to the public." This ruling was stimulated, mostly if not entirely, by a petition filed on December 2, 1970, with the FTC by Nader and Mrs. Cowan, in association with the Consumer Association of the District of Columbia and the Federation of Homemakers.

The work that led to Nader's petition was done by Mrs. Cowan, who is married to one of the lawyers who administers Project GM, an organization independent of Nader's personal empire, if not of his influence. Mrs. Cowan, who spent two years in the Peace Corps in Brazil, earlier compiled for Nader a research report on the Brazilian Indians, which still lies somewhere in his files. The FTC petition, Mrs. Cowan

says, "was totally Ralph's idea. He called me up and told me
to watch TV for a month and tape the commercials. . . . He
does this a lot—has a brainstorm and wants to act on it." Not
a television fan, Mrs. Cowan suffered through a month before the tube, and came away with the feeling, among others,
that women were not playing a very dignified role in commercials. "I think there's a good fairness doctrine case in the
way women are portrayed in TV advertising," she says tartly,
"always either in an apron or a strapless dress."

From her tape recordings and a file of advertisements from
the printed media, Mrs. Cowan compiled a list of advertising
claims and, in a series of letters signed by herself and Nader,
asked their makers to verify them with scientific data. She
wrote, in all, to fifty-eight companies, which had made a total
of sixty-eight claims she thought questionable. In a typical
letter, Mrs. Cowan asked Leonard Block, president of the
Block Drug Company of Jersey City, about two of his firm's
products, Nytol and Tegrin Medicated Shampoo. She asked
him, among other things, to substantiate claims that "Nytol
dissolves twice as fast as other leading sleep tablets," and that
Tegrin "leaves an invisible medicated area that keeps working for days." Alfred L. Plant, the vice-president of advertising, replied that "you may be sure that none of the claims or
representations cited in your letter for either Nytol or Tegrin Shampoo is exaggerated or unprovable." He did not furnish the laboratory data Mrs. Cowan had requested. (Only
three of the other firms furnished "scientific information" on
which advertising claims were based.) A few of her correspondents were afraid they might be victims of a hoax; it is
one of Nader's idiosyncrasies to write his letters on plain
paper, with no return address on the page. On the envelopes
of Mrs. Cowan's letters was the address of the Washington
office of *The New Republic,* which Nader in this case decided to use as a mail drop. The recipients found it difficult
to believe that Ralph Nader would not have stationery with

a printed letterhead and wrote to him suggesting that he might be the victim of a forgery. "I had the feeling," Mrs. Cowan says, "that Ralph knew exactly what was going to happen all the time, in terms of how the companies would respond. He had the foresight but he wouldn't let me in on it. I didn't resent that, I liked it. It's a good way to learn."

Robert Pitofsky, director of the FTC's Bureau of Consumer Protection, described some of the problems involved in regulating the advertising industry in an interview a few weeks before the new resolution was adopted. The decision to go ahead was by that time all but made. "One of the things we've learned," Pitofsky said, "is that it's very difficult to tie up a copywriter. You can make rules, deny them certain latitudes. But they'll find a way under or around—and, of course, the ad that you've banned has already made its impression on millions of people. So the echoes are available to a clever writer." A week or two before, Pitofsky had attempted in a speech before the American Association of Advertising Agencies, to prepare advertisers for what was coming. "Of course, there are going to be some situations in which the misleading claims for a product have been so outlandish, and the amounts spent on advertising so enormous that corrective advertising could be a mortal blow to certain brands," he told his glum listeners. "But that's because the false advertising created massive consumer deception—not because the remedy is not appropriate to the violation." His speech, Pitofsky says, was greeted with "polite silence. . . . They think the policy is a destroyer."

Nader doesn't think so. He immediately issued a statement saying that the FTC ruling, while it was encouraging, did not go far enough. He assigned one of his young lawyers (who has since taken a job in the FTC) to act as watchdog over the commission. The lawyer, Christian S. White, a huge man of twenty-six with a dragoon's mustache, would certainly give any timid representative of the soap industry reason for pause: to give himself more room, he has set the legs of his desk on Washington telephone directories he tore in half. Among other activities, White filed a petition with the FTC to ban phosphates from detergents, and he has worked with Mrs. Cowan on a similar petition dealing with enzymes. The petition on phosphate detergents was, of course, rendered irrelevant by the government's advice to go ahead and use such products.

The results flowing, directly and indirectly, from the report of the first Nader's Raiders have been more considerable than from those of some of their successors. A new style, altogether less rollicking, has overtaken the Raiders. It is a trend accepted by Nader and positively encouraged by the protective assistants who have gathered around him in the last couple of years. They are aware that a really serious mistake could discredit their work and perhaps even poison Nader's public image.

Robert Fellmeth, an unreconstructed conservative who has ground out more text than any other Naderite, approaches this problem with the certitude, and the revolutionary glee, of one who remembers the old days. "Now we're writing leading texts," he says. "Maybe we're too concerned about *accuracy*." It is one thing to be faithful to the facts—but, as other zealots learned before Fellmeth, it is another and altogether more delicious thing to be unanswerable.

11

Audacity—Always Audacity

The evils of bureaucracy do not afflict us.

RALPH NADER

The Center for Study of Responsive Law was housed on Dupont Circle during 1969 and part of 1970 in a crumbling brick mansion, gabled and turreted and dotted with unwashed windows. This first headquarters of the Nader organization had an air, at once tacky and vibrant, that suggested the zany righteousness anarchists and certain young lovers have in common. Inside, the Raiders roosted—aware, as one of them said, that they were the elite of a whole generation in search of a means of expressing a sense of honor. Ralph Nader, by his example of public emotion and rigid loyalty to a set of principles they believed to be their own, was giving them the means.

The world, with its symbols of alienation, was not far away. Across the street, in a tiny paved park that is the neighborhood's Skid Row, derelicts sprawled on benches, nursing wine bottles in paper sacks. Dupont Circle was the locus of the city's hippie community. Once or twice the drunks, or maybe the street people, walked through the center's unlocked doors to steal a typewriter—little realizing, as one of the Raiders remarked, that they were ripping off their liberators. In the shortened hair and the suits and neckties that for the most part they wore, the Raiders were easy enough to mistake for the enemy. Even in disguise, they might not have got by: there was too much expensive dental work in their smiles, too much confidence in their easy speech for them to be mistaken for anything but what they were, the children of a rich technocracy that had taught them to take acceptance and success for granted.

Inside, the scene was one of cheery chaos. Knots of Raiders sifted through the results of their research into the workings of business and the government, and a babble of graduate school disputation drifted down the stairways. The reception room, manned by militant girls, each with the manner of a Russian chauffeur who is really head of the KGB, was cluttered with cardboard boxes that served as files. Telephone messages, mostly several days old, were Scotch-taped on the door; posters, ranging from the ferociously anti-imperialist to what might be called drippy-lyrical, decorated the peeling walls. The effect was accurately described by Nader, who said that he and his followers strove for the unstructured. A middle-aged visitor, coming on the scene for the first time and wishing to make a pleasant joke, asked one of the miniskirted girls, "Are these the offices of Happenstance, Inc.?" The girl gave him a withering look, put her feet on the card table that was her desk, and resumed a discussion of the defoliant 2, 4, 5-T and its effect on the human embryo.

The old center's ebullience had something about it out of rhythm with Nader's parched seriousness, a quality akin to a socialite's season of good works. Nader had no expectation that most of the young people he attracted would have the necessary stamina. "I'm satisfied with a 10 percent hard core," he said in the summer of 1970, when the third generation of about one hundred Raiders was settling down to work. In his orientation lectures he told them, "Some of you will be lemons, some of you won't be able to take it. This is going to be like Parris Island, except that you'll have to be your own sergeants." He paid them $500 in living expenses for the entire summer—if they could not meet the cost out of their own, or their parents', pockets. He gave them complete freedom of action to attack the targets he selected. (They relished this liberty—and none more than Robert Fellmeth, Nader's favorite exemplar of the type, who gave one of his children "Quixote" as a middle name.)

Nader expected his followers to be motivated before they came to him, and he imposed on them the subtle discipline of his own example. Davitt McAteer, a youthful West Virginia lawyer, brought a group to Washington for Nader's guidance in preparing a report on the coal mining industry. Toward the end of a long session, McAteer began to feel that Nader's powers of concentration were outrunning those of his audience, and he suggested a Coke break. "Coke?" Nader said incredulously. "We don't drink Cokes." Later, walking down the street, McAteer suggested to Nader that all of his talk had been on methods and techniques; he asked if Nader could devote some time to inspiring the group. "Ralph was aghast," McAteer says. "He said, 'Look, if they're not committed now, there's nothing I can do. They have to feel this on their own.' Man, Ralph is really intense. He wants to know why you haven't done more, and he really means it."

Even the most committed had difficulty sometimes in grasping Nader's concept of priorities. He never made any public statement on, and very few private references to, the issues of race and war, the two questions that tortured the generation to which the Raiders belonged. When one young lawyer mentioned this in an interview, Nader learned of the remark before its publication and confronted him with it. Shaken by the experience, the young man searched out the reporter to whom he had spoken and disavowed his statement. To Nader, the youngster's statement was a flaw in perception. He has no time for frustrated pickets. "They can't get it through their heads," he said later, with asperity, "that they're on the sidewalk but I'm catching it at a more basic level. What is more intimately involved with civil rights and poverty than the invisible violence of the corporations? Who do they think gets cheated, diseased, crippled, and generally screwed if not the minorities and the poor?"

In the summer of 1969, Nader set the second company of Raiders to work on matters very far from the ghettoes and the Vietnamese battlefields, where their hearts were. Robert Fellmeth[1] returned to lead a task force into the Interstate Commerce Commission, the FTC's physical and spiritual neighbor, and with the help of six other young lawyers produced a study, *The Interstate Commerce Omission,* which maintained throughout its lengthy text the level of wit established in the title. Another group of Raiders led by James S. Turner produced *The Chemical Feast,* an expansion of a study of the Food and Drug Administration that Turner had begun the year before.

It was the third study of the summer, *Vanishing Air,* a report on air pollution by John C. Esposito, a 1967 graduate of Harvard Law School, and his younger associate Larry J. Silverman, that generated headlines. For the first time, they were not very favorable headlines. Nader had made the error of attacking a man who had a loyal media following of his own: Senator Edmund S. Muskie of Maine. As in the other assaults by the Raiders, Nader merely sponsored the attack,

1. The indefatigable Fellmeth has since produced a 3,000-page report on land policy in California. "We've accused half the state of bribery," he says happily, "and we've got the proof."

but the tone of Esposito's book was such an authentic echo of Nader's own style of inspired insult and reconsidered data that it made no difference. Muskie regarded it as a direct attack on his integrity, and so did many of the reporters who had covered Muskie's effort, in the poisoned presidential campaign of 1968, to save the dignity of the Democratic Party.

In his book Esposito suggested that Muskie had derived a great deal of mileage out of the pollution issue without really doing very much about it. ". . . [Our] Task Force—while giving him credit for his very limited successes—believes that Senator Muskie has failed the nation in the field of air pollution control legislation," Esposito wrote. As to Muskie's authorship of the Air Quality Act of 1967, with its emphasis on a regional, rather than a federal approach to pollution, the book said "that fact alone would warrant stripping him of his title as 'Mr. Pollution Control.'" Esposito, stating that Muskie neglected air pollution except when "it becomes a hot political issue," invited the senator to resign from the chairmanship of the Subcommittee on Air and Water Pollution "and leave the post to someone who can devote more time and energy to the task."

Nader and Esposito maintained they had attacked Muskie honorably, on his record. Muskie, in a mild public statement, said that he had done his best in the light of political realities and that his subcommittee had not acted "for the dark, secret, conspiratorial reasons suggested by the Nader Report." Leon Billings, a Muskie staffer, thought Nader's disclaimers were disingenuous. "If he can think that *Vanishing Air* was not a vicious attack on Muskie," Billings says, "then he is either incredibly naïve or he doesn't know the difference between a vicious attack and a robust criticism." Billings thought the Raiders' technique was similar to the tactics of the street youth at the 1968 Democratic Convention in Chicago—the exploitation of "an opportunity to make power insecure." Another Muskie aide, Eliot Cutler, heard echoes of revolution in a conversation with Esposito, on a friendly evening in a Chinese restaurant before the book was published. Esposito, he thought, had said something to the effect that in order to achieve political change, "you pick out the one man the people trust the most, and you attack him and destroy his credibility." Esposito, an intense thirty-one-year-old who does not consider himself a revolutionary, says this is "an absolute lie"—that he never thought or said any such thing.

The Muskie controversy diverted attention from the book's merit as a readable survey of an important question that Esposito and Silverman, as much as anyone, turned into the great public issue it afterward became. Muskie's staff compiled an eighty-five-page rebuttal of Esposito's book, identifying on each page what the staff regarded as an error or a distortion of fact. For the most part, the book's mistakes are minor, or a matter of interpretation. Some were regarded by Muskie's assistants as deliberate insults to the senator's motives. For example, the book made a good deal of Muskie's alleged collaboration with industrial polluters but included no mention of his bill to impose criminal sanctions upon them. Muskie introduced legislation early in 1970 to impose daily fines of $50,000 and prison sentences of up to five years on violators of the air quality standards.

Because the story concerned the front-runner for the Democratic presidential nomination, it was covered for the most part not by reporters assigned to Nader but by the men, a bit higher in the newspaper hierarchy, who wrote about the Senate and national politics. This was not, as Esposito discovered, an ideal public relations situation. Esposito thought that these reporters regarded his criticism of Muskie as a betrayal of the Old Left Establishment. "It was okay when we criticized bureaucrats, that was open territory," he says. "But there was some sacrosanct quality about Muskie or maybe

the liberal wing of the Democratic Party that we violated.
The newspapers were really stunned by our criticizing someone they perceived to be on the right side of the fence." One
avuncular reporter, he says, took him aside and said, "You
don't *do* this—you don't take the best person around and
criticize him in this town." Esposito thought this was an odd
departure from journalistic detachment.

The reporter, E. W. Kenworthy of *The New York Times,*
doesn't remember saying this, but he does remember being
annoyed with Nader and Esposito. "Nader and Esposito took
much of their time in the news conference and over and over
again in the book in having at Ed Muskie," Kenworthy says.
"I didn't give a damn about this, but I had only seven hundred words to write this story . . . and I had to devote almost
all my space to the attack on Muskie, thereby giving almost
no attention to the book's subject, air pollution. . . . I also
thought Esposito didn't document his charges against
Muskie. . . . I didn't see much point in charging collusion
with industry without evidence. I still don't."

Nader remained aloof from the controversy, except to defend Esposito and the accuracy of his work. A reporter who
happened to be assigned to both men found Nader willing,
after a good deal of verbal fencing, to concede that the report
might perhaps have gone too far. "I'll call Muskie up—about
something else," Nader told the reporter. He never did, and
tension persisted. The two men resumed a wary public
cooperation in December, 1970, when Muskie appeared as a
speaker at a conference on property tax reform sponsored by
Nader. "Ralph Nader has prodded me in the past," Muskie
said dryly, "and I'm sure that he'll prod me in the future."
Nader, seated behind Muskie on the platform, did not respond to the scattered giggles in the audience, or to the
courtly nod Muskie gave him. He has confined his subsequent attempts to influence Muskie to small tactical raids,

carried out by lieutenants—and for the most part out of sight of the press.

The turn of the decade, a psychological watershed for most of the nation, had an effect upon the Nader operation as well. "Ralph is at a crucial point," one of his young lawyers, Donald K. Ross, observes. "A newer, tougher game is developing. The old headline, press-focus game is going out. Ralph and his band of merry Raiders is going out." Nader would not entirely disagree. He is, he says, looking for the first time at the possibility of a mass organization of millions of people, tied to his methods, which he calls "the tools of citizenship," if not to him personally. "I want to get people thinking that [traditional political activity] isn't enough and they're just fooling themselves unless they're part of it," he says. Stage One was Nader, alone against the system; Stage Two was Nader and the Raiders, exposing sloth and venality. Stage Three, now being entered, will see the development of models of social and political action that can be applied by anyone.

Citizen action is now "primitive," Nader says; he honestly doesn't know if its quality can be improved. "You're fighting a lot of obstacles other than the powers you're confronting," he observes, "the personal way people live . . . weekends, six o'clock, their capacity to concentrate. . . . Every time somebody tries to change things, the proposal sounds dreamy because the problems are so overwhelming. And it is dreamy because it takes a good couple of million people to get this kind of involvement. . . . That's what we're going to try." Nader has already broadened his operation almost out of recognition. In addition to the Center for Study of Responsive Law, which remains the nursemaid of the Raiders and the sponsor of his reports, he has established the Center for Auto Safety, the Public Interest Research Group (PIRG), and a complex of other operations. There are fewer Raiders, more professionals. By the end of 1971, Nader had created a dozen mechanisms to deal with questions ranging from the antitrust system to air transportation to clean water to improved food to corporate responsibility. Nader denied his Center for Auto Safety jurisdiction over the question closest to his heart, the Corvair, by assigning responsibility for this issue to Gary Sellers and a former special assistant of William Haddon named Joan Claybrook.

The Public Interest Research Group is composed of a dozen young lawyers who operate almost entirely on gusto; Nader, who meets all of PIRG's expenses out of the proceeds of his lectures, pays the attorneys $4,500 a year each.[2] They are responsible to no one but Nader. "It's beautifully unbureaucratized," Nader says with delight, "just one stop—me to them." More than any other element of the Nader complex, the PIRG lawyers are practicing what John Esposito calls the new law: "It's law, it's journalism, it's street fighting, it's politics." At PIRG, the "new law" encompasses petitions to the regulatory agencies, investigations and tactical probings of the arcane workings of the Office of Management and Budget, advice to congressmen on such legislation as the Fair Credit Reporting Act, an orchestrated attack on the property tax structure—and even a bit of ghostwriting for receptive senators. "I'm writing a piece for Gaylord Nelson," confides one of the young lawyers, "and we hope he'll use it to kick off some investigations."

Gary Sellers, in a manic mood on the day he released Nader's letter to Senator Ribicoff, used the PIRG offices as a forward base. "You haven't got an answer from *The New York Times?*" he demanded of one of the PIRG lawyers. "Go over and hold Jack Morris's hand—*you have to hold Jack's hand!*" The lawyer, a gentle Texan named Peter Petkas, muttered, "I don't really feel qualified to hold Jack Mor-

2. PIRG was founded with the $280,000 Nader received in settlement of his invasion of privacy suit against General Motors.

ris's hand." By that time, Sellers was crooning into the telephone to another reporter, castigating Jerry Sonosky.

Out of PIRG has come the first glimmering of the third stage of Nader's work—the nucleus of a nationwide organization of students to lobby in the Nader style for the reform of society. Organizations of young people have been set up in Oregon, Ohio, Minnesota, and Connecticut; they will support PIRGs of their own to work on local problems involving the environment, consumerism, and the effectiveness of government. "This is clearly the most important development in the legal system since community legal services in the early sixties," says Donald Ross, one of the movement's organizers. "The bomb that's going to explode when this takes effect will just be fantastic. Today there are probably fifty to a hundred public-interest lawyers in the whole United States. We're thinking of thirty or forty *in each state*. . . . If that happens, it will be recognized as a legal revolution."

Nader solidified his idea for funding a network of self-supporting PIRGs—which would include scientists, economists, and political scientists as well as lawyers in interdisciplinary teams—in a casual conversation with a student he met on an airplane. When he returned to Washington, he was still in the grip of the student's enthusiasm, and he dispatched Ross and another lawyer, James Welch, on a cross-country tour to stir up interest and set the phenomenon in motion. In Oregon and Minnesota, Ross and Welch advised local activists, who managed statewide referendums in which students voted to pay a small yearly subscription as part of their university fees to support the PIRG. Welch ran a fund-raising campaign in Ohio, which brought in $75,000; in Connecticut, Ross, working with Connecticut Earth Action groups, raised about $40,000. The gross sum raised for this activity by mid-1971 approached three-quarters of a million dollars. Their next target is California, with its vast network of junior colleges, state colleges, and universities. Ross thinks that California may yield millions of dollars for the activists' treasury. "These organizations, like in Connecticut and Ohio, could become a sort of farm league for a super Nader organization," Ross says. "I hope that happens. . . . But you never know, Ralph is capable of dropping the whole thing." With his tendency to be a firefly over the meadow of issues, Nader has left Ross and Welch largely to their own devices—more so, in some cases, than they wished. During the months that Ross was in Connecticut, Nader turned up only once to help, arriving on Thursday and leaving on Friday. Welch, overwhelmed in Ohio by the demands of a state-wide youth movement that sprang up under the sun of Nader's reputation, pleaded with him to come in and give some inspiration. If the effort failed, Welch said, the papers weren't going to say James Welch fell on his face—it would be Nader's loss. Nader made several appearances after that.

Nader speaks of awakening the populace through activities like Ross's and Welch's, but he has difficulty fitting his own iconoclasm into the pattern of a mass organization. "Ralph steadfastly refuses to look at himself as anything but a person," Ross says. "He refuses to look at himself as an institution. That's part of his attraction, of course, but it weakens the overall organization." When the Nader organization began to form, there was a good deal of speculation that Nader would be bureaucratized. "The danger," he said then, "is not bureaucratization but impotence." To all appearances neither has happened, but there are tinges of both. Nader keeps the power of decision entirely to himself, so there is at the same time in his activities a lack of orderly procedure, and an abundance of rigidity, both of which, ironically, he abominates in equal measure. It may be that the candle of the original rambunctious spirit went out at the end of the summer of 1970, when the old center was torn down to make way for the Dupont Circle Station of the Washington sub-

way. Nader rented a suite of offices over a storefront a few
blocks away. The new headquarters, carpeted wall to wall
and air-conditioned, is populated by unsuspected ghosts: the
Nixon-Lodge campaign staff had its headquarters there in
1960.

A few weeks before the move, Nader hired Theodore Jacobs as executive director of the center. In addition to being
Nader's best friend, Jacobs is a born chamberlain. He is a
tidy man, gentle in speech and careful in his enthusiasms.
Manipulating a keyboard telephone, he stands between
Nader and the world, absorbing the fury of the attacked,
offering solace to the ignored, always speaking the absolute
truth within the limits of what he believes Nader would wish
him to reveal. When they were at Harvard Law School,
Nader thought Jacobs was a stick-in-the-mud (or so Jacobs
believed); later, when Jacobs was working in a New York
law firm, the unemployed but perfervid Nader would drop
in, and, lifting a contract or a tax return between thumb and
forefinger, would ask, "Why are you wasting your time on
this?" Finally Nader needed him for the qualities he had
mocked. Through Jacobs' office almost everything passes, and
it is the one still place in Nader's cacophony of causes. Another Nader associate believes that only Jacobs could fill his
function, because no one else has enough confidence in his
relationship with Nader to carry on the necessary work in
the long silences of Nader's absences, or the patience to keep
track of which enthusiasm Nader has assigned to what lieutenant.

For almost half of Nader's public career, most of what has
been done in his name has been done by others. More and
more, Nader—who detests structure and money above all
things—has been driven to raise money in order to support
the organization that has grown out of his causes. The Nader
who used to tear up checks sent to him by admirers now
spends the greater part of his time on the lecture platform.

His fee for a speech is $2,500; in 1970 he made upward of 150 speeches, some of them free and some at a reduced fee. He loses from the total a booking agent's fee of about 25 percent, but a reasonable estimate of his recent yearly income from this activity might be $200,000.

He still lives on $5,000 a year, using the balance to support his activities. "I really cringe when I walk up to the podium," Nader says. And he does: his long body curves in on itself, like that of a boy playing catch who is afraid of the ball, and his hands with their huge fingernails, yellow and as big as nickels, work nervously. "I just push myself to do these things," Nader says. "If you think you should do it, then you desire to do it. That's the whole key to doing what I'd really rather not be doing."

Despite Ted Jacobs' best efforts to strike a balance between spontaneity and order, the Nader organization remains not so much an administrative entity as a fellowship of the spirit. All energy is directed upward, like prayer. There is little communication among the parts. Everything must pass through Nader, and when he is not available, action is often suspended. The apparatus is organized, as one of its members says, on the principle of the wheel. "It's gotten so now," he says, "that there are too many spokes—it jams up at the hub, which is Ralph. . . . One of the problems is that Ralph is so seldom here." This system is partially a function of Nader's passion for secrecy, partially of his belief that too much structure kills the spirit of those involved in it.

He recognizes the problem with blithe good humor. Of the unhappy Raiders of 1970, who staged a small rebellion in their confusion over what was expected of them, Nader says, "They had so much freedom that they began to crave a hierarchy." Probably they will not get one from Nader. "Everyone has a sort of love-annoyance relationship with Ralph," says Donald Ross. "He's a wonderful person, so you make allowances for him that you wouldn't make for anyone else."

Like most of Nader's followers, Ross says that he is, for the moment, a true believer—and there is a practical as well as an emotional reason for this. "I realize," he explains, "that I couldn't go out, climb up on a box, and cry, 'Follow Donald Ross!' "

Nader's disciples, living like their leader on salaries below the poverty level, bear some resemblance to the figures of the early church. In their reports, they produce a scripture that lacks the grace if not the fire of the Gospel, and they forage for souls in the public places of an empire that tolerates but does not wholly understand them. Sometimes Nader comes across one of Caesar's men who, with a quick look behind him, draws with his toe the outline of a fish in the dust. One such is Gordon Sherman, heir to the Midas Muffler fortune; through the Midas International Foundation, he gave $100,000 out of the half million and more contributed to Nader's work in 1970 by foundations and private donors.[3] Another half-million dollars was received from these sources in 1971.

A growing source of income is the sale of the reports; Richard Grossman estimates that *Vanishing Air* and *The Chemical Feast* have sold about 150,000 copies each, with sales of *The Interstate Commerce Omission* at 75,000. All royalties go to the center.

In 1971, exhausted by his speechmaking tours, Nader decided to go directly to his constituency for funds. Through

3. Donors to the Center for Study of Responsive Law in 1970 were: Midas International Foundation, $100,000; Laurence Wein Foundation, $1,000; Leonard and Rose Sperry Fund, $1,000; Jacobi Society, $1,000; Jerome Levy Foundation, $10,000; Norman Foundation, $25,000; Samuel Rubin Foundation, $10,000; Wallace-Eljabar Fund, $20,000; Field Foundation, $10,000; Stern Family Fund, $41,000; New World Foundation, $9,300; Florence Rogers Fund, $10,000; Public Safety Research Institute (a Nader organization), $5,000; Bedminster Fund, $3,000; Abelard Foundation, $7,500; New York Foundation, $5,000; Ottinger Foundation, $3,200; Public Welfare Foundation, $10,000; Sierra Club Foundation, $5,000; Joseph Gluck Foundation, $6,000; Sunflower Foundation, $2,000; nine anonymous donors, $44,300; and a total of approximately $25,000 in contributions under $500 each.

a new organization called "Public Citizen," he asked 200,000 persons (whose names were drawn from the mailing lists of such magazines as *Newsweek, Evergreen Review,* and *Consumer's Report*) to support his work with small contributions. Nader hoped that the appeal, backed up by a national advertising campaign, would bring in about $300,000 a year. From June through October, 1971, Public Citizen collected about $100,000. The ideal result, of course, would be complete freedom from reliance on the kind of Establishment guilt money exemplified by foundation funds.

Ironically enough, the Nader organization had its origins in an offer of money from the Establishment when Eli Evans, an official of the Carnegie Corporation of New York, saw a newspaper reference to Nader's plan to set up a group of young lawyers to lobby and litigate in the public interest. After two days of unreturned calls, he reached Nader by telephone and said, "I saw your ad in *The New York Times* and I wonder if we can help you." Nader did not rise eagerly to the offer; he had had unproductive negotiations with other foundations and did not want to talk to Evans and his associates at Carnegie unless there was a serious possibility that a grant would be made. Foundations, which are tax-exempt and therefore theoretically apolitical, have difficulty in giving money to individuals like Nader who are involved in lobbying and other political activities.

Carnegie's officials thought they could properly support some of Nader's nonpolitical activities, but they suggested that it would be easier to do so if the funds could be given to an organization that was separate from his public personality. After descending into a period of silence, Nader came back with a prospectus for the center, and with papers granting it tax-exempt status. When Carnegie asked him to tidy up a bit more by appointing a board of trustees, Nader furnished a list with himself as managing trustee. Members of the board are his sister Laura, two professors from the

University of Michigan named Paul W. Gikas and Layman
Allen, and Edmund A. Shaker, a Canadian lawyer who is a
Nader relative. "I talk to them once in a while," says Nader,
describing the relationship of the trustees to the work of the
center. "They help us once in a while. There are no meetings. You see, I'm the managing trustee, so there's a differen-
tiation." ("The best thing about our board of trustees," Harrison Wellford says cheerfully, "is that you don't have to see
them at all.") Carnegie gave the center $55,000 in 1969 to
carry out a two-year study to produce a handbook or a series
of pamphlets "describing the operations of the government
and the ways in which an ordinary citizen may affect policy
and register complaints." Eli Evans, in a lighthearted moment, said that one of the principal benefits of Carnegie's
grant was to provide the elusive Nader with the money for
an office telephone and someone to answer it.

There are disabilities attached to operating with tax-
exempt money. The center is precluded, under its tax ex-
emption, from any political activity "other than making
available the results of non-partisan analysis, study, or research." Nader has an office in the center, but he takes a
touchy view of what he should do in it—when writing testimony and lobbying on the telephone he uses his rooming
house or the PIRG offices. "There are a lot of people around
town who'd just love to pull Nader's tax exemptions," says a
Senate aide. Ted Jacobs expects that there will be more after
Fellmeth gets started on his study of the Congress. Nader, in
order to protect the center's apolitical status, is sponsoring
this particular project as an individual, compartmenting
Fellmeth while he works on it from all of his organizations.

Nader's search for a hard core of activists has not been notably successful. "We are looking for the tigers," he admits.
Out of almost three hundred Raiders, he has found no more

than six who meet his standards for permanent association. "It's tough," Nader says, "to get the full range of qualities for this kind of work—the value system and the sense of equity and the stamina, the hard work and the inability to get discouraged or despair, the ability to subordinate personal problems to professional dedication, the ability to square your work with your spouse, the ability not to be tempted, the ability not to make blunders. The ability to work with people and not have ego problems. . . . And to be smart, even brilliant."

This is a demanding formula, and it is plain that Nader believes in it. He has a way, when he is intense, of aiming his body at his listener, as if it were a gun for firing ideas. Few can fit this job description, which is, of course, a description of Nader. For the most part the people he attracts are brilliant, but they are hardly more than boys. "Ralph always asks us how hard we work," says one of his most effective and least reverent lieutenants, "and we always lie." It is impossible for this young man to cut himself off from art and friendship and girls and sport. "Ralph is the most *alive* guy I have ever met," says another associate. "But—Jesus!—he and I are alive in different ways." It is not that Nader is unaware of the needs of ordinary people, merely that he regards appetite as irrelevant. He seems unaware even of the possibility of problems arising from the new appetites of young people. One of his summer workers mentioned to a *New York Times* writer, in the offhand form of her generation, that she had not only smoked marijuana, but had also used LSD and mescaline before she worked for Nader. When he read the story in the paper, he was flabbergasted. "Mescaline! It was the last thing I would ever have thought," he said in wonderment.

Of all appetites, that for money is most puzzling to him. "Some of these people want to do good in the world for $18,000 a year to start," he says contemptuously. Those who do find their interviews with Nader at an abrupt conclusion.

The money question, Nader says, is the principal reason for the total absence of blacks in his organization. He offered to set up an independent black public-interest law firm, paying its members his usual $4,500 a year and giving them a free hand to pursue whatever issues seemed relevant to them. He tried also to find a black lawyer for the center, offering a higher salary than usual. He had no takers. "They're tired of poverty," Nader explains. Young women, few of whom have joined Nader at a professional level, don't mind economic discomfort as much as the idea of being under the control of a male. When Nader tried to set up an all-female law firm, the women he contacted were afraid of the ridicule they would attract from their militant sisters. It was a new experience for Nader to be regarded as a sexist and member of the power structure.

There are other difficulties of a more fundamental nature. "Young marriages are a problem," Nader observes. He is not hostile but cool and objective, an expert discussing a management problem. "Young wives are the leading assets of corporate power. They want the suburbs, a house, a settled life. And respectability. They want society to see that they have exchanged themselves for something of value." Young marriages among Nader's followers are certainly put under considerable strain. The men work long hours, they are subject to sudden assignments that may take them away for weeks at a time, they are absorbed in their work.

Most of all, they are passionate about Nader. To one young woman, this worshipful tendency seems almost, as she says, a sort of intellectual adultery, an intrusion into her husband's emotions. Some damage is inevitable: a young man, being interviewed by the author late at night, told his wife three separate lies when she called him as many times to ask him to come home; it was obvious that she did not believe him. After the third call, he rushed for a taxi and rode across town, actually trembling with anxiety. "It's interesting," says another young man, recently separated from his wife. "A lot of people who work for Ralph are separated. The wives love him, how couldn't they? But after a while those late-night phone calls stop being so charming."

These are not matters that are discussed with Nader, or that he discusses with his followers. A good deal of intensity, and even a lot of banter, marks their conversation—but it is confined to issues. "Ralph keeps his distance, he lets you know he's judging you," says one of his associates. "Then one day you cross the barrier. And he trusts you absolutely ever afterwards. His voice on the phone—everything—changes." Nader does not like to think that the people he trusts—trust, for Nader, being the equivalent of affection—can have weaknesses. One of his young lawyers, after a long trip marked by a great deal of acrimony, confessed to Nader that he was depressed and worn out. "Don't ever say that!" Nader told him. "Even if it's true, don't ever say that you're psychologically worn out!" There is nothing cold in Nader's treatment of his people; it is the heat of his convictions that attracted them in the first place, and the depth of his impatience. These qualities are not always directed outward to the whole human race, while the searchlight crew stands beside him in the darkness. "When he's most impatient and critical, I feel closest to him," Larry Silverman says, "because it's *personal*."

It is Nader's very sensitivity, in fact, that seems to get in the way of communication. Few venture to trouble him with bad news or inflict hostile opinion upon him. The people who are closest to him, in the opinion of one young man, are the least critical. "There's a tendency not to upset him," he observes, "a tendency to protect him from things which might upset him." Nader hears very little of the negative things said about him by outsiders. Insiders seem to regard it as a failure of loyalty to question his judgment. Even when they do, he can be unyielding. "A lot of what Ralph is," says an associate, "can be traced to the GM experience where peo-

ple told him he was crazy and he went ahead and prevailed.
It gave him a lot of faith in his own sensitivity and judgment, which of course is completely justified. But there's a
stubborn streak in any successful idealist."

The result of this tendency, in the view of another
associate, is that "the problem of frank feedback to Ralph is
very serious." Nader is a defensive man, and this quality can
be an uncomfortable one to live with, especially for very
bright young people who have been conditioned through
many years of excellent education to believe that outspoken-
ness is not merely a virtue, but an obligation. "I want to say
sometimes," one of them comments, " 'Please, Ralph, relax!
Everyone here is on your side! Relax!' But he can't." Once a
diligent devil's advocate, he has given up this role. "It's like
water off a duck's back," he says.

No doubt these undercurrents are unimportant, measured
against the inspiration and the opportunity Nader gives his
followers. They regard him with a respect and affection bordering on the metaphysical; he has quite literally changed
their lives by inviting them, if not into his confidence, then
at least into the force field of his personality. "Before Ralph
was there," Davitt McAteer says, "there was something wrong
with me. My mother knew it, I knew it. I was trying to do
good without knowing the technique. Ralph is incredible—
he seems to know instinctively how to go about things." John
Esposito, who is one of the earliest of the followers, has been
stunned by the range of Nader's ideological creativity ever
since their first interview in 1966. "I had never talked to anyone in any situation with whom I agreed more," Esposito recalls. "He talked about a lot of things which have become a
part of the language. . . . I hadn't even *heard* these phrases
then."

It is possible that Nader leaves emotion out of his conversations with the like-minded because he takes their
emotional approach to issues for granted. No one who works

with him finds him humorless; there is affection for his quirks. It is endearing that he would like to find offices with no air-conditioning, or that he is triumphant in the discovery that the Washington office of a business newspaper has no Xerox machine, because this strengthens his case against installing one at the center. It is comical that he neglects to pay an assistant for half a year, or complains that another, to whom he has allotted $5,000 to overthrow the public image of a corporation that budgets millions for advertising, is spending too much money. His mordant contempt for the Establishment's self-regard is a delight; when Silverman told him he had been solemnly analyzed by a group of university professors, Nader replied, "That's the leisure of the theory class." His witticisms pass through the organization in a flash; it is possible to hear the same remark repeated a half-dozen times in as many conversations.

In the summer of 1970, a small group of that summer's Raiders were not able to make the connection between Nader's personal remoteness and his concern for mankind, as represented by themselves. There was a minor revolt, involving perhaps fifteen of the young people. "They wanted to see more of Ralph," Jacobs explained. "And when they did see him it wasn't too satisfactory. He's shy and I guess they puzzled him because the work hadn't set them on fire. They saw him as an apparition." The youngsters wanted more communal activity; they suggested to a befuddled Nader that he ought to organize softball games and play touch football and have outings along the Potomac. "They wanted a *feeling*, a personal friendship type of thing," Nader says. "One of them said, 'The center's *cold*.' I said, 'You haven't got any complaints—you've got the subjects that interest you, you've got independence of operation, and you've got no policy restrictions in terms of how you're going to express yourselves. So why are you complaining?' . . . The point is, I tend to overestimate their capabilities."

The interlocking operations of the center and the Raiders have continued to produce a series of closely researched, tendentious reports. From the original book on the FTC to Wellford's *Sowing the Wind* to Mark Green's lawyerlike study of the antitrust system, *The Closed Enterprise System,* and David Zwick's lively *Water Wasteland,* the reports have reflected Nader's unsparing view that business and government are allied in a system of greed and deception that is ruining the nation's natural resources and perverting its social purposes.

Nader believes that American institutions may literally be insane. His followers, in their studies, document an accretion of small decisions and petty deals that, they maintain, provide the framework of policy and authority for the plunder of the consumer. Wellford speaks of "agribusiness," an alliance of the Department of Agriculture and other arms of the government and the food industry, which he believes frustrates laws such as the Wholesome Meat Act and injects poisons into the food chain. A similar theme runs through the other books. American life, they think, is based on a straight trade—political power in return for business profits, and vice versa. This is not a new picture of the lobbying activity, but it is a darker one than most people, especially lobbyists, are used to. Only an occasional hero—Ralph Nader almost always, Gaylord Nelson or Philip Hart occasionally, and frequently some lonely (and ignored) scholar—moves through this landscape of Byzantine corruption. The America of the reports is poignant with the despair of youth; it is a Paradise Lost. This portrayal of the nation can be convincing, but it is somehow not always moving. There is too much detail, and much of the detail is selective. As Nader's favorite writer, Alfred North Whitehead, said of the author of the original *Paradise Lost*: "Milton, I think, knew too much finally for the good of his poetry."

Neither Nader nor anyone connected with him is afflicted

by equanimity. "To opt for neutrality is to opt for the status quo," says Gary Sellers. There is, of course, a kind of neutrality in identifying problems without really doing anything about them. That has been Nader's essential function, and that of his followers. It is a frustrating role for an activist. Being a writer of reports, Larry Silverman observes, made him "feel like an artillery officer, firing cannons off into the night." Nader has decided, apparently, that the barrage has lasted long enough; he hopes now to send in the infantry.

His battle plan envisages an army of citizens, equipped with information and resolve, marching on the capitals of their exploitation. Nader is not altogether sure that such a crusade is possible in America. Neither he nor his followers are free of the germ of elitism. "Almost by definition there's a certain elite quality here," John Esposito says, "because we are better educated than the general population." With his technologist's vision, Nader believes that he and his followers are setting up a model that can be copied by lesser individuals. "It takes exceptional people to set up a production line," he says, "but once you get it set up the demands on the full range of human abilities aren't as great. . . . Once the breakthroughs are made, the work can be done by people with lesser attainments or work habits."

Nader's view of the common people is almost that it is a baffled beast, baited by affluence and conditioned by the symbols of jingoism. When construction workers in New York confronted leftist youth in 1970, it was no surprise to Nader. "The construction workers were a perfectly predictable product of our educational system," he said. "They're breaking heads to defend the system, but the system is killing them. . . . They worry about kids destroying the flag, but they, their bodies, are being destroyed by industrial practices which take nothing into account but profits. . . . Workers have been corrupted to use the flag as a fig leaf—not, according to my understanding of American history, the purpose of the flag. . . . I would say to the workers: 'Stop immediately this terrible emphasis on symbols. Don't fight over symbols, but over reality!' "

Nader's sorties against the system have had, themselves, a symbolic air. This is true partly because of the smallness of his resources, as measured against those of his adversaries. If he has a million dollars, or even two, at his disposal, General Motors (as he is fond of pointing out) has gross receipts of more than $2 million an hour, twenty-four hours a day, 365 days a year. It is not reasonable to expect Lowell Dodge, the director of the Center for Auto Safety, to accomplish a great deal in the face of this competition. Dodge is a self-effacing lawyer of thirty-one who went to Hotchkiss, Yale, and Harvard Law School. Like many other Naderites, he is a former civil rights activist, with time in Mississippi and North Carolina. And, like many of his colleagues, he would really rather be helping Negroes than consumers. "It became fairly clear that the blacks . . ." he says, breaking off a thought. "I didn't succeed in getting a job in any civil rights organization I was interested in, so I ended up working for Ralph." Dodge's operation is the most obscure of Nader's public enterprises, although it is the one most closely connected to the issue that launched Nader. Its prime purpose is to keep an eye on the National Highway Safety Bureau. Nader believes, with the expansiveness that comes over him when he speaks of the accomplishments of his followers, that the bureau is all the better for it. "Why is it the most active and open bureau in government?" he asks. "It's because we've put most attention on it."

"Lowell is in here a lot, examining files," says Frank Armstrong, director of the bureau's Office of Compliance. "Basically, what Ralph Nader does is forward letters from consumers to us. A lot of them are bitching letters. We go through all of them on the chance of finding something substantive." The monthly computer printout from all consumer letters received by Armstrong's office is about six inches thick. Sometimes the computer turns up a fault consistently enough for it to be suspected of being part of the design. When that happens, Armstrong opens an investigation. "We are a little like the FBI," Armstrong says. "We never close a case." Nader and Dodge believe that investigations ought to be pressed with more vigor.

In one case where he felt this was not happening, Nader obtained a federal court order requiring the bureau to complete its investigation of the three-piece Kelsey-Hayes wheel on three-quarter-ton trucks manufactured by General Motors between 1960 and 1965. The wheels, Nader alleged, had a tendency to "disintegrate suddenly and explosively." Four months later, in November, 1970, the bureau ordered General Motors to notify 150,000 owners of the defect, and the Justice Department asked the courts to impose a $400,000 civil penalty on the corporation. A suit by General Motors to enjoin the government from this action was dismissed. But General Motors, in a series of legal maneuvers, has continued to resist the bureau's action. Near the end of 1971, the matter was still before the Federal District Court for the District of Columbia—and the defect notice had not been issued to owners of trucks equipped with the Kelsey-Hayes wheel. "It's a moot question whether we would have continued on Kelsey-Hayes without the outside pressure. That was Ralph, mostly," says Robert Brenner. Brenner has his doubts that the government should yield to this kind of pressure when the fate of a smaller business than General Motors is involved. "It's a complex business, applying the regulatory powers of the federal government. What would we gain by driving American Motors out of business? That's what [a major recall campaign] might do to them."

These considerations do not concern Nader, and he does not think they are a proper concern of the government. "[Corporations] should be *driven* out of business if they cannot provide decent environmental conditions," he told the Muskie subcommittee in early 1971. The dictum applies across the board—to makers of unsafe cars as well as those responsible for dirty skies.

The Center for Auto Safety has fewer than a dozen employees, and not many of them can be paid out of a budget running to only $1,000 a month. Dodge can issue press releases and compile data for the auto companies to challenge. But he is a feeble instrument, without official standing, and subject to charges of pettiness when he attempts to assert what he believes to be the public interest. When the air bag restraint system, a pet project of Nader's, was to be tested at an Air Force facility, Brenner informed Dodge that there was no room for him in the crowded laboratory because the Air Force had limited the number of observers to ten. The inflation of the bag takes place in ten milliseconds, so there is very little to see with the naked eye. Brenner told Dodge he could see the slow-motion films whenever he wanted. "Lowell thought we wouldn't invite him because of his connection with Ralph . . ." Brenner says. "I told him, 'You only want to be there so you can be photographed. You won't learn a damn thing.' But I don't think I allayed his suspicions."

In collaboration with an engineer named Ralf Hotchkiss, Dodge has written a book called *What to Do with Your Bad Car,* or, for short, "the Lemon Book." It is hoped that sales of the Lemon Book will bring in enough money to expand the activities of the Center for Auto Safety. Grossman printed 75,000 copies and a book club ordered another 125,000. The book contains chapters of advice, both practical and legal, to those who have purchased faulty new cars on how to pressure the dealer and the manufacturer. It leans heavily on Nader's file of letters from unhappy motorists. Hotchkiss, who describes himself as a "gadgeteer," interviewed about thirty mechanics and automotive engineers before writing the chapters on mechanical faults and tires. Nader contributed the introduction and a good deal of editing. The Lemon Book is not very highly regarded even by friends of the cause. David Swankin, director of the Washington office of Consumers Union, notes that his organization, which regularly pays part of the budget of the Center for Auto Safety, declined to publish the book. "If it had been submitted as a Ph.D. thesis, a lot of our engineers would have flunked it," Swankin explains.

Suffused as it is with amateurism, the Center for Auto Safety is no present threat to the forces it confronts. Its infrequent triumphs come about through the injection of Nader's name and his personal participation—and that is an increasingly rare event. The diffusion of Nader has led to a certain cynicism. "Letters go out from his offices," says a sympathetic student of the Nader phenomenon, "and people ask the question: Is Ralph really behind this? If he is, watch out." If he is not, the stimulus is correspondingly less.

The Project on Corporate Responsibility, otherwise known as "Campaign GM," illustrates the dynamics of the Nader reputation. Campaign GM was never a Nader operation, but it owes some of the results it achieved in its first assault on Detroit to the impression that it was, somehow, an instrument of Nader's will. The enterprise was launched by two young lawyers who had been roommates at Harvard, Geoffrey Cowan and Philip W. Moore III. After finishing law school (Cowan at Yale, Moore at the University of Chicago), they conceived the idea of a project to open the management of large corporations to public scrutiny and public influence. They raised $40,000 and, as a first step, looked around for prominent people to stand for election to the General Motors board of directors. Their first choices were Nader, John Kenneth Galbraith, and John Gardner. All declined—Nader because his lawsuit against General Motors was, at the time, still pending.

Nader nevertheless agreed to talk to Cowan and Moore, and on September 29, 1969, he met them for tea at the Peking Restaurant in Washington. Cowan and Moore expected a brief meeting. It went on for hours. Moore was surprised by Nader's grasp of political tactics; Cowan had imagined that he would be wholly monkish. "I was surprised by Ralph's sense of humor, the way he was relaxed and sort of gossipy," he says. Nader gave them ideas for resolutions, identified issues, provided lists of people to approach for help.

Moore was taken aback by such quick acceptance. "The line he took," Moore says, "was, if I was so confident, okay—go ahead. But he hardly knew me." What Nader did know, of course, was that he, in his larger war against General Motors, had absolutely nothing to lose in the skirmish that Moore and Cowan were eager to lead. It was perfectly logical that he should lend his name and his advice to the effort. Had a less attractive character—say, an ambitious senator—made this effort to attach himself to Project GM, its leaders might well have suspected they were being co-opted. No such caveat could apply to Nader.

On February 7, 1970, Nader held a joint press conference with Cowan and Moore to launch Campaign GM. This event gave birth to the enduring suspicion, which is not altogether unjustified, that Campaign GM is, in Cowan's phrase, "a front for Ralph Nader." Cowan thought that if they had to be associated with anyone in the public mind, Nader was the best of all possible choices.

At the General Motors stockholders' meeting in Detroit on May 21, the Project on Corporate Responsibility offered a proposal to establish a Shareholders' Committee for Corporate Responsibility to report on the company's efforts to produce cars that are safer, nonpolluting, and cheaper to repair. Their chief effort was directed toward the election of three new directors to represent the public interest. Under Nader's tutelage, their candidates had metamorphosed from Galbraith, Gardner, and Nader into a more symbolic slate—a woman, Betty Furness; an environmentalist, René Dubos of Rockefeller University, and a Negro, the Reverend Channing Phillips, whose name had been placed in nomination at the Democratic National Convention in 1968. As they had expected, both their candidates and their issues were resoundingly defeated. On the question of seating the new directors, Campaign GM received (partly through the block votes of several universities owning GM stock) 5,691,130 votes from 53,495 stockholders; this represented 2.44 percent of the total vote. They did slightly better on the Shareholders' Committee, getting 2.73 percent of the vote. Campaign GM itself held 12 of the 285,700,000 shares of General Motors stock outstanding, so they regarded their showing as a moral victory.

Cowan and Moore thought that Nader might have helped to achieve a higher total by coming to Detroit for a rally designed to persuade stockholders to cross over to the cause. They ended with Robert Townsend, former chairman of Avis, as the principal speaker. "They wanted me to go to Detroit," Nader said equably on the day of the stockholders' meeting. "I said I wouldn't do it. Oh, how they bitched and moaned—but tomorrow they'll tell me how well they handled it." A few days later, he coolly critiqued the performance. "They ran it like a Gene McCarthy campaign," he said. "Before it was over, they saw for themselves that that wasn't the way to do it. Some of them won't do it again. I expect that."

Cowan and Moore, and most of their colleagues, stayed around to try again. Between the stockholders' meetings of 1970 and 1971, the people at Project GM decided they wanted to separate the project's image from Nader's. "We wanted to travel our own road," Cowan says, "and not be identified with Ralph. Maybe that helped us." They had, in any case, better luck attracting the proxies of institutions that, Cowan thinks, "were maybe scared by the idea that we were a Nader front."

From their perspective, the showing they made at the 1970 meeting turned out, finally, to be something more than a moral victory. General Motors, by the time its 1971 shareholders' meeting rolled around, had appointed a Negro, the Reverend Leon Sullivan, to its board of directors. It had deposited $5 million in black-controlled banks around the country; increased its fund for the development of a pollution-free automobile by $26 million (to a total of $150 million); appointed a new vice-president for environmental affairs; named a six-man committee of scientists, including a Nobel Prize winner, to advise the corporation on technology and the environment, and appointed some of the outside members of its board of directors to a public policy committee to review General Motors' social impact.

In the light of all that, the stockholders at the 1971 meeting gave Project GM a considerably smaller percentage of the vote than they had done the year before; the percentages on three proposals ranged from 1.11 to 2.36 percent. The results of the 1971 meeting were generally interpreted as a vote of confidence in the management of the corporation. Cowan is not altogether certain that the confidence is well placed, or that General Motors should savor its victory too soon. "The kind of response GM made could be cosmetic," he says. "Our impression is that they don't intend to make it substantive. But they may find that they've invited a monster inside the tent. With this machinery in motion, they may not be able to control what follows."

James Roche controlled the visible monster with great firmness; Cowan asked three of the five questions permitted to Project GM, and Roche cut off his microphone each time. Cowan thought that that was perfectly appropriate, even though he believed Roche and the management of General

Motors were less inclined to think that the Project GM people were tools of Ralph Nader than they had been in 1970. At one point during the meeting, which lasted for nearly seven hours, Roche said, in response to a question, "We are a public corporation, owned by free, white . . ." Amid derisive laughter and cries of "Right on!" he finished his sentence: "Yellow, black people all over the world." The next day, Nader chuckled over the incident. "What an incredible slip of the tongue!" he said. Cowan was not so certain. "I think Roche did something courageous in appointing a black to the board, and I think he's ahead of some of his peers on these issues. I do think he's made a real attempt to help blacks. I felt sorry—I didn't think it was our place to point all these things out when he made that slip of the tongue—but I felt sorry for him." Nader himself avoids all personal contact with his adversaries; his equipment is the high-altitude bomber, not the bayonet. His policy of aloofness might be reduced to the following maxim: Exposure to the humanity of the powerful corrupts the reformer. It dulls the edge of outrage to see James Roche—gray-haired, a grandfather, an honest man baffled by his times—hooted for a cliché that has been leached of its meaning.

On the eve of his retirement, Roche acknowledged that it is very difficult for General Motors to make its meaning plain, or even acceptable, in the face of Nader's criticism. "I think it's necessary for corporations such as ours to continue to emphasize the importance of the economic system under which this country has reached its present enviable position in the world, so there is a better understanding of it against the attacks of those who would like to destroy it . . ." he says. "Unfortunately, what we have been dealing with is a highly emotional subject, and also a technical one. And it's one thing to make a charge, for example, that the automobile accounts for—you name the percentage—of the pollution, and it's another thing to identify the pieces of that and the technical problems that are involved, and what progress has already been made. This has been our great problem. The charges of the critics get the headlines. The answers kind of get put back in the want-ad section."

Roche despairs of Nader's baleful approach to the problems of the auto industry. Nader argues that the industry, with its enormous wealth, should be able to solve any problem of a technical nature virtually overnight. Roche, who has spent his life at the center of technology, has less faith in its possibilities. "Mr. Nader likes to propound the problem and then say that everybody is derelict because they didn't come up with it ten or fifteen years ago," Roche says with asperity. "If we could legislate knowledge, or if we could legislate technological progress, that would be fine. But we haven't found any way to do this." If he could buy a solution to the problem of polluted exhaust emissions, Roche says, he would do so tomorrow.

The punishment Nader has in mind for an economic system that has not produced the solutions he thinks it is capable of producing is, in Roche's opinion, abolition of the system. Roche accepts the necessity for government regulation of auto safety, but he thinks that the deterrents of the criminal laws and market pressure are sufficient to keep the industry awake to its obligations. "We've got these mechanisms built into our society without the things he's advocating, unless he's looking for an entirely different system of government. And that may be what the objective is," Roche says. "I don't think Mr. Nader agrees . . . at all with our present system of competitive enterprise. I think he likes to make the statement that he is trying to work within the system, but the things he is doing are not, in my judgment, working within the system."

Even on intellectual grounds, some of Nader's closest associates have difficulty keeping up with his punitive attitudes. "I honestly don't think you have to punish people to achieve reform," Gary Sellers says. "On this I disagree with Ralph in a modest way." Sellers disagrees with Nader on little else. If any of Nader's lieutenants can claim the title of truest believer, it is Sellers. He is a tiny man of thirty-five, glowing with perspiration and yeasty with secrets. Beneath a shock of limp hair, his mobile face is punished by a combination of anger and cunning and intelligence; he carries the brain of a Florentine courtier and the instincts of a revolutionary in the body of a flyweight boxer. If Ted Jacobs is Nader's George Marshall, Sellers is his Patton. "To work for Ralph," Sellers says, "you have to be willing to sacrifice your personal relationships for what is right. It's the only skill I have. I can't make bombs—I couldn't sleep nights with bombs in the house." Regarding himself, as he says, as Nader's foil, he ravishes personal relationships with abandon —and not always among his enemies. Another Nader lieutenant, during the course of a heated telephone conversation with Sellers, threw a bad spine out of joint and spent a week in the hospital, in traction.

Sellers, the son of a Michigan surgeon and winner of varsity letters in swimming and lacrosse at the University of Michigan, worked for the Washington law firm of Covington & Burling for two years after he was admitted to the bar. Nader met him when he was a legislative attorney at the Bureau of the Budget, and the two soon recognized the kinship of their opinions and methods. Sellers resigned this job in 1969, he says, after his superiors advised him not to talk to Nader, who has always regarded the Bureau of the Budget (now the Office of Management and Budget), with its control over funds and programs, as the jugular of the government. After only a week in the employ of a law firm headed by Thomas H. Kuchel, the former Assistant Minority Leader of the Senate, Sellers had a call from Nader, who asked him to come to work for him. At the Bureau of the Budget Sellers had been working on the administration's draft of the Coal Mine

Health and Safety Act of 1969, and Nader wanted him to watch the bill as it went through Congress.

Sellers almost immediately embarked on a curious double career. Securing an introduction from another congressman, on a Saturday afternoon Sellers dropped in on Congressman Phillip Burton, a Democrat from California who is a member of the Subcommittee on Mines and Mining. Impressed with Sellers' expertise, Burton took him home with him, and the two spent the Fourth of July weekend going over the draft of the coal mine bill. Sellers almost immediately joined Burton's staff as a legal consultant, charged with responsibility for the bill. "I was also working for Ralph," Sellers says. "Sure I was. If someone wants to think that's a conflict of loyalty or ethics, let 'em. Goddamn it, I didn't do it for my employer, I did it for myself. If they want to prosecute me, let them try." Both Nader and Burton pay Sellers what he describes as "a minimal salary."

Sellers regards the whole history of the Coal Mine Health and Safety Act as a conspiratorial scenario—the forces of privilege and reaction, represented by the mineowners and congressmen who are in thrall to them, against the reformers, represented by Burton and Sellers, with Nader in the background. Sellers did not have the manners of a shy newcomer, and he believes that Burton regarded this as an asset. "Phil Burton realized that something valuable had come into his office," Sellers says; "[I was] someone who would work for a minimal salary and be violent in my opinions." Sellers represented Burton at the hundred or more staff meetings involved in drafting the bill, and he provided the congressman with information and arguments at key points. He conceived a great admiration for Burton. "He's an irascible bastard," Sellers explains, "but, man, is he good, a backbone of steel. There were at least two dozen opportunities to disfigure that legislation, and he stood them all off."

Sellers is himself a fierce defender of positions, and he

shares Nader's contempt for decorum. "Gary is always saying
I won't accept this or that, or *I* won't stand for this," another
House staffer says. "It's a temptation shared by a lot of people to ask, '*I* would like to know who the hell elected *you*!'"
At the House-Senate conference on the coal bill, Sellers says,
one congressman asked Burton to restrain Sellers, who had
been crossing the table to proselytize the Senate staff. "I said,
'Gee, is this a search for the truth or isn't it?'" Sellers says.
Burton did not insist. Sellers had been out of town for two or
three days before the House-Senate conference, and he says
he returned to find that "a whole series of prior agreements
had been compromised" in negotiations between Republican
and Democratic committee staffers: "I said, 'I can't accept
some of this.' Everyone from both sides reviled me and said
that my objections would cost us all or most of the strength
we'd put in the bill. I held out anyway, and the fact of the
matter is that the bill the President signed was stronger in
five of the six contested areas." Sellers and Burton were
champions, among other matters, of a provision to require
lighting in underground coal mines, and one to reduce the
silica content in rock dust. Throughout the negotiations,
they held out for the word *shall*—mandatory rather than voluntary safety standards.

Even after the passage of the act, Sellers was not persuaded
that the government took the word *shall* seriously enough. In
March, 1970, Burton and two other congressmen, Ken Hechler of West Virginia and James G. O'Hara of Michigan,
joined with a West Virginian coal miner named John Men-
dez in a federal suit to require the administration to enforce
the provisions of the act. Gary Sellers wrote their petition.
They charged that the government had not, as required by
the act, published regulations on respirable dust or carried
out spot inspections of mines found to be liberating excessive
quantities of methane and other gases. Twelve miners, Sell-

ers says, died in uninspected mines during the period in which inspections were not held. He believed that their families had grounds to sue the government for cash damages.

It was, Sellers believes, the first suit ever filed by members of Congress to require the executive branch to enforce a law. Sellers was convinced that there was a clear legal precedent for the suit under the Federal Tort Claims Act. He thought that death or injury in an uninspected mine was analogous to the same fate suffered by the victims of a shipwreck when the light in a lighthouse operated by the federal government burns out and is not, through the government's negligence, replaced. The U.S. District Court for the District of Columbia left this intriguing legal theory unresolved when it refused to consider the suit on grounds that the government had promised to enforce the law.

The lawsuit was filed, significantly, not against the United States government as an impersonal force, but against Walter Hickel, then the Secretary of the Interior; Elliot Richardson, Secretary of Health, Education, and Welfare, and an obscure federal official named Henry Wheeler, who is director of the Division of Health and Safety of the Interior Department, the agency charged with administration of the act. "The act invested rights in coal miners," Sellers says. "When this administration wouldn't enforce it we said, 'All right, we'll go into court, and every miner who dies will have recourse against the federal government. . . .' " The effect of that decision would have been salubrious in terms of Nader's, and Sellers', vision of the federal bureaucracy. "If [the] lawsuit would do nothing else," Sellers says, "it'd get those bastards out of their nice antiseptic buildings and down in the coalfields where people are dying. The next time one of them doesn't do his job, he'll know he has to spend two months down in Kentucky, defending himself in court. It's almost as good as putting him in jail. Get him out and he can't function. People should show their power—that's what I've learned from Ralph. Hit these cats with everything society allows."

Sellers has continued to operate in Congress as Burton's assistant and Nader's agent. It is not a role that more traditional figures in the House are comfortable with; they continue to deal with him, Sellers says, but warily. It is not easy to escape him. During the drafting of the Occupational Health and Safety Act of 1970, Sellers was convinced that a cabal involving congressmen and their staffers, the AFL-CIO, and the U.S. Department of Labor was forming to defeat the purposes of the act. Meetings were being held to which he was not invited. Sellers found out about them anyway. "When you can't reach a lot of key people in the morning and their secretaries are vague, you know there's a meeting," Sellers says. "Where else could they be? So I'd go down the halls, opening likely doors, until I found the meeting. Then I'd sit down, smile, and spread out my papers." Sellers was not always quite the outsider he pictures himself, however.

Sellers did, in fact, sit down secretly with the Establishment during the drafting of the Occupational Health and Safety Act. A year later, this episode still resounded with resentment and misunderstanding. It was at Sellers' suggestion that a meeting between administration officials and the bill's prime movers in Congress was arranged. On the administration side were Under Secretary of Labor James D. Hodgson (now Secretary) and Solicitor of Labor Laurence Silberman (now Under Secretary). The House delegation included congressmen William A. Steiger of Wisconsin and William D. Hathaway of Maine and a small group of aides. Sellers represented the absent Burton.

The purpose of the negotiations, according to Laurence Silberman, was to produce "a complete bill that would theoretically slide through the House." Neither the AFL-CIO nor the Chamber of Commerce, the two groups chiefly inter-

ested in the legislation, was informed that a compromise was
being worked out. At the end of the negotiations, Silberman
and Hodgson thought that an acceptable bill had been
drafted and that their congressional counterparts had agreed
to support it. Word of the compromise, however, leaked to
the AFL-CIO before the labor organization's liaison among
the negotiators had a chance to break the news. Labor's reaction was very spirited. "The AFL-CIO," Silberman contends,
"threatened to drum some of those congressmen out of their
seats." According to Sellers' more urbane view of the matter,
"the AFL-CIO wanted to make its own compromises."

By the time the bill came up for discussion before the
Democratic caucus of the House Committee on Education
and Labor, the AFL-CIO had made its position plain to most
of the caucus's members. The Democrats decided that they
could not support the compromise bill. Outside the caucus
room, Sellers ran into Laurence Silberman. According to Silberman, Sellers gave him a smile and said, "Sorry, you're
double-crossed." This was Silberman's first hint that the deal
reached in the negotiations would not be honored. He
reacted with what Sellers describes as "rage and astonish-
ment." Silberman thought, and still thinks, that Sellers, having made a deal and then broken it, should have resigned
from Burton's staff. Sellers never thought that any firm deal
had been made, and he contends that he was in no position
to control the Democratic caucus in any case. In the end, a
bill very similar to the compromise version—but "softened,"
in Sellers' opinion, so as to be closer to the original administration position—passed the House.

If Sellers was not prepared to resign on what Laurence Silberman judged to be a matter of principle, he has been ready
to support Ralph Nader in bewildering changes of position
arising from Nader's own reluctance to betray his principles.
Both Nader and Sellers worked zealously toward the passage
of a bill to establish an independent consumer protection

agency in the government. The establishment of such an agency, as a superbureaucracy to oversee the behavior of business, is among Nader's enduring objectives. But he has twice opposed legislation that would have set up such an agency—both times on grounds that the enabling law had been eviscerated by Congress.

The date of the first such occasion was December 1, 1970, when a bill to create a consumer agency came to a vote on the floor of the Senate. Nader and Sellers were in the gallery, sending messages to senators and their assistants. In a press conference only a few days before, Nader had characterized the bill as one of the most significant of the decade. As the Senate debate progressed, Nader perceived that the bill was moving farther and farther away from his concept of perfection. He scribbled a statement and handed it to reporters in the press gallery. Morton Mintz, one of the reporters, had noticed that Nader and Sellers were disturbed. "Pretty soon somebody handed me Ralph's handwritten statement which said this was the most atrocious piece of legislation he'd ever seen," Mintz recalls. "I almost fell out of my goddamn chair. How could it be so terrible when a day or two before it had been so wonderful?"

Nader places responsibility for what he sees as a gutting of the bill squarely on its floor manager, Senator Abraham Ribicoff. Nader and Sellers had attempted to have strengthening amendments inserted in the bill when it was before Ribicoff's Subcommittee on Executive Reorganization, and failed. Then Senator Philip Hart let Nader know that he would introduce amendments on the floor that would limit the number of presidential appointees to the new consumer agency. Hart would have created a degree of congressional control over the agency by authorizing the President, the Speaker of the House, and the Senate Majority Leader to appoint three members apiece to the agency's nine-member executive board. Hart proposed other amendments, to increase the power of the new body to represent consumers in court against other government agencies, and to make it more directly reliant on Congress than on the President for funds.

Ribicoff thought that he had met Nader's major objectives in the committee version of the bill. Ribicoff had an agreement, notably with Senator Jacob Javits of New York, not to accept amendments on the floor. Javits and other Republicans wished to prevent the creation of an agency that might be too independent of the President. Nader believed he had an assurance from Ribicoff that he would accept Hart's amendments. Ribicoff did not do so, and all of Hart's proposals were defeated. Hart, in the end, voted for the bill even though he had been unable to amend it. Nader would not compromise. He saw the weakening of the bill on the floor as the first in a series of maneuvers that would destroy his concept of a consumer agency altogether. He thought Ribicoff had betrayed him. "I can see why Ribicoff changed his mind," he said, "but I think I should have been informed of that. I saw the bill getting whittled, whittled, whittled. Then it reached the Rubicon. . . . All I could see was chipped in the Senate at every step, chipped in the House at every step, and then the Republicans would have exacted their final ounce in the [House-Senate] conference. So I had to come on strong." Mintz and other reporters thought that Nader, on this occasion, had come on a little too strongly in his sudden attack on Ribicoff. They used Nader's statement at the end of stories describing the bill as a step forward in the protection of consumers. Sellers, meeting Mintz the next day, told him he thought he had written a pretty terrible story. The bill was killed, in the end, on a vote in the House Rules Committee.

On October 14, 1971, legislation to create a Consumer Protection Agency was revived and passed the House of Representatives by a vote of 344 to 44. Nader, after supporting an earlier version of the bill, abruptly withdrew his approval. The legislation, he said, had been "stripped of its integrity and effectiveness" when the House rejected an amendment to give the Consumer Protection Agency broad powers to intervene in all formal proceedings on consumer questions and the power to review and investigate the activities of regulatory agencies such as the Federal Trade Commission. Nader complained of another broken promise; Congressman Wilbur D. Mills of Arkansas, he said, had given him "a blanket endorsement" of the amendment and then had voted against it without forewarning.

Sellers regards himself as Ralph Nader's intuitive twin. "I don't have to twist my personality to fit his," he says. "I respond emotionally as he does, usually." Sellers' operations are certainly closer to Nader's natural technique than the frank atmosphere of Nader's daylight activities. Like Nader, Sellers stays up much of the night, often in Phil Burton's office, taking incoming telephone calls. He cajoles a reporter for the *Los Angeles Times* to hold out against cuts in a five-thousand-word story he has filed on the Corvair, sympathizes with an engineer who, after cooperating with Nader, finds to his surprise that he is not considered employable by an auto company, talks cryptically to Nader ("Let's back up over that—I'm, uh, not exactly alone"). When he is on the phone, his brittle voice softens into another tone, as if he might be speaking to a child or a girl. "I assume," he says to his visitor, who is sitting across the desk with an open notebook, "that when I'm on the phone it's off the record. I mean, you could really do us in—phone calls in the night."

Sellers has Nader's extraordinary tenacity, his capacity for turning an issue into something like a wolf pack that surrounds an adversary and sends its members snapping out of the darkness from all directions. As an adjunct of his general attack on the Corvair—and General Motors, and the Ribicoff subcommittee—Sellers filed a complaint with the

Michigan Bar Association against two General Motors lawyers, whom he named, and who he said were "signing off on lies" in the corporation's lawsuits in connection with the Corvair. "These cases are filled with the stench of their lies!" he cries. "Even if it's not the ultimate penalty, disbarment, even if it's only the inconvenience, the trouble, the embarrassment of answering, it should have a cleansing effect on the company." If Sellers, who in the tradition of selfless lieutenants is an aspect of Nader, has any motto at all, it must be Danton's *"De l'audace, encore de l'audace, et toujours de l'audace!"*

The English meaning of the key word is subtly different from the French. It is in the break between meanings, of course, that ideals incubate and idealists operate. That is why they elude definition, escape judgment—and sometimes, when the hour is right, compose their contradictions and do precisely the things they have deplored in their enemies.

"We've got to go deeper . . ." Nader says. "This country is in a battle between—what are the old formulations?—freedom and knowledge, or whatever. Right now it's a struggle between justice and suicide." The workbench of Nader's justice is his organization—cluttered as it is, and clamorous. The craftsmen vary in their skills and in their methods, but they are all part of the process.

12

The Unknown Variable

If my father had not met Ralph, and been encouraged
by Ralph to run, I think he wouldn't have run. . . .
Ralph was the magical unknown variable that could grab
victory from the jaws of defeat.

JOSEPH A. ("CHIP") YABLONSKI

Late at night on Saturday, May 3, 1969, four men met in the
empty offices of a law firm at 1730 Rhode Island Avenue,
N.W., in Washington. They came separately through the deserted streets, and in such secrecy that even two years afterward their most trusted associates did not know the details of
their discussion, or that a chain of circumstances began on
that soft spring night which would end in the murder of one
of the men.

Three of the men had agreed to talk to an outsider about
matters they had almost never discussed outside the safety of
their family. They were Joseph A. ("Jock") Yablonski, a
high official of the United Mine Workers of America; his
brother, Leon, a UMW international representative, and

Leon's son, Steven, in whose office they were meeting. Jock and Leon Yablonski were the sons of a Polish immigrant who had died in a mine accident. They had gone into the mines themselves when they were teen-age boys. They had spent their lives in the union. Now they were preparing to discuss the union's shame with an outsider who was not a union brother and who, in fact, had never in his life done hard manual labor.

The outsider was Ralph Nader. If he was not a miner, he had shown himself in the press, and in more private ways, to be a friend of miners. He had publicized their plight—one of every two, he wrote, suffered from black lung disease; one of every thirty was injured each year. He had given his support to a wildcat strike of West Virginia coal miners who in 1969 marched on the state capital, demanding a law that would make black lung disease compensable under the workmen's compensation laws. He had denounced the government, and the coal operators, and finally the United Mine Workers of America, for insensitivity to the suffering of miners. "I saw this emerging as an immensely significant thing, right from my first black lung article," he said later. "The tip-off was the dissident workers. In a tight-run union like that, they could wildcat." With nothing to gain, Nader had done something. The Yablonskis, who knew better than Nader what odds he was fighting, and what dangers he was inviting, respected his efforts.

Steven Yablonski, a member of the law firm Rowley & Scott, had worked with Nader on some antitrust questions. They had formed a friendship, they were about the same age, and they thought alike about a lot of things. One of the things they discussed was the United Mine Workers Union and the state into which it had fallen under John L. Lewis's successor, W. A. ("Tony") Boyle. Nader learned that Steven Yablonski's uncle and father were officials of the union; as

Steven carried Nader's views to his family, and his family's opinions to Nader, both sides became interested in a meeting. Finally one was arranged.

There was no agenda; the Yablonskis had no thought that they might join forces with Nader. They had traveled a considerable psychological distance even to talk to him. "Ralph was asking my uncle if the information he had exposed about the UMW was a true reflection of conditions in the union," Steven Yablonski recalls. "My uncle, of course, said that it was." There was a long discussion that seemed to be leading nowhere except back to the sense of outrage they all felt about a union that at best seemed to care little for its members, and at worst seemed to have fallen into the hands of criminals.

Tony Boyle was up for reelection that year. It was taken for granted that he would win another five-year term. Boyle called himself John L. Lewis's handpicked successor; he controlled the union's funds, its presses, and its organizational machinery, which included many violent men who owed their jobs to Boyle. No candidate with ability or reputation had risen to challenge him. Almost no one thought of Jock Yablonski—thirty-five years a faithful member of the hierarchy, a former president of District 5 (Pittsburgh), a member of the international executive board, acting director of the UMW political arm, the Non-Partisan League—as a candidate. Yablonski himself had toyed with the possibility, but he had never discussed it outside his family; his relatives were not encouraging: it was an expensive, exhausting, dangerous run that he had virtually no chance of winning. Yablonski had no plans to be a candidate when he met Ralph Nader for the first time.

Jock Yablonski came to the meeting with a high opinion of Nader. "My dad had a tremendous respect for Ralph Nader," says his son Joseph A. ("Chip") Yablonski. "It transcended anything he did in the Mine Workers or for the miners. The whole idea of the impact this one guy had had, taking on GM—one dedicated guy doing that inspired in him unlimited faith." On the night of the meeting, Yablonski's respect began to turn into what several of his friends testify was his later feeling about Nader; Yablonski's friends always use the same words to describe this feeling: mystical faith.

After the meeting had lasted for a couple of hours, Nader paused and looked at Jock Yablonski. With no preliminaries, he asked him if he would run against Boyle. "Ralph came right out and asked my uncle if he would consider running," says Steven Yablonski. "I was a little staggered, to tell you the truth. I guess my uncle was surprised, too." Yablonski hesitated. Nader told him, in his intense way, that if he did decide to run he, Nader, would give him, as Steven Yablonski remembers the phrase, "all-out support." No one asked what that meant. Nader made no specific promises.

Finally, Jock Yablonski looked at Nader and said, "If I do run, Ralph, they'll try to kill me."

Steven Yablonski thought that his uncle's remark was a little melodramatic. Nader said, "They wouldn't dare—you'll be in a goldfish bowl."

Nader turned the conversation to practical matters. Under what conditions would Yablonski run? Yablonski said he would need, at a minimum, the public backing of Nader, of Congressman Ken Hechler of West Virginia, and of the three doctors who had led the fight in West Virginia against black lung disease. Yablonski had made no decision when he came into his nephew's office because he had little hope of winning the union election. When he left in the early hours of the morning he still had made no decision, but he had been given hope.

Over the next three weeks, Yablonski and Nader met on at least nine occasions, sometimes in Steven Yablonski's office, sometimes in a room at the Holiday Inn on Scott Circle. The

meetings usually began shortly before midnight and sometimes lasted until five o'clock in the morning. In all, about
seventy-five hours were devoted to these secret discussions.
Yablonski had still not made a final decision. He was still
consulting his sons and other members of the family, and
still measuring the risks against the slim likelihood of success. He did not, in fact, consent to be a candidate until May
25 or 26—only three or four days before the formal announcement of his candidacy.

During the meetings with Nader, Yablonski defined his
objectives. He wanted to cleanse the union, restore its democratic procedures, turn it once again into a militant fighter
for the health and safety and wages of the members. Those
were Nader's objectives, too. But, in his case, the election was
merely part of a larger operation. He had already installed
Gary Sellers on Capitol Hill to watch over the Coal Mine
Health and Safety Bill. In West Virginia, he had put out
lines to the miners through the black lung campaign. Also in
West Virginia, Davitt McAteer had begun his Raider-style
study of coal mine safety; McAteer had recruited his own
team of students and brought them to Washington to be in-
structed and inspired by Nader; he had raised $9,280, of
which Nader contributed $20. "I think Ralph saw my dad's
candidacy as a vehicle for passage of the Coal Mine Health
and Safety Act," Chip Yablonski says. "To that extent he
used my dad, but I don't find anything particularly improper
about that."

Yablonski appointed Chip, who had resigned his job as an
attorney at the National Labor Relations Board, as his campaign manager. Nader deputized Gary Sellers to deal with
the Yablonskis. There was still no specific discussion of what
precisely Nader was going to do to help. Nader talked about
strategy: how to use the press, how to awaken John L. Lewis,
how to stir the rank and file of the union by showing the violence Boyle's men had done to their bodies and their pride.

Yablonski thought Nader was a genius. In his mind Nader became, as Chip Yablonski says, "the magical unknown variable that could grab victory from the jaws of defeat."

The one point on which all the Yablonskis, and all the members of the campaign staff who were close to Jock Yablonski, agree is that Yablonski would not have run at all in the absence of Nader's persuasion. Yablonski thought Nader was in all the way. The more he saw of Nader, the more he thought he had a chance to win. By the time the campaign actually began, Yablonski was convinced that he could defeat Boyle. He held fast to this conviction until the end. "Obviously Ralph couldn't make Jock win," says Fred Barnes, a young newspaperman who was Yablonski's press secretary. "He couldn't have won that election with a hundred Naders." Nader does not agree. "In fact Yablonski would have been elected had it been a clean election," he says. It was not a clean election, and all the intricate plans could not make it so.

Nader approached the issue as he approaches all others—in the newspapers. On May 23 he wrote a letter, published that day in the Washington papers, to John L. Lewis. Lewis was eighty-nine years old and dying. "The union you built," Nader wrote, "has deteriorated into a state of sycophancy toward the coal operators on such crucial matters as health and safety." Moreover, Nader wrote, Boyle was plotting to take for himself Lewis's seat on the board of the United Mine Workers' welfare fund. Boyle, he predicted, would accept the $60,000 salary that went with the post, a salary Lewis had always declined.

The old man might have been expected to regard this letter, from a Princeton boy who had never spent a day on a coal face, as a piece of effrontery. Evidently he did not. Later, when Jock Yablonski telephoned him, Lewis said he wanted to sit down with him and talk. Yablonski, knowing Lewis, took this to mean that he was not hostile to his candidacy.

Someone told the Yablonskis that Lewis had read the letter and thought the charges were generally true. The Yablonskis began to believe Lewis would support Jock, but he died on June 11 before he had spoken out.

On May 29, in the Pan American Room of the Mayflower Hotel, Yablonski announced his candidacy for the presidency of the United Mine Workers of America. There were guards at the door. Nader sat at the back of the room. Yablonski was a balding, powerful man with very clear gray eyes under heavy brows; his face was so deeply creased that it seemed the lines in his cheeks and forehead might have been cut with a knife; he had huge hands and a rasping voice. In comparison, Nader seemed almost languid.

Reading from a prepared statement, Yablonski said, "I participated and tolerated the deteriorating performance of the [UMW] leadership—but with increasingly troubled conscience. I will no longer be beholden to the past. . . ." He spoke of his "deep awareness of the insufferable gap between the union leadership and the working miners that has bred neglect of the miners' needs and generated a climate of fear and inhibition." He referred to the "shocking ineptitude and passivity of the union's leadership on black lung disease." He added a description of the larger meaning of the union:

> . . . Unions represent men and women who are part of communities, are citizens of states and a nation. The public environment affects the well-being of miners and their families. What good is a union which reduces coal dust in the mines only to have the miners and their families breathe pollutants in the air, drink pollutants in the water and eat contaminated commodities? What good is a union that achieves an acceptable wage rate and then condones the reduction

of that wage by frauds and abuses in the marketplace
and waste or corruption of government?

The cadences and the ordering of issues were unmistakable. Ralph Nader, mingling his own ideas with Yablonski's,
had written the statement of candidacy. Not even that fact,
which was generally known to the reporters present, controlled their skepticism. One of them asked Yablonski why
he had been silent so long; only a few weeks before, he had
been traveling with Boyle in West Virginia, introducing him
with what *The Washington Post* called flowery speeches before audiences of the miners Yablonski now said Boyle had
betrayed. Yablonski quoted John L. Lewis: "When ye be an
anvil, lay ye very still; when ye be a hammer, strike with all
thy will." Earlier in May, when he was already in touch with
Nader, Yablonski had accepted appointment from Boyle as
acting director of the Non-Partisan League, one of the most
powerful posts in the UMW. Yablonski said that he had decided that Boyle must go on June 21, 1966, when Boyle asked
for, and received, Yablonski's resignation as president of District 5. (In retrospect, some of the Yablonskis believe that
Boyle, even at that early date, feared Jock Yablonski as a
rival for the union presidency.) Yablonski gave the details of
his criminal record, which he expected to become an issue in
the campaign. He had broken into a slot machine thirty-nine
years before and served eight months in jail. He was par-
doned by the governor of Pennsylvania in the fifties.

Chip Yablonski believes that Nader's presence at the press
conference destroyed some of his usefulness. He did not
know that Nader was going to turn up; the arrangement, he
thought, was that Nader would call reporters and tell them
about the conference, saying only that it was "something big
involving the Mine Workers." "The whole idea went down
the drain," Chip Yablonski says, "the idea that he would re-

main aloof and retain all his credibility with the press as an arch-critic of the United Mine Workers. All that went by the boards. He became associated with one of the candidates and anything he said thereafter was regarded as a partisan statement. I was really surprised." Nader is surprised at Chip's naïveté; that first public appearance with Yablonski was the major contribution he wanted to make. "I drafted his statement . . ." Nader says. "I wanted to launch him and I wanted to identify my sympathy with his cause. It was very important that he get immediate and good press coverage. . . . He was unknown. Everyone had extreme skepticism about his motives, really extreme, because everything coming out of that union was subjected to skepticism. But I believed him. Here was a man who really had changed. He was never anything like as bad as the other people he had associated with on the board. . . . Jock had everything to lose."

Nader's public identification with Yablonski did, in Chip Yablonski's opinion, "provide the magnetism" for Joseph Rauh, a highly regarded lawyer, to join the campaign as counsel. Nader paid the salary of a Harvard law student named Beverly Moore, Jr., who worked in Rauh's office as a campaign aide throughout the summer. Gary Sellers, already working eighteen hours a day on the coal bill, was assigned to help out with ideas and tactical advice, and as a speech writer. There were misunderstandings from the beginning as to Sellers' role. "Gary worked his heart out," Nader says. "The only thing I can say about Gary is that to get the simplest thing done required moving mountains," Chip Yablonski says. "I just didn't have the time to go through the tortuous procedure of trying to find him, trying to talk to him, arrange meetings. I'd just go out and do it myself." Sellers was aware of the problem. "I had to make the decision to work on the coal mine bill," he says. "Which was more permanent—a federal law or a campaign for union office? I was up till two o'clock night after night, just persuading people to keep their knees together. The industry's employees who would be covered by the Act were the same ones Jock wanted to help." More than once, Sellers brought Yablonski to Capitol Hill to tell congressmen and their aides the realities of the mines.

When Chip Yablonski took over management of his father's campaign, he was twenty-eight years old. He was inexperienced and, as Nader concedes, "Gary didn't make any secret of the fact that he thought Chip was making some errors, some serious miscalculations." At a meeting in Rauh's office in the early stages of the campaign, Sellers suggested that Chip Yablonski be relieved of his duties. Not unexpectedly, Chip's father did not agree. Sellers, who thought that a more experienced man was needed, concedes that Chip Yablonski "turned out to be excellent . . . but there was no indication of it at the time." Although he realizes his suggestion produced wounded feelings, Sellers is surprised that these should have persisted. "Wow," he says, "isn't it funny how tiny little things will loom large to people?"

The campaign was, from the beginning, a violent one. A pre-nomination rally for Yablonski in Shenandoah, Pennsylvania, was disrupted by the Boyle forces. Yablonski charged that the union's leadership was trying, through strong-arm tactics, to prevent his getting the endorsement of fifty locals needed for nomination. He was knocked unconscious by a Boyle supporter in a hotel room on June 28 in Springfield, Illinois; his arm and foot were numb for weeks afterward. Yablonski accused Boyle of manipulation of the pension fund, intimidation of the membership, rigged elections, and worse. Sellers thought that Yablonski might win because of the absence of his opponent. "I thought the FBI would get in and just drag Tony Boyle away," he says. "If half of what Yablonski said was true, it was only a matter of time." Even Chip Yablonski thought that Boyle might resign. "It was sheer folly to have believed that," he concedes, in retrospect.

These optimistic estimates of Boyle's reaction to Yablonski's charges ("Tony Boyle is going to be a cellmate of Jimmy Hoffa") did not reckon with the resourcefulness of the UMW hierarchy. In one twenty-four-page issue of the *Mine Workers Journal*, there were thirty photographs of Boyle. Yablonski's candidacy simply was not mentioned. Yablonski eventually secured a federal court order forbidding the UMW to use its newspaper as a Boyle campaign instrument. Other court orders forced the UMW to give Yablonski access to union membership lists that had been withheld from him and to mail his campaign literature. A group of miners sued the union's leadership for $75 million, charging conspiracy to defraud them of their pensions through fiscal mismanagement and manipulation of union funds for private gain. Yablonski, as a footnote to his charge of general corruption, said that Boyle and two other high UMW officials had, among them, nine relatives on the union payroll who were paid $399,331 in salaries and expenses in 1967 alone. The Department of Labor announced in November, 1969, that the UMW pension fund had "never been adequately disclosed in the annual financial report," as required by law.

Early in the campaign, Joseph Rauh asked the Labor Department to investigate irregularities, including the UMW's refusal to distribute Yablonski's campaign literature, failure to afford a reasonable opportunity for the nomination of candidates, the use of union dues to support the Boyle slate, and threats of violence. On July 23, Secretary of Labor George P. Shultz informed Rauh that he had referred the allegations of violence to the Justice Department for investigation. The other points, he said, had been settled either by private suit or by events. A subsequent FBI investigation of the assault on Yablonski in Springfield and of the disruption of the meeting in Shenandoah produced no evidence that the government regarded as sufficient for prosecution. Shultz said that "the Department of Labor, as a matter of policy, has never initiated or conducted an investigation of an election prior to the actual conduct of an election."

Under the Landrum-Griffith Act, the department could seek internal union remedies, investigate, or set aside the results of the election after it was over and conduct a new one under the supervision of the Secretary of Labor. After Rauh pleaded with the department once again to investigate, Shultz said on July 25: "The developing circumstances of this case may . . . lead us to consider this matter further after the nominations are closed on August 9." On December 6, Shultz refused another demand from Rauh for an investigation. Congressman Hechler informed Shultz that the Boyle forces had printed 50,000 extra ballots. After the election, on December 23, W. J. Usery, Jr., an Assistant Secretary of Labor, refused Yablonski's request to impound the ballots. The Labor Department never found evidence that ballots had been tampered with "on a mass scale."

"The most fascinating thing about the whole affair," says Nader, "was the depth of the sickness of those law enforcement agencies, like the Labor Department. Just unbelievable!" Under Secretary of Labor Laurence Silberman, who at the time of the UMW campaign was Solicitor of Labor, maintains that "there was no statutory power for the federal government to do anything [to intervene in the election]." Although the Landrum-Griffith Act gave the department authority to investigate an ongoing union election, this had never been done. Such an investigation, Silberman explains, "is basically unfair, because it would almost certainly affect the results of the election—and the impact would be problematical; it might well have helped Boyle."

Silberman thought that Rauh's argument was not that the Boyle forces could be proven to have done wrong, but that these were the sort of people who could be expected to do wrong. "I sat in the room with Silberman," says a Labor Department official, "and heard him say to Joe Rauh, 'Please, just give me one piece of evidence.' But they couldn't do it." Silberman says, "I certainly thought all along that this was a classic 'bad guy' situation—exactly the kind who should, in our system, be guaranteed due process."

Gary Sellers was disgusted by Silberman's legalistic approach. "I really underestimated Larry Silberman for his insensitivity," Sellers says. "Jesus Christ, what a beast!" Sellers and Nader believe that part of the reason for the Labor Department's aloofness was the "political influence" of the UMW. "That is ludicrous," Silberman says. "The position of the UMW was, and is, virtually that of a pariah *vis-à-vis* this administration." A high Labor Department official puts it more colorfully: "The Boyle faction is lower than whale shit at the bottom of the Pacific as far as we're concerned."

According to Sellers, Nader himself made a number of appeals to the Labor Department on Yablonski's behalf. Neither Shultz nor any of his deputies remember having any dealings with Nader or anyone connected with him on the subject of the UMW elections or Yablonski. Nader had his only meeting with Shultz while the UMW elections were in progress. He and Shultz discussed the Walsh-Healey Act. Shultz's executive assistant, David Taylor, recalls that Nader was emotional about what he suspected were widespread violations of Walsh-Healey, which lays down standards for safety in work places. "By the end of the conversation he was trembling, indignant about this . . ." Taylor says, "but he never mentioned Yablonski."

The tensions between the Nader forces and the Yablonski staff, meanwhile, continued to increase. Yablonski had always been short of money, and he decided to organize a committee to raise funds. At a meeting in Rauh's office, it was suggested to Nader that he might serve on the committee or write a public appeal. "I just said," Nader recalls, "that I don't raise money for anyone." Nader had, in fact, attempted to interest

John D. Rockefeller IV, recently elected secretary of state in West Virginia, but no contribution was forthcoming. The Yablonskis did not want financial help from Rockefeller, whose very name they regarded as a liability to a candidate for union office. Later in the campaign, when Rockefeller offered to endorse Yablonski's candidacy, he was turned down. Chip Yablonski, like Fred Barnes and other Yablonski staffers, believes that Nader was upset because Yablonski was not using more of his own money in the campaign. "I didn't think that Ralph or anyone else had a right to expect my father to walk away a pauper," Chip Yablonski says. It was agreed, finally, that Nader would write some sort of letter that could be used in the fund-raising campaign. Nader never wrote the letter, but he permitted the use of his name in an advertisement appealing for contributions.

Nader's aversion to fund-raising was understandable to Yablonski's family and staff. They had greater difficulty in comprehending a second refusal. Chip Yablonski wanted to set up a network of poll watchers on election day, and he asked Nader to write a letter appealing for student volunteers. Chip Yablonski drafted and redrafted a letter for Nader's signature; he says that he carried ten different versions to Nader for signature. After Nader had approved one version of the letter, Sellers demanded the revision of a phrase that implied that Nader was endorsing Yablonski's candidacy. "It was an explicit endorsement of Yablonski as a person," Sellers explains. "Ralph has never done that." The change was made, but it delayed the mailing of the letter by forty-eight hours.

Sellers never considered the possibility that young poll watchers responding to Nader's appeal might be in danger as intruders in a union affair that had been marked by violence. "It may be revealing about me . . ." Sellers says, "but I didn't think that was a realistic possibility at all. I don't think about things like that." In the end, Nader said that he would not sign the letter, but that it could go out with his name printed at the bottom. By that time it was very late. "There was some foul-up with the mailing," Sellers says, "some strange Thanksgiving weekend or something, and maybe they didn't get it out as early as they should have." Chip Yablonski says, "It was useless. . . . We got back a dozen responses from five hundred letters."

These were not minor incidents, and they created an atmosphere of doubt. There was, perhaps, something about idealistic, elite Harvard lawyers and tough-minded trade unionists that could not mix. Beverly Moore says, "Yablonski was a pretty impressive guy—or should I say, 'for a coal miner?' " Chip Yablonski believes that Nader did not understand the realities of the situation. "But I don't think anybody did," he adds. "Ralph felt you could hammer away at the UMW [in the press] and it would fall. . . . You can have the greatest access in the world to the big-time press, but you don't reach 90 percent of the membership. . . . There's suspicion in Appalachia—people would say, 'What's he in this for? What's he really trying to do? He's going to get rich out of this somehow.' A lot of people felt that way about Ralph, and they feel that way about us today."

The breaking point came in July, shortly after the Boyle forces published an election bulletin on Yablonski. The labor movement has preserved a vocabulary of slander from its early days of persecution and struggle. This vocabulary was used to level charges against Yablonski that he had abandoned his first wife and their child, that he was a convicted felon, and a great deal more.

"Ralph and Gary read this smear sheet," Chip Yablonski says. "*And believed it.* . . . I watched Ralph and Sellers as they read it. Watching Ralph's face, Ralph acted as if he'd been had, that we had foisted my dad off on him." Chip made no effort to discuss the smear sheet with Nader; his father had been forthright about his criminal record, and the

rest was distorted. "I don't know what you say," Chip Yablonski says. " '*Surely you don't believe that?*' You don't say
that to Ralph." Nader insists he did not believe the charges
in the smear sheet. "You only have to sit down with the other
guy to know that you wouldn't give him credit for anything," Nader says.

Nader did sit down with "the other guy." This was Michael Budzanoski, president of UMW District 5, who collab-
orated with the editor of the *Mine Workers Journal,* Justin
McCarthy, in writing the election bulletin. Nader and Sellers met in July with Budzanoski in a room in the Sonesta
Hotel in Washington. "I've never seen such hate . . ." Sellers recalls. "He had suitcases full of stuff he kept pulling out.
He kept contradicting himself. He had these vicious cartoons
he wanted to show Ralph and me. It was horrible. . . ."

Nader and Sellers did not tell Yablonski in advance about
their meeting with Budzanoski. Chip Yablonski never had
any information about the meeting at all from anyone in
Nader's camp. Sellers told Yablonski about the meeting after
it had taken place. "I told Jock, 'Look, it's better to listen to
him,' " Sellers says.

Yablonski, his son believes, regarded the meeting between
Nader and Budzanoski as a betrayal. "He was hurt—hurt,"
Chip Yablonski says. "I don't think my dad felt that Ralph
could have believed what Budzanoski told him. On the other
hand, I do. I do." After these events, Chip Yablonski did not
see Nader again, although he talked to him on the telephone
a few times. Soon even that contact ceased. Nader, with no
explanation to the Yablonskis, simply withdrew himself from
the campaign into which he had launched them. From July
onward, he made few public statements about the UMW or
the election.

"Jock Yablonski," says Fred Barnes, "felt seduced and
abandoned."

Nader refuses to believe that this is true. He maintains

that Yablonski had no grounds for disillusion. Nader says he never gave any credence to the charges in the smear sheet. The Yablonskis simply believed, he says, that he was going to play a greater role than in fact he ever intended. "I guess they mistook a launching for a marriage," he says. "What they never realized, and what they probably could be forgiven for not understanding, is that we never intended to be deeply involved in this. All we intended to do was to make sure that he had a solid launching, which was done very intricately, and provide him with a student [Beverly Moore], and be available for any consultation or any help. But never more than that. From that misunderstanding flows all these consequences." Nader points out that he was involved with more than a hundred summer Raiders, with seven other projects, with auto safety. "It just stands to reason I wouldn't have been able to do all these other things," he says.

Chip Yablonski understood from the beginning that Nader's contribution would be pretty much as Nader describes it. "The way I see Ralph's *modus operandi*," he explains, "is that he gets in, gets something started, and then walks away. He's provided the impetus, and he goes on to bigger and better things. . . . After he read that scandal sheet, I continued to be in touch but I never really expected much. When I looked at the balance sheet I just took Ralph off as an asset."

It was some time before Jock Yablonski could do that. He brooded over Nader's withdrawal. At one point he said to Barnes, "Ralph is really mad at me. Why has he turned against me?" Nader will not believe that Yablonski believed these things of him; they had breakfast together after the Budzanoski incident, and Nader detected no resentment. Within the family, no one doubted Yablonski's resentment. Only three days before he died he made a final, bitter judgment of Nader's retreat. At a family council, Chip tried to persuade his father that the Yablonskis had expected more help from Nader than he had promised to give. Jock Yablonski leaped to his feet in anger. "You don't know what you're talking about," he shouted. "I expected a hell of a lot more out of Ralph than I ever got."

Yablonski lost the election by 46,000 votes to 81,000. Pensioners as well as working miners had been permitted to vote. In some districts controlled by the Boyle forces, he was defeated by such margins as 273 to 1. "There's just no way anybody can be beat that bad," Chip Yablonski says. "Let me just say this: If Ralph had wholeheartedly committed himself on just one thing—observers—the election would have been damn close. . . . All we were asking for was observers, just to make sure that the ballots cast were the ballots counted." After the election, Yablonski charged that there had been two hundred separate irregularities in the balloting. He said that Boyle, at the head of a union that was "riddled by fear," was guilty of "stealing the election by fraud, coercion, and intimidation." He again asked for a Labor Department investigation and was again refused.

After the campaign, Yablonski returned to his home in Clarksville, Pennsylvania. Yablonski was exhausted and disheartened by his experiences; failing outright victory, he had hoped to force a close enough result that the election would be voided and a new one conducted under government supervision. His campaign had persuaded a great many people, including much of the UMW's cynical rank and file, of what Nader had perceived in the beginning—that Yablonski was a man who had changed, who wanted to change his union. "I'm sure this union will never be the same again," he had said during his campaign.

On New Year's Eve, three men jimmied open a door in the Yablonskis' house. Armed with a .38-caliber revolver and a .30-caliber carbine, they went upstairs in the dark and murdered Yablonski, his wife, Margaret, and their twenty-five-year-old daughter Charlotte in their beds. Chip Yablonski's brother Kenneth found the bodies on January 5, 1970, when he drove out from Washington, Pennsylvania, where he lived, to see why no one was answering the telephone. One of the killers confessed to the FBI that he and his accomplices had been stalking Yablonski for six months, from the beginning of his election campaign. They were paid a total of $5,200 for the murders by a man they knew only as "Tony."

The UMW said at once that there was no connection between this "Tony" and Tony Boyle and posted a $50,000 reward for apprehension of the killers. Within forty-eight hours of the discovery of the bodies, the Department of Labor sent 230 investigators into the field; they interviewed 4,400 people at a cost of $500,000. The department subsequently filed suit in federal court to set aside the election, saying that the UMW had intimidated Boyle's opponents with "penalty, discipline, improper interference, or reprisal."

George Shultz, testifying before the Senate Subcommittee on Labor, said that "our investigations did not disclose a sufficient basis for allegations that violence during the election campaign affected the outcome of the election." Shultz added, "If threats and allegations alone were to bring the government into a union election, intervention would be so massive and widespread as to justify counter-complaints of excessive government action. And, let me repeat again, we do not know that there is any connection between the election and the murders." Nader thought that this statement was a cold-hearted outrage. "In a civilized country," he said, a few days after Shultz had testified, "George Shultz would be in jail."

Yablonski was buried with his wife and daughter in the midst of the Pennsylvania coalfields, on a bitterly cold day in January, in the presence of his sons, his brother, and those of his friends who could attend. Ralph Nader did not go to the funeral. He did not call Chip Yablonski or write to him. On the night that the murders were discovered, he telephoned

Davitt McAteer, who had organized a small group of students on his own to poll watch for Yablonski in West Virginia. "On the night we learned of Yablonski's death," McAteer says, "that was the only time Ralph had nothing to say. It seemed he just wanted to hear a voice. He kept saying, 'What's happening?' He was shocked, shocked."

For months after Yablonski died, his friends continued to wear his campaign button. It was printed with black lungs—the symbol of Nader's issue—and the words *Stop Murder*.

13

The Place That God Forgot

Ralph says things like, 'Your minimal goal is to replace
the management of Union Carbide.' Oh, he's serious all
right.

LARRY SILVERMAN

Ralph Nader has never been to Anmoore, West Virginia. He
is nevertheless an absentee citizen of that bleak Appalachian
town—and, in the eyes of many of its residents, a savior. "I'd
like to say one thing to Ralph Nader," says Dale Hagedorn
of Anmoore. "I'd like to thank him for being."

That is a comely sentiment, for it was Nader's existence,
rather than anything he himself did, that made it possible for
the people of Anmoore to change their lives. It was the people themselves who made the change, using their own imagination and their own tiny resources, though in the last stage
of their struggle they were helped by two remarkable young
men from the Nader organization. The young men, Larry
Silverman and William C. ("Willy") Osborn, were not acting according to any master plan drawn up by Nader. Like

the townspeople, they were improvisers, and they were almost as poor. What Silverman and Osborn introduced into the situation, in addition to their ingenuity and energy, was their power to invoke Nader's reputation against an adversary that had, through neglect rather than design, turned Anmoore into a victim of a town.

The adversary was the Union Carbide Corporation, a $3-billion enterprise that happened to have a plant on the outskirts of Anmoore. Nader's purpose in sending Silverman and Osborn into West Virginia was to expose and humiliate Union Carbide. If Nader touched flesh and blood in Anmoore, it was because of what the town symbolized, rather than what it suffered. But the fact that he was, as usual, in pursuit of an abstraction made little difference to the outcome, and no difference at all to the townspeople. "I have never met Mr. Nader," remarks Mayor Buck O. Gladden, "but I'll say this: he has helped a town that nobody even cared to hear about before."

Few towns can ever have needed help more than Anmoore, a hamlet of 905 persons lying in the mountainous northwest corner of the state, a few miles east of Clarksburg, a few miles west of the Appalachian Front, in a cluster of villages bearing lovely frontier names: Lost Creek, Jane Lew, Nutter Fort, Tenmile Valley. These are old places. Anmoore, with its simple houses skewed on a barren slope, is new. Anmoore exists because Union Carbide established a plant there, in open country a decent distance from Clarksburg, in 1904. There were few people nearby when the plant opened; they came later, in the Depression and during the war, attracted by the smokestacks and the promise of jobs. Eventually there were enough of them to make a town.

The plant, operated by Union Carbide's Carbon Products Division, manufactures ferroalloys and graphite products, including nuclear reactor graphite. It is a dirty process, as the management of Union Carbide always realized. "The reason

we went to Anmoore," says Philip Huffard, Jr., the company's director of environmental affairs, "was because it was a
no place. It was nothing. We knew we'd have this lousy situation. *But there were no people there.* . . . It was the place
that God forgot."

Huffard's "lousy situation" is a pall of fly ash and particulates from the stacks of the plant. Bits of debris, some of it as
large as butterfly wings, gather in drifts on Anmoore's dead
lawns. This debris kills trees and flowers. It blackens the
shingles on the houses, filters inside, soils furniture, clothes,
wallpaper. "It will eat the paint right off a car," says Mayor
Gladden. And, of course, it is breathed with the air and swal-
lowed with the food of every person in Anmoore. No film
maker could have created a scene better expressing Nader's
vision of the hostility of industry to human life.

Anmoore has always been desperately poor. The local
school, though still in use, has been condemned for nearly
thirty years. There is a simple town hall and firehouse, a few
small stores, and a paved main street. The other streets, running up the steep hillsides, are dirt. In the wet Appalachian
winter they turn to mud, deeply rutted by the spinning
wheels of automobiles. From December to April, these
streets have, until recently, been impassable. The dead and
the sick were brought out over the mud on children's sleds to
the hearse or the ambulance parked at the foot of the hill.
Sewage ran in open ditches beside the dirt streets; bags of
garbage, thrown into the ditches, caused them to overflow. In
spring, because the town could not afford to buy gravel or
even dirt fill, the sewage was shoveled out of the ditches to
fill the ruts. Each year the mud contained a larger proportion of sewage. The children walked through this mixture on
their way to school.

Buck Gladden, a gaunt and slow-spoken man in his forties,
had never been a politician. After he got out of the service,
he married a girl from Anmoore, pretty and smart. He works

the night shift as a grinder in the mold shop at a nearby plant of the Continental Can Corporation. By night he breathes the fine dust that flies off his grinding wheel, by day the air of Anmoore. He has one cold after another and he can't get rid of them. The Gladdens' four children were all in the hospital, one at a time, between Good Friday and Thanksgiving, with what the doctor called bronchial pneumonia; their treatment cost $2,000 in addition to the charges met by group medical insurance.

During the winter following this spell of sickness, Gladden looked out the window of his house one morning and witnessed something that changed his life—and, as it turned out, the life of Anmoore. "I saw a little girl slogging along in this slime," Gladden remembers. "She lost her boot, it was sucked right off of her, and she had to put her little foot, in a white sock, right down into it. I thought of her sitting in school all day like that, and that was when I decided to run for mayor."

Gladden was elected in June, 1969, by 198 votes to 139, defeating Victor Gonzalez, who had been mayor for eighteen years, ever since Anmoore was incorporated as a municipality. It was a bitter campaign. Gladden's opponents derided his promises to pave the streets, replace the antiquated streetlights, improve the inadequate water supply, provide better police protection. There was no money to do any of these things. The municipal budget was $19,000 a year. Union Carbide's real estate taxes, paid through the tax collector of Harrison County, accounted for about $9,000 of the total. Few believed that Carbide could be persuaded or obliged to pay more. The plant manager sometimes gave the town a few loads of crushed brick for the streets and, as part of a community relations program, contributed fifty dollars a year to the school patrol and a few dollars to the Little League baseball team.

No pressure had ever been brought on Union Carbide to

pay more taxes or help the town in other ways. In part, this was pride—the townspeople would not ask for charity. Mostly it was a superstition, as one resident says, that if Anmoore was unfriendly enough to raise taxes, the plant would simply move away. "This may sound funny to you," a Union Carbide worker says, "but most people around here figured that Carbide would do just about anything it wanted to, and there was no use fooling with them. They feared that outfit." Only one in five of the town's labor force worked for Union Carbide. The rest were employed somewhere else but had to come home to Anmoore. "Most places on Sunday, you come home from taking the children to church and you sit down to dinner in a white shirt," Gladden says. "You can't do nothing like that here because your shirt'll turn black right on your back. The kids can't go out and roll in the yard. If they do, they come in looking like they've been down in a coal mine."

Gladden accepted the pollution of the air as a fact of life. He didn't think much could be done about it, but he did believe something could be done to ease the burdens of living inside the black cloud that the plant spilled over the town. "I understand that they're in business to make a profit," he says, "but they ought to show a little compassion for the town." Soon after his election he went down to talk to Max Burkett, the plant manager. It was his first contact with a plant manager who wasn't also his own employer, and he was pleased by the results. "Mr. Max Burkett was a real man," he says. "He was sincere, down-to-earth, an ordinary fellow to talk to. I think if he had lived, things would have got better." Max Burkett died of a heart attack soon after his talk with Gladden. "When Mr. Burkett died," Gladden says, "relations with Carbide died." He had no further contact with the plant management for several months—until he began to lead the town council toward an action that would cost

Union Carbide a great deal of money—and later, an embarrassment that would shake not just the Anmoore plant, but the whole great corporation.

The embarrassment was being prepared in Washington by a young Naderite named Larry Silverman, who was at work on *Vanishing Air*. Silverman regarded the book, which he coauthored with John Esposito, as a collection of horror stories. Although it devoted only ten pages to the air pollution caused by Union Carbide, Silverman believed that the activities of this corporation comprised the most horrible of the horror stories. Philip Huffard, who doesn't think that Union Carbide is more guilty of pollution than a lot of other companies, understands this point of view. "If you say *chemical,* what word comes next to mind?" he asks. "*Smell.* Then you proceed to *bad.* The chemical industry ranks high as a polluter. If you can go after it, you can get the others."

That, roughly, was Silverman's view. When the book was finished, he approached Nader with an idea: single out one large corporation with a bad pollution record, and hit it everywhere. "We wanted to make this company a watchword as a warning to others," Silverman explains. It was a formula Nader had no difficulty in approving, though he had, at the time, scarcely heard of Anmoore.

In comparison with some of Union Carbide's operations in other places, the situation in Anmoore was mild. A hundred miles to the south, in Alloy, West Virginia, the corporation operates a ferroalloys plant that produces more visible air pollution than New York City. About the same distance to the west, at Marietta, Ohio, Union Carbide was under attack by the public, and by the federal government, because of a cloud of sulfur dioxide emitting from another plant. There were similar situations elsewhere in the United States, and in Canada and Brazil. The corporation, as it was soon to realize, was in an indefensible position. It was especially vulnerable because, unlike many other chemical corporations, it had invested millions of dollars in an advertising program designed to make it highly visible to consumers.

Huffard, with wry hindsight, sees the tactical advantage "the Discovery Company" gave to its attackers. "Union Carbide was the only chemical corporation to have, together with the pollution problem that is typical of the industry, a 20 percent turnover in consumer goods," Huffard says. "I think we were a just and logical choice, and if I had been Mr. Nader I would have made the same choice."

When Larry Silverman began his foray against Union Carbide, he was twenty-five years old, a graduate of Saint John's College at Annapolis and of the University of Pennsylvania Law School. Many of Nader's young people are adventuresome, but most appear somehow to be playing hooky from the upper middle class; one feels that they will sooner or later go back where they belong. Silverman is Huck Finn himself. Under a mass of red spunklocks, his bespectacled urchin's face glows with mischief. He is tall, well over six feet, and bony and gawky. He dresses like a fifth-generation millionaire: a frayed double-breasted overcoat, baggy trousers, rumpled jacket, ruined shoes. All his style is in his mind. Of all the young people who have attached themselves to Nader, Silverman is the only one who is unquestionably more intelligent, more fluent, more inventive than Nader himself.

Silverman and Nader saw Union Carbide as a natural target, and one they could attack with limited resources. Nader, in the perfunctory way in which he is wont to launch great enterprises, told Silverman to see what he could do. He gave him $5,000 to conduct a one-year campaign against a corporation with global resources and an annual advertising budget of more than $1 million.

He gave him, also, Willy Osborn, another twenty-five-year-old who had recently joined Nader after a period as a storefront lawyer for VISTA in Boston. Osborn, tall and slender, with a tidy toothbrush mustache, is a Princetonian and the eldest son of a family that is listed, to his discomfort, in the Social Register. He is as dogged and lawyerlike as Silverman is elfin and impatient of detail. Silverman and Osborn, between them, had six months' experience in the practice of law. Characteristically, Nader trusted to luck that they would develop into a team. He was barely acquainted with either of them. He knew little of the detail of their work, which they improvised from day to day, but he found some vicarious enjoyment in their escapades. "What you guys are getting out of this," he told them after one particularly satisfying coup, "is the moral equivalent of sex."

That was very nearly all that Osborn received for his work. Nader had agreed to pay him fifty dollars a week, but to Osborn's mystification, never sent him a check. After several months, Osborn learned that Nader was making a speech in Bethany, Pennsylvania, and traveled there from West Virginia to ask for some money. He did not have sufficient funds even to return to West Virginia.

After the speech, Nader and Osborn spent a couple of hours talking in Nader's motel room at the Pittsburgh Airport; it was Osborn's first long exposure to the blaze of Nader's midnight eloquence. "I was so entranced," Osborn says, "that I left without remembering about the money." With one of his last dimes, he called Nader from an airport pay phone and explained that he was broke. "Ralph said he'd put some money under the door for me," Osborn recalls. "I went back up and found twelve dollars—two wrinkled old fives and two ones, all folded up—pushed under the door." At about the same time, when Silverman had spent four thousand dollars of his original five in six months of hectic activity, Nader exploded. "Where is all that money going?" he demanded. "How can you spend so much?"

Silverman and Osborn were led to Anmoore by a passage, four paragraphs long, in *Vanishing Air,* describing a skir-

mish that was being fought against Union Carbide by Dale
Hagedorn and his wife, Leonise. By what Silverman describes as "very circuitous means," he got a copy of a
newsletter, devoted to the corporation's pollution in Anmoore, which was printed in the Hagedorns' home. Hagedorn, a freelance commercial artist, illustrated the one-page,
typewritten publication with biting caricatures of Union
Carbide officials. The Hagedorns called their newsletter
"Carbon Copy," and they sent out some five hundred copies
to politicians, the newspapers, upper executives of Union
Carbide, and other interested parties whenever they were
more than usually annoyed at something the company had
done. So far as the Hagedorns could tell, Union Carbide simply ignored them and "Carbon Copy," but this was not altogether true. "Frankly," says James S. Freeman, the company's
director of public relations, "I had never heard of Anmoore,
West Virginia, until Mr. Hagedorn came along." The newsletter was dutifully read, and neatly filed, at Union Carbide's
New York headquarters.

When "Carbon Copy" was mentioned in *Vanishing Air,*
under Nader's imprimatur, the Hagedorns began to think
that they had a chance of reaching the outside world with
their message. They had been complaining for years about
the pollution. They had written to the governor and their
congressman. Mrs. Hagedorn, at the head of a delegation of
housewives, had dumped a large mound of sooty laundry on
the plant manager's desk. They got no response from the
company until they put out the first issue of "Carbon Copy."
"It no sooner hit the street," Hagedorn says, "than management hit our front door." They were invited to the plant
manager's office to talk things over. "We put on our best
clothes and went down there," Hagedorn says. "They have a
tendency to ruin everything. As we got up to leave, the plant
manager said, sort of, that Carbide was awful big and we
were awful small. That *did* it." Thereafter, the newsletter

came out on a regular basis, and the Hagedorns began looking around for allies.

When reinforcements arrived, in the persons of Silverman
and Osborn, Anmoore had already won the first round of its
fight with Union Carbide. Buck Gladden had discovered that
West Virginia municipalities were empowered to levy a general tax on business enterprises, amounting to thirty cents
for every hundred dollars of gross income. He brought the
town council around to the view that this tax should be imposed. When news of his plan reached the plant management, Gladden says, they called him up to tell him they were
very concerned. "They don't like to hear tax," he says tersely.
"We had a meeting with the Carbide people, and we more or
less sat back and let the plant make the first offer, which was
$10,000. We wanted $25,000." After a good deal of negotia-
tion, the town council voted the tax, but specified that no
one taxpayer should pay more than $20,000 in a single year.

The $20,000 ceiling was designed to reassure Union Car-
bide. The corporation, as Huffard points out, had always
avoided creating company towns. Now they had one, on
somebody else's terms. "We didn't try to run local
governments," Huffard says. "We hoped they would mind
their business and not ours. As you go along, you learn."
One of the lessons Huffard thinks Union Carbide might
have learned earlier, to its social profit, is to help communities like Anmoore before being dragooned into doing so.

But that was not company policy—indeed, with Union
Carbide operating until recently as a loose system of autonomous fiefdoms, each responsible to central management for
profits alone, there was no company policy. No Carbide executive in the field had any incentive to volunteer for anything
that cut into his assets. "Our plant managers are not likely to
say to a fellow who comes in and asks for five dollars, 'Why,
that's unrealistically low! You need fifty,'" says Huffard.
"We would have fired a man with judgment like that."

Larry Silverman and Willy Osborn had, as a starting advantage, the resentment created in Anmoore and elsewhere by decades of Union Carbide's bad judgment. A good deal of groundwork had been laid by ordinary people, and not only in Anmoore. But these people had been working in virtual silence. Nader's men had access to the national press; the Buck Gladdens and the Hagedorns could not even command the support of the local newspapers.

Gladden's frustrations, he says, had radicalized him long before Silverman and Osborn turned up on his doorstep. "I've sat home and watched these people fighting the so-called Establishment, and my idea always was that they were a bunch of rioters," he says. "Maybe I was wrong about that. Just like my children are being taught right now that the law is there to protect you. This is the biggest joke going. If one man in the government is supposed to help you, and he doesn't, you're supposed to be able to go right up to the President. I've done that, and I've found that sometimes they won't even answer your letter. The newspapers are supposed to protect the people if everything else fails, but you don't see much about Carbide in the Clarksburg papers. It has to be *The New York Times,* someone who comes hundreds of miles to talk to me. These men are supposed to protect the little people. But I've found out they won't do it. If that's the Establishment, then I'm against it."

Hagedorn says that he was overawed by the effect Nader's name had on a situation he'd thought could never change. "Our aim," he says, "was to prove that Union Carbide had to pay attention to people. When Nader came into it, they were maybe convinced that they have to pay attention or somebody will show up. Ralph Nader was the last person in the world they wanted to show up."

The people of Vienna, West Virginia, across the Ohio River from the Marietta plant, had been trying to fight Union Carbide through the Establishment for almost five

years. It was, as a federal official remarks, like attacking the
Russian Army with slingshots in January. In 1965, a taxpayers' committee in Vienna wrote to Senator Jennings
Randolph, the West Virginia Democrat, complaining about
emissions from the Marietta plant, which rolled across the
Ohio and filled the town with a sulfurous cloud. A field investigation by the National Air Pollution Control Agency
(NAPCA) followed, and NAPCA decided to invoke the federal law on interstate pollution. In late 1965 an abatement
conference was held, and the participants adopted stringent
standards requiring Union Carbide and twenty other industrial polluters in the area to clean up their emissions.

Enforcement was left, as the law provided, to the states
rather than the federal government. Because almost all of the
dirty plants in the Marietta-Vienna area were in Ohio, the
government of that state was left with responsibility. Very
soon, Ohio officials wrote to the Secretary of Health, Education, and Welfare, asking that the recommendations of the
abatement conference be set aside until Ohio was able to
provide further data on the extent and nature of the pollution. NAPCA kept trying to get this data. Union Carbide refused to furnish it. William Megonnel, an assistant commissioner of NAPCA, recalls that J. S. ("Sam") Whitaker of
Union Carbide came to Washington to explain the corporation's position. "Sam said that his company objected to dealing with a federal agency as a matter of principle," Megonnel
says. Whitaker thought that NAPCA should confine itself to
dealing with state officials in Ohio. Finally, in 1969, Megonnel got Ohio's entire file on Union Carbide. It consisted of
one sheet of paper.

NAPCA decided to have another abatement conference in
Vienna-Marietta. All the corporations sent representatives,
except Union Carbide. Sam Whitaker sat in the audience.
Megonnel ran into him in his motel and invited him to join
in the discussions. "No," Whitaker said, "I like the position

I'm in now." The conference, invoking the Clean Air Act, required Union Carbide to furnish data on its emissions under penalty of a federal fine. It also required that all the plants in the area reduce sulfur emissions by 40 percent before October 20, 1970. When the deadline rolled around, it was discovered, Megonnel says, that every company in the area, except Union Carbide, had made some improvement.

Here, in real life, and on the record, was an example of Nader's dark sequence of corporate violence, governmental impotence or worse, and victimized citizens. It was a delicious target. Willy Osborn and Larry Silverman, at home in Nader's vision of the Establishment, stepped first of all into the lion's den, visiting Union Carbide's headquarters in New York. Silverman noticed, on his way in, what a splendid place it was for pickets; the Union Carbide skyscraper on Park Avenue, all chaste steel and glass, is surrounded by a broad pavilion, big enough to hold almost any number of demonstrators. Nader lost no time in vetoing any idea of picketing the corporation. It was a wasteful activity, he told Silverman; later, when some Canadian activists considered marching on the American Embassy in Ottawa, to protest Carbide's pollution in Quebec and Ontario, Nader nipped the plan in the bud. "You'll have G-men from both countries all over you," he said.

Inside Union Carbide, Silverman felt that he was visiting a totalitarian state in microcosm. "It's a despotic organization, like all corporations," Silverman says. "People are living in fear. I began to think that the plant manager's position is one of the most brutal ever contrived in human history. He's the administrator of brutality at the local level. [He] gets all sorts of nervous habits." The management of Union Carbide looked on Silverman and Osborn, two skinny boys in old clothes, as a serious threat. The corporation, says one of its officials, couldn't decide whether they were saboteurs or germs. In either case, Union Carbide decided to isolate them. The vice-president for law, Frank Lyon, Jr., told them they could not speak to any Union Carbide employee unless they had his permission to do so. They told Lyon that they couldn't reveal the name of any Union Carbide employee who spoke to them in confidence. Silverman was a little scared by his own bravado as the vice-president gave him a cold stare. "My heart was really pounding," Silverman confesses. Silverman and Osborn conducted their interviews in the presence of a company lawyer and a tape recorder.

After several days, they found they had learned very little about the corporation that did not confirm their original conception of it as an insensitive, cumbersome, antihuman entity that was lusting for profits. Any attempt by the corporation to plan for the onslaught it saw coming would have been largely a waste of energy, because Silverman and Osborn had no plan of their own. "In a way, I had no clear idea of what our long-term aims were," Silverman confesses. "I think they overestimated us in general." If that was true, it was also true that Union Carbide seemed to Silverman and Osborn, and of course to Nader, a good deal more resourceful and truculent than it really was. "All corporations are self-oriented, it's their nature," Philip Huffard says. "When you compare that to someone who is not self-oriented, and totally not, like these two kids of Nader's, then some of your motivation will fall away. They say that Carbide is in confrontation. We're really such a bunch of chicken-livered old ladies that we're dying to conform."

That is not an argument an activist can use, even if he believed it. In Anmoore, Silverman and Osborn got in touch with the only people in town to whom they were not total strangers—Dale and Leonise Hagedorn. The Hagedorns, in a meeting at their house, introduced them to Buck Gladden, the chief of police, and the members of the town council. From that, there developed a meeting of about 150 townspeople. Silverman thought it was the first meeting of its kind in the town's history. At the end of it, about fifty people lined up to sue Union Carbide for abatement of its smoke, and for punitive damages. Some of them, a few months later, were not altogether sure that this was what they had done. "Was that the paper we signed at the meeting with Willy and Larry?" Mrs. Gladden asked her husband. "Must've been," he replied. In the end, the Hagedorns, represented by a young lawyer from the Appalachian Research and Defense Fund ("Apple Red") in Charleston, filed a class action against the corporation, asking a federal court to enjoin Union Carbide from further pollution of the air, and for $100,000 in compensatory and punitive damages. Apple Red, which was funded by the U.S. Office of Economic Opportunity, gave Silverman and Osborn office space during their stay in West Virginia.

Osborn devoted a good deal of effort, in the months that followed, to attempts to instigate other lawsuits like the Hagedorns', but with no success. "The principle of reparations can be told to these people," he said. "We can have a wonderful lawsuit." Osborn decided, in the end, that the risk for the people involved was more important than the principle. In Boomer, the town next to Union Carbide's Alloy plant, he found a retired worker who was willing to go to court. The Alloy plant is a scene out of Dante. Its buildings, only fifty yards from the highway, are invisible under a thunderhead of smoke pouring out of stacks and through the blackened walls of the buildings themselves. Deep inside the smoke, what seems to be a tiny red flame can be seen; on closer approach, one sees that the fire is, in reality, as large as a burning house. A respirator, worn in the yard where silica is hauled to the plant's fifteen furnaces, clogs and shuts off the breath in precisely seventeen minutes. By Carbide's own measurement, each cubic meter of air around the plant contains 400 micrograms of soot. This is four times the level that the federal government says causes children to experience "an increased incidence of respiratory disease" and five times the level that can lead to "a noticeable increase in mortality among the elderly and middle-aged." The Alloy plant emits a total of 70,000 tons of particulates a year, or about five times as much as the city of San Francisco.

Osborn's man had emphysema; he believed it was really silicosis. He had started operating a crane at the Alloy plant in 1934. In those days, cranes were steam-driven, with a firebox in the cab; the temperature in summer would rise to 135° Fahrenheit. "For thirty-five years I handled silica with a crane," he said, "took it out of these great big stockpiles in a twenty-five-yard bucket, and dropped it someplace else. Sometimes it looked like a atomic bomb going off—you couldn't see the bucket for the dust, and it took five, maybe ten minutes for the dust to settle. I figured it was all right or the company wouldn't let me do it." In the early days he didn't wear the crude respirators then available because they filled with his sweat in a matter of minutes and were useless. Even improved respirators clogged up quickly in that atmosphere; a filter lasted about twenty minutes before it became so filled with silica that a man couldn't breathe through it. Supervisors made no attempt to force the men to wear respirators, as required by company rules. "You couldn't work with a respirator, and the company knew it," he said. He had had some terrible experiences. Once another worker, daydreaming, stepped behind his crane while it was moving. Nobody knew where he was until later, when they looked under the huge machine and found his body, all packed into a bloody bundle.

Emphysema is not compensable under West Virginia's workmen's compensation law. Even if it were, his company pension would be reduced dollar for dollar for any state compensation he received. The company pension stops on his death. Union Carbide never acknowledged that he had occupation-related emphysema. A friend of his, a man of about forty, explained his own situation. "Two months before I had to leave that plant, Doc told me my X rays was as clear as a bell," he said. "I said, 'Well, I was just wondering why I was so short of breath I can hardly take a step.' And old Doc said, 'You're doing everything you can about that already.' I said, 'What's that?' And Doc said, 'You quit smoking.' Doc told me it wouldn't do me any good to move out of here. I thought I might get my breath better in Arizona or one of them places. Doc told me I was allergic to polluted air."

Osborn, taking notes on a pad held on his bony knee, didn't push these men toward a lawsuit. He simply explained that he believed the pollution was a violation of their rights under the Fifth, Ninth, and Fourteenth Amendments to the Constitution, and a probable violation of other federal laws. Twice his age, Osborn's host listened respectfully to his careful explication, delivered in a voice bred by several generations at Princeton. The man was filled with a kind of bitter enthusiasm. "I wonder to myself why I dislike this outfit, and to be honest with you, I do dislike them," he said. "It's the power they have and how they use it." He'd seen everything fail before Carbide's power—the state police, the government at Charleston, even the union, which didn't do much to protect its members; the union had let a relative of the plant manager become a crane operator before he did, all those years ago, being more interested in currying favor than in protecting the seniority of a union man.

He walked Osborn to the door, a long slow journey of twenty feet for a man who could hardly breathe. His wife, a motherly woman in a spotless housedress, sat on a straight chair on the sun porch, her worried face turned away a little so that she looked into the corner. "On the lawsuit, I'm interested," he said. "But, Willy, there's no way they can touch my pension, is there? Things have changed an awful lot since I saw them go out and take a man's camera and film away

from him—on the highway, not on their own property. On
the highway." Osborn told him they'd have to be sure about
the pension before they went ahead. No lawsuit was ever
filed, with Osborn's participation, in Alloy.

Silverman and Osborn found it slow going in West Virginia for a while. Then they persuaded Buck Gladden that
Anmoore ought to remove the ceiling from the tax it had imposed the year before on Union Carbide. The town council
did so, opening up the possibility that Anmoore would
henceforth receive as much as $100,000 a year in taxes from
the plant. The day the new tax was passed, one of the corporation's lawyers showed up at the office of the state tax
commissioner in Charleston. "It would be editorializing to
describe the lawyer's attitude," an official in the tax commissioner's office says. "He was sitting at a desk, going through
papers in a very determined way, while his secretary took
notes."

Two days after the Anmoore council voted the increased
tax, an auditor from the tax commissioner's office showed up
unannounced to examine the town's books. His manner was
cold, suspicious—and, Gladden thought, threatening. A reporter from one of the Charleston newspapers happened to
be there, and she called up Charles Haden II, the tax commissioner, to ask for an explanation. The auditor's visit was
a routine check for information, in response to a request by
Union Carbide. The auditor had been sent out by a subordinate, without Haden's knowledge. "It was innocent enough,"
says Haden's deputy, Ronald G. Pearson, "but it sure looked
like harassment to the people in Anmoore." Pearson pulled
the auditor out of the Anmoore town hall forthwith. A few
months later, when Gladden was running for reelection, the
same auditor turned up again for a surprise inspection of the
books. Again he was told to clear out by Haden's office. Both
incidents looked to Gladden, and to Silverman and Osborn,
like the heavy-handed use of Union Carbide's power.

Silverman and Osborn were sitting in the council room when the new tax was voted. At one point, it looked as if the proposal was going to be shelved in an extraparliamentary maneuver by one of the village officials. Willy Osborn rushed up to the table and said, "You can't do that legally, can you?" The measure came to a vote, and was passed. "When we got back to Charleston," Silverman says, "we were suddenly local celebrities. People had known we could stir up trouble, but they hadn't known that we could get anything accomplished."

Silverman and Osborn were not the first earnest Northern youths to descend on the West Virginians since the plight of Appalachia had come to the attention of the idealists. But they brought with them something new—a whiff of the great world. Alerted by Nader's name, reporters from *The New York Times* and *Newsweek* and *The Wall Street Journal*, among others, traveled to see them and their local allies. The result was a bombardment of publicity, all of it unfavorable to Union Carbide, and most of it illuminated with the honest human interest that marks almost any report on the upright people of West Virginia. The poetry of the situation sometimes outsang the facts. *The New York Times* ran a story about a statue of Saint Anthony, outside a church in Boomer, that had been eaten away by pollution from the Alloy plant. The statue was replaced by a new one, enclosed in a glass case to protect it from the fouled air.

The pastor of Saint Anthony's, the Reverend Roy A. Lombard, was amused by the nationwide response of the reverent to the story. "Father McDonald, my predecessor, had a tin lamp hanging over Saint Anthony," he says, "and to tell the truth, maybe rust dripping off the lamp did more damage than the pollution." Father Lombard, a bouncy cleric who makes his charitable rounds on a motorcycle, with the legend "God's Angels" stenciled on the back of his black leather jacket ("The Holy Ghost came through with the idea"), says a tombstone salesman in Charleston told him that statuary in the cemetery near Alloy had to be sandblasted every few years because it was dirtied by the air. "Maybe my idea for the glass case will catch on," the priest says, evoking a vision of graveyards of angels, madonnas, and lambs turned into shop windows for the Life Everlasting. Father Lombard resists suggestions that his parish ought to sue Union Carbide for damages to Saint Anthony's statue and the church. He has noticed that people in mountain parishes, breathing only the most crystalline air, cough just as much as his parishioners in Boomer when he's preaching his Sunday sermons.

The stories in the national press—even *Business Week* published a tough exposé of Union Carbide's pollution problems—gave the struggle of the West Virginians an importance that surprised them, and it cemented their trust in Silverman and Osborn. "It overawed us," Dale Hagedorn says. "It turned my thinking around. These kids have a feeling and a caring. I think a lot more of Ralph Nader because of Willy and Larry."

The two youths, so different in background and personality, turned out to be a powerful combination. They established two main lines of action: cooperation with local individuals and groups in what they came to regard as a pilot project in legal and community action, and intense lobbying in Washington. Working with the taciturn West Virginians made Silverman more shy than bearding the Establishment. He went to call on Hubert Humphrey, just reelected to the Senate after his defeat in the 1968 presidential campaign, and told him the Union Carbide story. He was astonished at what a good listener the garrulous Minnesotan turned out to be. "I more or less told him," Silverman said afterward, "now's the time to get aboard." When William Megonnel protested that he couldn't be like Nader but was obliged to be impartial toward Union Carbide, Silverman told him, "I know that, Mr. Megonnel, but here's a chance to do what you've always wanted to do! You'll never have a company like this in such a position again."

The West Virginians, however, were less aware of Nader's power than of Union Carbide's. The manager of the Alloy plant used to call its smoke "black gold" and remind the people of the Kanawha Valley how much they owed his company. After decades of joblessness, his listeners were not so certain that he wasn't right. Silverman and Osborn believed, and wanted to make the workers understand, that their work was, quite literally, killing them.

Silverman and Osborn saw the unions as a natural mechanism to be used against the corporation. They went to a meeting of a local in Alloy and listened to a two-hour discussion on whether a crane operator should be a union man. "They're dying off!" Silverman says. "You wonder, can you work with this kind of institution?" After listening to Silverman's plea for a united front against Union Carbide, the union president asked them to leave the meeting, because they were not members, and wait outside for a decision on their proposal. Osborn and Silverman sat in their car, with a heavy rain beating on the roof, for a long time. Then they were called back inside. "They said, 'Well, we've decided to back you a hundred percent,'" Silverman recalls. "Sweet words." At another union meeting, in Marietta, they were touched when the members passed the hat for them and gave them a handful of dollar bills and small change to carry on the fight.

Silverman and Osborn had less luck with the high leadership of the unions. Their problem was the same one Nader had had with the United Mine Workers—they were outsiders, with the wrong background, the wrong accent, the wrong appearance. Silverman thought all that should not matter if they had the right ideas. Their prime idea was a coalition of all the international unions representing Union Carbide em-

ployees to hit the corporation hard on issues of occupational
health and safety.

In the spring of 1971, there was a meeting of the Union
Carbide unions at the Sonesta Hotel in Washington. On the
first day, Osborn turned up, armed with a draft resolution on
health and safety, and attempted to persuade the meeting to
adopt it. He ran into a stone wall of suspicion and hostility.
One high official from the International Union of Oil,
Chemical, and Atomic Workers flabbergasted Osborn by
coming to the defense of Union Carbide. By this time the
corporation had yielded to public opinion and government
pressure and agreed to clean up its Marietta plant, along
with most of its other factories. Why hadn't Nader given
Union Carbide any credit for this? "This guy didn't like the
resolution and everyone was parroting him," Osborn says. "I
was taking reams of shit from these guys. They said that in
twenty years I'd be making $100,000 in some big corpora-
tion, so what was I doing crashing a workers' meeting. I
finally left."

The next day, Silverman spoke to the group at the Sonesta. He got a cool reception and some unfriendly questions.
Finally a union official from Marietta named Bill LaRue
stood up and said, "These guys have done a great job. They
cleaned up the plant and saved our jobs." After that, the atmosphere was calmer, and Silverman and Osborn tried a little lobbying on behalf of their draft resolution. "It was like
being pickpockets," says Silverman with a grin, "Willy working one side of the room and me the other." But their
resolution was ignored.

Shortly before this meeting, Silverman had been carried
by his enthusiasm into an embarrassing encounter with some
officers of the Oil, Chemical, and Atomic Workers. He had
discovered that there were abnormally high concentrations
of mercury in the urine of some workers at a plant owned by

the Allied Chemical Corporation in Moundsville, West Virginia. Silverman ran into an executive of Allied Chemical at a meeting and, as Osborn says, "laid this data on him." The Allied Chemical man was visibly upset. "Larry came away thinking he had exercised power on this guy, and he felt good," Osborn says. But word of the conversation got back to the union, which had shared the information about the urine samples in confidence, and its officials regarded Silverman's intellectual prank as a breach of trust.

Union Carbide's resistance was broken, finally, by the only force with sufficient power to do it—the United States government and, in its wake, the government of the state of West Virginia. After the corporation failed to meet the deadline for reduction of sulfur emissions from its Marietta plant, the administrator of the Environmental Protection Agency, William D. Ruckelshaus, issued recommendations that, in effect, forced them to do so forthwith. Union Carbide, under the threat of a fine, had submitted a plan to reduce sulfur oxides by 28 percent by September, 1972, and by 74 percent by September, 1974. Ruckelshaus, in return, ordered the company to buy low-sulfur coal to fire its electrical generators so as to reduce sulfur oxides by 40 percent immediately. Sulfur emissions were ordered reduced by 70 percent by April, 1972. Ruckelshaus also ordered Union Carbide to build taller smokestacks by April, 1972, so as to control downwash of the plume, and to reduce fly ash by 25 percent by September, 1971.

It was a tough action, and Larry Silverman thought that he had inspired it, at least in part. A day or two before issuing the order, Ruckelshaus—who, incidentally, is a Princeton classmate of Nader's—summoned Silverman to a meeting in his office. Silverman, caught while traveling, was wearing a jacket with a large hole in the sleeve. "I was worried about walking in there," he says. "Ralph would have said, 'What the hell are you doing, worrying about a hole in your coat?' "

Ruckelshaus drew his chair up next to Silverman's and said, according to Silverman, "What do you think ought to come out of this office on this Marietta matter?" Silverman told him, and when the order was issued two days later, it coincided with the advice Silverman had given Ruckelshaus. "Later on, Ralph asked me how many twenty-five-year-olds have a chance to achieve that kind of results," Silverman says. "It was pretty inspiring." One of Ruckelshaus's assistants, Richard D. Wilson, maintains that the Environmental Protection Agency would have acted against Union Carbide at the same time, in the same terms, even if Ruckelshaus had not seen Silverman. Ruckelshaus's order to the corporation had been drawn up before his meeting with Silverman, and it was not changed afterward, according to Wilson.

It is, in fact, a misnomer to describe Ruckelshaus's letter to Union Carbide as an "order." There are no penalties under federal law if the corporation does not comply. In the absence of compliance, the government can call a public hearing by state and federal officials—with federal officials in the minority—to determine the facts. Six months after that, the government can file a suit in federal court to force compliance. Appeals, of course, can consume years.

According to Philip Huffard, that sequence of events is unimaginable. Union Carbide has made the decision to clean up its pollution. The corporation, Huffard says, will meet the deadlines at Marietta. The cost for installation of wet limestone scrubbing devices to remove sulfur dioxide from high-sulfur coal will be $10.5 million. Anmoore will be 99 percent cleaned up, in conformity with state regulations, by June, 1973. In Alloy, again in response to state regulations, 90 percent of particulates will be eliminated by the fourth quarter of 1974. Huffard points out that the corporation started to solve Anmoore's "black cloud" problem in the middle of 1969, and that 95 percent of the particulates from the power station at Marietta were eliminated between 1955 and the end of 1970. "There are few extenuating circumstances for being a polluter," Huffard concedes, but he thinks that what Union Carbide did before it came under pressure demonstrates that the company was aware of the problem and working on it. "The tone of Union Carbide today is, Don't get yourself in a pollution mess," he says.

As to whether Carbide would have gone as far as Ruckelshaus told it to go without compulsion, Huffard is not certain. "In time, yes," he says. "In the same time, no. If there had been no pressure, I guess maybe you'd never do it." In 1971 Union Carbide budgeted $43.1 million, or more than 25 percent of net income, on pollution control; in 1972 the figure will rise to $64 million, or about 40 percent, assuming that profits remain at the same level ($159 million in 1970). There are a lot of things Union Carbide would rather spend its profits on than pollution control. The corporation's profits, figured against its assets of $3 billion, amount to 5 percent. "We'd do better to buy savings bonds," Huffard says. "The point is, our resources really are limited." Huffard understands that Nader cannot consider such factors. "Gandhi didn't get India where it is by saying the British were half right," James Freeman observes, with remarkable insight into the methods of his enemy.

Nader had a chance to castigate Union Carbide's imperialism soon after Ruckelshaus had issued his guidelines for the Marietta plant. The corporation announced that it was contemplating laying off 625 workers in order to comply in the short time available to it. Nader immediately labeled this plan "economic blackmail," and called on Senator Muskie to hold hearings to explore, among other things, criminal sanctions against Union Carbide for making "false statements" to the government and the public on environmental questions. F. Perry Wilson, president of Union Carbide, told Muskie in a letter that "we tried to make it clear that if all other efforts failed, we would regretfully have to shut down parts of the operation in order to comply." Wilson said his corporation would "exert every effort to avoid this solution."

Muskie did not move at once to announce hearings before his subcommittee, and Nader and Silverman were not pleased by his inertia. They had a new stimulus, in addition to Nader's routine interest in the cross-examination of corporations in public. If, indeed, more than six hundred jobs were lost at Marietta, it would be possible to accuse Nader of losing them through his attack on Union Carbide. "If he's going to take credit for slaying Union Carbide," a Senate aide observed, "he'll have to take responsibility for consequences like starving workers. Right?" Muskie's staff thought that if they could persuade Union Carbide to retreat from its threat of layoffs, they would accomplish all that was important. One of Muskie's assistants suspected that Nader's demand for hearings was a transparent device for putting the senator on the spot again, as had been done with *Vanishing Air*.

Nothing that followed allayed his suspicions. Silverman, acting on Nader's instructions, made the rounds of the potential presidential nominees among Senate Democrats, urging them to make a public statement calling on Muskie to convene hearings. He received polite audiences from Hubert Humphrey and staff assistants of some of the others, such as Edward M. Kennedy. Did Silverman think that this tactic—asking U.S. senators publicly to embarrass another senator who was the front-runner for the presidential nomination—would succeed? "It will super succeed!" said the irrepressible Silverman. There was, however, no public statement and no private pressure on Muskie from his colleagues. In the end, Muskie scheduled hearings on the general problem of pollution control and its effect on employment—and, at one of the first hearings, invited Nader and Silverman to testify.

This was the hearing at which Silverman thought Muskie, smothering his witnesses' fervor with senatorial courtesy, had outradicaled him.

In the long course of their campaign against Union Carbide, almost nobody else outradicaled Silverman and Osborn. Much of what they attempted did not wholly succeed. They never gained a real foothold where the power counted in the labor unions. A key element in their strategy, the blizzard of embarrassing lawsuits they originally envisaged, never materialized. Plans for a newsletter, bearing Nader's picture, to be distributed to all Union Carbide employees (complete with an invitation to inform on the company about its internal practices), was still in the planning stage after the main battle had been won through the action of William Ruckelshaus.

An ambitious attempt to expand the battle into foreign theaters came to almost nothing. Nader sent a young man on a confidential mission to Brazil to gather material on Carbide's pollution there, but the envoy, untrained to gather this sort of data and defeated by a strange culture, came back empty-handed. Silverman and Osborn raised a small storm of publicity in Quebec, when they traveled there to attack Union Carbide in a town called Beauharnois. Osborn spoke, in French, to a meeting of about two hundred of the townspeople; he astonished the audience with his fluency until he got to the end of a translation provided by a Quebecois sympathizer. Osborn thought, as he stumbled gamely through the rest of his speech in Princeton French, that his listeners felt more comfortable.

Earlier, he and Silverman had made Dr. Victor Goldbloom, Quebec's minister for environmental affairs, uncomfortable by asking him, during a midnight meeting in his office, why exactly he had negotiated an agreement on pollution control with Union Carbide that was the least stringent in North America. "Just who *are* you?" Goldbloom asked them. He found out when the Canadian newspapers, and later *The New York Times,* carried interviews in the Nader style, castigating him and the agreements. These had been negotiated in December, 1970, after all the bad publicity in West Virginia, and Silverman was certain there was a connection. "They're learning," he said of Union Carbide, "but I'm not sure it's what we want to teach them."

Goldbloom refused to renegotiate the agreements, on the grounds that he had given his word, and therefore the word of his government, to abide by them. Union Carbide pointed out that it was spending $4 million on two dust-collection systems at its ferroalloys plant in Beauharnois. Goldbloom told the newspapers Silverman and Osborn were "a pair of self-appointed judges."

Nader, in an antic mood, had told Silverman and Osborn that he would pay them a bounty of $10,000 for every member of the Union Carbide board of directors they forced to resign. Nader himself took a hand in this effort, accusing James M. Hester, a Union Carbide director who is president of New York University, of "seriously compromising if not disgracing" his university by "silent complicity or knowing participation in company air pollution policies." Nader called on Hester to resign; Silverman and Osborn, who had written Nader's letter, thought he might. Hester replied, in a letter to Nader, that he was staying on in his directorship: "In my opinion [resignation] is not the way to reform our institutions." Hester did not receive Nader's letter until after he replied to it; he had read Nader's letter in *The New York Times.*

Whatever tactical failures they may have suffered, Osborn and Silverman achieved a major strategic success. They did it on their own, out of their own imagination and sense of outrage, and with virtually no resources other than the right to invoke Nader's name. Critics in Washington remarked that they had entered the fight when it was in its last stages and reaped the credit for long years of effort by obscure citizens who had a great deal to lose and virtually no hope of victory. No one with whom they dealt in West Virginia said that. Without the burst of national publicity that Silverman and Osborn engineered, the whole venture would have been in doubt. "Carbide's chief incentive," as a federal official conceded, "was bad publicity."

Ralph Nader, at the beginning of his career, told Drew Pearson what had drawn him into the fight for auto safety. "If, at the end of his life, a person was asked if he would rather have made a million dollars or saved hundreds of thousands of lives," he said, "I wouldn't have to hesitate." Silverman and Osborn, obscured in their own accomplishments behind Nader's reputation, may well have achieved an ambition that increasingly eludes Nader. He has never been eager for human contact. His ideas and his rhetoric and the structure that grows ever more complicated around him have, in only five short years of fame, moved him out of sight of the human race. Like a President or an archbishop, Nader enunciates principles and excoriates the wicked. But he does not, and for the most part his empire does not, touch the lives of people.

Silverman and Osborn showed that this need not be the case. They brought Nader's name into Anmoore and breathed its foul air on his behalf. As a result, the air itself was changed. If, as Nader says, there is a technological solution to everything, it is also true that such solutions are only achieved by human passion. Dale Hagedorn was awed by the power of Nader's name. To a child, walking to school over pavement laid down by Buck Gladden atop Anmoore's streets of sewage, the fact that Larry and Willy searched out this lost town, and lived in it until it was free of filth, might seem the greater miracle.

14

In the Tents of the Righteous

Indians in the woods saw things that the white man never saw because the Indians were trained to see them. We can do the same in our technological society.

RALPH NADER

The decor of the main ballroom of the Hotel Pierre in New York features gilt cherubim in flight across a smudged ceiling, and clumps of dusty ostrich plumes atop Doric columns made of plaster. It is a room that strove for the vulgar and achieved the gauche.

Ralph Nader, wearing a tuxedo, entered the Pierre ballroom on the night of April 18, 1971, with the air of a man who had rented out his soul for the evening. He was there to receive $10,000 and a Steuben glass plaque, symbolic of the annual Max Berg Award, bestowed upon the person judged to have made "a major achievement in prolonging or improving the quality of human life." The award was made by the David and Minnie Berk Foundation, which had hired the ballroom, complete with an orchestra playing show tunes, for ceremonies to follow a five-course dinner.

A few moments before, Nader had emerged from another of the Pierre's public rooms, where cocktails and an astonishing variety of canapés had been served. On Nader's arm was Mrs. Minnie Berk, a tiny old lady with a sweet face and jolly voice. Mrs. Berk and Nader seemed to be delighted with one another. Ted Jacobs, following them in a crowd of dinner jackets and sequined gowns, spied an acquaintance and gave a happy guffaw. "Welcome to Ralph's bar mitzvah!" he cried.

There was about the affair an atmosphere of clannish festivity. About four hundred persons had paid $175 a plate to honor Nader and the late Max Berg. Mr. Berg, as the printed program explained, had lived a life of quiet philanthropy, rescuing Jews from Nazi Germany, helping poor children through college and summer camp. The foundation established by Max Berg's brother, David Berk, and his wife, Minnie, with the help of other members of the Progressive Synagogue in Brooklyn, had done many good works, including the establishment of a clinic in the East Village "to provide free medical care and human kindness to sick and disturbed youths." The Max Berg Award had previously been won by two Nobel Laureates, Dr. George Wald, the Harvard biologist and peace movement activist, and Dr. Arthur Kornberg, synthesizer of the DNA molecule, and by Dr. Michael DeBakey and Dr. Adrian Kantrowitz, the heart surgeons.

At each table, seating ten persons, were inexhaustible supplies of French claret to drink with the smoked salmon, pâté de foie gras, chateaubriand, and a pretty ice-cream dessert. The guests rose between courses to fox-trot, and even rumba, to the reedy strains of the band; the dancers had a cheerful competence, like people who had mastered the steps on many a rainy afternoon in the Catskills. Nader, scrubbed and curly and a foot taller than anyone else at the head table, did not dance. But he kept laughing at the grandmotherly sallies of Minnie Berk. Now and then he would turn serious as George Wald told him about his encounters with policemen to whom a peacenik was a peacenik, Nobel Prize or no Nobel Prize. Gradually he was infected by the good spirit of his hosts. "Look," said one of the wives, "Ralph is on the verge of forgetting that he's wearing a tuxedo."

After the dessert, David Berk silenced the band and took possession of the microphone. "I hope while you ate you read something in the program about Brother Max," he said. "Every word is true." He spoke for a few minutes about the dinner, congratulating those who had planned it. "Is there a Ralph Nader?" Berk asked. "Until I met him I wasn't sure. I thought he was the product of a P.R. man's dream. . . . Ralph, we may be members of the Establishment here, but we're very glad you've decided to be with us."

George Wald, a short man, shining with scholarly innocence, bald in front with long white hair falling over his collar, followed Berk to the microphone. "Our friend Ralph has become an American legend," Wald said. "I don't like to use the word crusader, because we know too much about the Crusaders. But by the time Ralph Nader is through he will have prolonged more lives and improved the quality of life more than all the other award winners put together. It all works because Ralph Nader asks nothing for himself. Just now he told me what his young lawyers are paid—$4,500 a year!—and he doesn't take more than that for himself. That's less than the floor recommended for welfare mothers."

After-dinner cigars were burning all over the room; there was a murmur of conversation, like the throb of an engine deep in the hold of a cruise ship, as Wald's voice came through the amplifiers. "Forty-five hundred dollars a year— *what?*" said a man through a cigar. "Ssshhh," said his wife.

David Berk called Nader to the podium. He moved across the dance floor, with Minnie Berk on his arm again. At the microphone, Mrs. Berk gave him the check for $10,000 and said, "Lean over, Ralph." She gave him a kiss on the cheek. There was a burst of applause, a lot of affectionate smiles.

Standing among the saxophones, trumpets, and guitars left behind by the band, Nader looked out over the audience. "Automobile accidents in this country cost as much every year as the gross national product of Brazil," he said. After the orotund delivery of David Berk and George Wald, Nader sounded more staccato than usual. The incongruous setting—cupids overhead, people sleepy as pythons after too much food and drink, and Nader himself dressed in a dinner jacket and standing in a spotlight on a bandstand—seemed to wrench him out of his harshness. Nader's speech, with only minor adjustments of hyperbole, could very well have been a sly comedy routine, and it was possible to wonder when the first stand-up prophet of doom would start making the night-club circuit.

"The Congress is now reduced to almost a whimpering body, impotent even to examine the budget," Nader said. "If we had a criterion for insanity of institutions, ours would be committed. We have the technological capability to reduce automobile injuries by 75 percent even if we didn't take one drunk off the highway or prevent one accident. Any culture that subjects its children to ugliness and gloominess is one that has foreshortened their sensitivity. Something drastic must be done about the reordering of power in this country. Ask yourself what you can do, and do it."

A guest wondered how many shares of General Motors stock were represented in the audience. "If I had a paper napkin," he said, "I'd make out a questionnaire." Another man said, "For two hundred bucks, write on the cloth napkin." The band came back, and people started dancing again. The waiters, having served dinner with that mixture of expertise and contempt which is the New Yorker's union card, had vanished. A few of the guests went off to the bar to arrange for drinks to be brought into the ballroom.

Nader, sipping ice water, stayed up until two o'clock, chatting with his neighbors at the table of honor. At 6:59 A.M., having already made several telephone calls, he appeared in the lobby of the Pierre and jumped into a waiting taxi with two companions. "What time is your plane? I want you to know I've been sitting here for twenty minutes," said the cab driver. "It goes at 7:25," Nader said. "Just the right amount of time to get there." The driver said he guaranteed absolutely nothing. He wanted to tell Nader about the chances he had taken with other fares who had even less time. Nader ignored him.

"I figured it all out," Nader said to his companions as the taxi roared crosstown under yellow traffic lights turning red. "The drinks before the dinner were $2 each. Then there was the food, the orchestra, the wine—everything. A minimum of $20,000." He held up his check, signed by Minnie Berk in a large, clear hand. "This will pay for two lawyers for a year," he said, "so that makes up for the shindig." He seemed wonder-struck by the prodigality of the David and Minnie Berk Foundation.

Nader was beginning a week of speaking engagements that would take him back and forth across the country—Cleveland, New Jersey, Minneapolis, Tulsa, Chicago, back to Ohio, out to Colorado. He was raising money, giving five or six speeches a day, rising at five, going to sleep at two in the morning. He travels in the rumpled suit he stands up in, carrying a small bag for clean shirts and linen. Under his arm he carries a large stack of manila envelopes. People have given him briefcases, but he turns them into files and leaves them behind. His office in Washington is a wilderness of cardboard boxes, filled with documents and books. When he leaves it, he takes some of the clutter with him in the envelopes, which he never lets out of his hands. He carries them with him to the lectern when he speaks, places them on a table by his head when he sleeps, holds them in his lap in cars and airplanes. The envelopes are like the medicine bag of a Sioux; their contents are secret, they are never opened, they stay next to the warrior's body.

The taxi driver made it from the Pierre to LaGuardia in eighteen minutes. "I wish I had time to tell you how good that time was," Nader said, and loped for the gate. Aboard the plane to Cleveland, Nader accepted breakfast—an omelette and sausages, sweet rolls, acid airlines coffee, and a small container of orange juice. "Hey, fresh orange juice!" he said. "Do you realize it would take only six months of reeducation for the people of this country to be conditioned to drink pure orange juice?" He peeled the label from his companion's orange juice and put it in his pocket. "I may write to these people and express a citizen's appreciation," he said. "Think what they have to contend with to sell this stuff right off the tree, without sugar." He would not eat the sausages or drink the coffee. The stewardess, harassed and not happy to be on a breakfast flight, brought Nader the glass of milk he had requested on three separate occasions. Nader pointed at the sausages: "Bad stuff," he said, with a lift of the eyebrows. The stewardess gave him a brilliant smile. "Thank you, sir!" she replied, and hurried away.

Nader is not a gallant customer. He stifles taxi drivers because they have nothing of interest to tell him. With stewardesses and waitresses he is relentless: to offer him a Coca-Cola is to invite a detailed analysis of the harm done to the human body by this drink, filled with sugar and caffeine. The suspicion he feels for American food transfers to those who serve it; he glowers at the sore-footed women in restaurants and at the jaunty miniskirted girls in the aisles of jet airplanes as if they are, all of them, unwitting Borgias. "The only thing you should be proud to serve on this whole airplane," he said to one puzzled stewardess, "is the little bags of nuts. And you should take the salt off the nuts."

When his breakfast tray was taken away, Nader uncapped a felt-tipped pen and began to go through *The New York Times* and *The Wall Street Journal,* marking stories and scribbling file references on them. By the end of the week, his pile of envelopes had expanded to include fifteen or twenty newspapers, filled with valuable information to be clipped when he returned to Washington. He carried the whole bundle with him, along with the envelopes, wherever he went.

Nader was pursued, throughout the week, by a news story in which he saw no humor at all. Gore Vidal, in the issue of *Esquire* then on the newsstands, had written that Nader ought to be, and could be, the next President of the United States. To make room for Vidal's article, the editors of *Esquire* had canceled a profile, written by the author several months before. Nader was convinced that the magazine had not printed the profile because the editors feared reprisals from large industrial advertisers. He said as much at a news conference in New York.

When he learned of Vidal's article, he regarded it as a prankish reprisal for his public criticism of the magazine. "They've got some unknown writer to do this. They're using me!" he cried. The editors permitted him to write a brief, angry disclaimer, which was buried in the back of the magazine over a picture of Nader to which a large black mustache had been added by the art department.

Vidal's article was, in fact, very praising; apparently the novelist quite seriously believed that Nader should be at the head of affairs in this country. Nader did not want to be associated with *Esquire*'s exercise in antic bad taste. He had never talked to Vidal, though a member of the New Party, Marcus Raskin, had asked him to run as the party's presidential candidate. Nader refused. When, at a news conference in Cleveland, he was asked about the *Esquire* story, he was still seething with resentment. "I'm not interested in public office," he said. "The biggest job in this country is citizen action. Politics follows that."

Like a presidential candidate, Nader has only one speech. He gives it without notes, his body arched over the lectern, his voice, which is rather thin, pitched at a conversational tone. His lips touch the microphone, like a singer's. He receives 50 invitations to speak in a typical week and accepts about 150 a year at $2,500 per speech. The total includes a few free appearances and some at a reduced rate. The free speeches and the cut-rate ones are supposed to be shorter, but he is rarely able to finish in less than an hour and forty-five minutes. Often he runs over two hours and will then take half an hour or forty-five minutes of questions from the audience. To some of his listeners, the length is stupefying. "My God," whispered a baffled professor at a Southern college, "does he always go on like this?" Nader would like to go on even longer. "Some day I'm going to say to one of these colleges," he says, " 'Six hours without interruption, or no speech.' "

Nader is interested in what he is saying. His *leitmotiv* is, of course, the depredations of industry and the connivance of government. He is a never-failing spring of startling statistics. One ounce of water pumped into each chicken sold in the United States would cost consumers $35 million a year; GM took in more money in 1970 than any government in the Western Hemisphere except the United States; America ranks thirty-third in the world in male life expectancy, twenty-second in female life expectancy. He makes no concessions to the audience. There is no rhythm or structure in his speeches. He merely stands up before a packed house and imparts information. "It's like watching somebody scatter leaflets from a balloon," said the Southern professor.

The audience sits absolutely silent, never applauding except when Nader mentions the Vietnam War, which is rarely, and never laughing, except when he mentions Vice President Agnew, which he had begun to do with increasing frequency. At the end of the long speech, Nader does not signal that he is finished by any final grandiloquent phrase, or even a change in inflection. He merely gathers up his envelopes and slouches away from the lectern. There is a moment of silence. Then, always, tumultuous applause, a standing ovation that can last for as much as five minutes. As often as not, Nader stands with his back to the crowd, oblivious to the clapping and shouting and whistling. It is a phenomenon, the professor said, that ony Marshall McLuhan could explain.

The effect of Nader's rhetoric, which is almost always addressed to the young, seems to be akin to that produced by a light show. The author, passing through audiences after seventeen of Nader's speeches, asked a total of ninety-one persons if they could quote verbatim any one of the hundreds of phrases they had heard. None could do so. "Man, I don't know whether you can understand this," a young girl said, "but we're here to get the *feeling* of this cat. I already knew what he'd say."

In Cleveland, Nader gave full-dress speeches in the gymnasium of Cuyahoga Community College to four audiences of about two thousand people. This institution, even more than most of the out-of-the-way colleges that invite Nader to speak, is an expression of the building as a machine. It is located in the central city, its administrators explain, to serve the people of the central city. Surrounded by concrete, its buildings are gray, massive, unadorned; the exterior shines with glass but there is no natural light inside. Straight corridors lined with raw cinder blocks lead past blank plywood doors, the color of schoolroom desks. There are no odors and, during classes when the doors are shut, almost no noise. Along the halls, Negroes in dashikis and Afros and shades stand in silent groups. Although blacks seem to make up the majority of the student body, few of them appeared in the gymnasium for Nader's speeches.

Nader dislikes speaking in gymnasiums, with their cavernous spaces and their poor public-address systems and their bleachers along the walls, so that most of the audience is seated sideways to the speaker. Television cameras are almost always on hand, with powerful lights shining in his eyes. His eyes are sensitive to light. He looks downward as he speaks, fiddles with the microphone, moves imaginary objects over the top of the lectern. It takes him thirty minutes or so to feel the presence of the audience, and he talks in a jerky, disconnected way until the vibrations begin to reach him through the lights. Partly it is a physical problem; he cannot see the audience until his eyes adjust to the glare of the television lights. Once he can see, he becomes more fluent and inventive. Although he always says roughly the same thing, and in the same terms, he varies phrases, and invents new ones, and remembers facts as he goes along. When he makes an important point, he stamps his left foot, in a large scuffed shoe, the lace broken and knotted.

In Cleveland, before he addressed his first audience of high school students, a blond dumpling of a girl wearing red, white, and blue hot pants leaped from the first row and handed him a bunch of yellow wild flowers. A television man scrambled, his camera balanced on his shoulder, to record the scene. Nader took the flowers and stepped back, unsmiling. The girl, grinning happily, stepped close to him. Nader turned away and mounted the stage, still holding the bouquet. He took the flowers to the lectern with him.

"I want to level with you," Nader said. "This country's in trouble and we all know it. We have a society in America that treats teen-agers as children. Everything emphasizes this juvenile nature, it's a psychological climate. Who caters to this illusion? The corporations. Hundreds of millions go into cosmetic advertising. For what? To focus on the neuroses that the ads cultivate. You've got to fight this. Don't be lulled into thinking that you can't seize power through citizenship. On the athletic field you never give up. You've got to do the same in the citizen action arena. You shouldn't throw in the towel on the field of life itself. So what if you have these little teen-age problems? You should ignore them and concentrate on what's important. This is not the time to fool around, wasting countless hours watching television or chitchatting. Not when the future of civilization is at stake. Don't waste your time on these ridiculous problems. You can make a whale of a difference right where you are. You have numbers, brains, and now the vote. We need your sensitivity. Special-interest groups have their team. We must field our team."

The youngsters, bussed in from high schools all over Cleveland, listened in silence to Nader's phrases, delivered in Dutch-uncle tones with pointed forefinger. He spoke of a college student who was going to swim the Cuyahoga River that day as a stunt to raise money for the Ohio Public Interest Action Group. OPIAG, the student movement being organized for Nader by James Welch, was attempting to raise a million dollars. "The swimmer is going to wear a rubber suit," Nader said, "and he's well advised, if he doesn't want to dissolve before he sinks." The youngsters laughed for the first time. Nader told them that the Cuyahoga River, choked with industrial wastes, had been declared an official fire hazard and had in fact burst into flames on at least one occasion. He mispronounced the name of the river several times, drawing titters from the audience. Later he said to a companion, "How do you pronounce that? *Kee*-a-hoga is not it, I gather." In the next three speeches, he said *Ky*-a-hoga.

At lunch in the faculty dining room, a woman said, "Oh, Mr. Nader, you've become the modern gadfly!" Nader, lifting a spoonful of tomato soup, said, "It's okay to be a gadfly, but when you're attacking pesticides you have a conflict of interest." A group of organizers for OPIAG sat down with

Nader after lunch. He listened patiently to their problems, which were mainly concerned with the impossibility of raising a million dollars for a reform movement in a conservative state like Ohio. "Look, Ohio is one of the most polluted states in the Union," he said. "This state has a historic tradition that appeals to individualism, which is now being manipulated by the vested interests. This is a very symbolic work you're doing, even if it isn't one hundred percent successful. If it can be done here, it can be done anywhere." Later, to a small audience of community leaders, he said, "OPIAG will never be a bureaucracy. It will be lean and hungry. Fight for it. This country was not founded by a Silent Majority and it won't be saved by a Silent Majority."

Nader had been met at the plane that morning by a girl from OPIAG, who shook hands briskly with Hays Gorey of *Time* magazine, traveling with Nader, and began explaining the day's schedule to him. She thought that Gorey, a sandy-haired man who wears glasses, was Nader. Despite all the television programs and all the newspaper photographs, Nader is not often recognized when he travels. Nader's other greeter in Cleveland, James Lowe, Jr., public relations director of WEWS, the local Scripps-Howard television station, had no trouble spotting him. Nader was committed to appear on a WEWS talk show in the afternoon, and Lowe stayed with him all day, ferrying him around in his Lincoln and worrying about the schedule. Nader, between speeches, kept ducking into phone booths and offices to do his telephoning. Lowe, staring at his watch, spent an unhappy day, pacing outside the phone booths into which Nader had folded his bony frame. "This guy's telephone compulsive!" Lowe cried.

Lowe finally got Nader to the station, more or less on time. "We're ready to tape," Lowe said. "Can I use your phone first?" Nader asked. He sat down at Lowe's desk and began dialing. On the desk was a photograph of an Indian ascetic lying on a bed of nails. "Do you think this is possible?" Nader asked a companion. The man said he'd seen the trick in India. Nader was in the presence of new information. "Wait a minute," he said into the phone. "You mean they really do it—it's not an illusion?" When he had all the information he wanted on fakirs, he took his hand off the mouthpiece and finished his conversation.

He was interviewed, for a WEWS show called *Inner Circle,* by Dorothy Fuldheim, a Cleveland celebrity. Mrs. Fuldheim, said to be seventy-eight years old, wore bright red hair and a green pants suit; Lowe said that she had interviewed Adolf Hitler and had once said to Jerry Lewis, on the air, "What do *you* do, young fellow?" She is a combination of grandmother and cutthroat. Neither Nader nor Mrs. Fuldheim's partner, a handsome and retiring man named Fred Griffith, got to say very much. But Lowe was happy with the show. "I promise you," he said, "Nader really comes across electronically."

That evening, after a flight to Philadelphia, Nader spoke at Trenton State College. He was met at the airport by two young men and a girl in a battered car. "How long is the ride to Trenton?" Nader asked. "About forty-five minutes," said the driver. "If they say forty-five minutes, you know it's an hour and a half," Nader said. He buckled himself into the back seat and, with his envelopes on his lap, went to sleep. To save his voice, Nader refuses to converse in moving automobiles. "What they consider an hour and a half's leisurely conversation in a noisy car is equivalent to a speech," he says. He goes to sleep at once, his chin on his chest, his head bouncing, oblivious to the conversations going on around him.

The drive, as Nader predicted, took almost two hours. At the college, he was shown into the offices of the campus newspaper, where a girl offered him a Coca-Cola. "I'll use the bathroom instead," Nader said, leaving the girl with a paper cup in her hand. The college librarian, a stooped graying man, approached Nader with an urbane smile. "I wonder if you'd just autograph the college's copy of your book, Mr. Nader," he said. "No," Nader said, and turned his back. The librarian blushed; his hands, holding the book, trembled. Nader's companion said, "He never autographs anything. He has something against it." The librarian said, "I thought he'd make an exception for—for an *institution*."

Nader's scheduling, which is arranged by his agent in New York, is always slightly awry, so that he is consistently late for speeches. Two thousand students had been waiting for an hour in the college's old auditorium. As Nader entered, a photographer with a large white beard flashed a strobe light in his face from a distance of about two feet. Nader recoiled and threw his arm across his eyes. "Come *on*," he said, "have a little consideration." The photographer laughed. "You'll get a lot of that inside," he said, backing up before Nader as he advanced into the auditorium and shooting more flash pictures.

Nader had already made four speeches that day on five hours' sleep, counting his nap in the car, but he showed no sign of weariness. There was no television coverage, and only two weak lights, erected by the campus film unit, shone into his eyes. The auditorium was packed with youngsters sitting on the floor and in the aisles, boys and girls with their arms around each other.

Nader liked the audience. "Senator Phil Hart has estimated that the cost of corporate looting in this country is $45 billion annually," he said. "It costs $200 million to make one C5A for the Air Force, and we spend $125 million on the Federal court system. The government puts $30 million a year into subsidies on the sale of tobacco overseas. You may well ask what sense of priorities creates such a situation. If there were a Communist behind every smokestack, exhaust pipe, and swordfish, we'd wave that flag and go after pollution wherever it is. Someday we'll have a legal system that will criminally indict the president of General Motors for these outrageous crimes. But not as long as this country is populated by people who fritter away their citizenship by watching TV, playing bridge and Mah-Jongg, and just generally being slobs. It could cost consumers $35 million a year just for the water pumped into chickens to increase their weight. Annual style changes on automobiles cost $1.7 billion. Men are spending over a billion dollars a year on cosmetics. Men! They've got quarterbacks on TV dabbing on perfume to show that it's virile to smell good. I don't think you people are going to put up with this, not this generation. You can act, you've shown that you can act. If students hadn't acted I believe we might now be in a war with China instead of playing Ping-Pong with them." He ended, as he usually does, with the reading of the address of the Public Interest Research Group, where students can write for information and help in forming their own PIRG.

Outside, where a light rain was falling, the bearded photographer was waiting. Nader walked across the campus in a knot of young people, paying no attention to a boy who said, "Mr. Nader, you're wonderful, but you're wrong about Volkswagens." The photographer scrambled for position, leaping hedges and vaulting onto the hoods of cars to take his flash pictures. Nader, walking faster, said, "That's enough. No more pictures." The photographer laughed again. "Just a job," he said. "You've done it, if indeed you are a press photographer," Nader replied. "I am indeed. Associated Press. I can prove it if you like," the photographer said. "Just go away," Nader said. "Okay, bastard," said the photographer, with three quick bursts of strobe light.

Nader's old gift for talking to strangers ("Everyone I meet knows something I don't know," he told Ted Jacobs when they were at Princeton) has all but left him. After his speech at Trenton State College, he decided to spend the night in

Princeton. He was seated in a booth in a restaurant after midnight when the waitress, made timid by Nader's cross-examination as he ordered a ham and cheese sandwich on whole wheat bread, approached him. "Sir, I'm sorry," she said, "but there's a man in the next booth who has a bet on, and he wants me to ask your name." Nader said, "Lewis Smeltzer," and took another bite of his sandwich. When he finished eating, he beckoned to the bettor, a stocky man with carefully combed black hair, wearing a double-breasted blue blazer. "I thought you were Ralph Nader," the man said. "You're right, so don't pay off the bet," Nader said. "Now I don't know whether to believe you, but here's my card," the man said with a laugh. Nader looked at the card. "Anchor Corporation?" he asked. "What does that do beside come in last?" The man said he sold mutual funds. "Believe it or not, I'm one of your admirers," he said. Nader turned his head away and called for the check; the man stumbled away in embarrassment. With Nader were Lallie Lloyd and Claire Townsend, Princeton freshmen who had worked for him the summer before. "Did you notice that guy, how he was leering at Lallie?" Nader asked.

Earlier, in search of Claire Townsend, Nader was recognized as he walked across the darkened campus by a long-haired student. Nader fell into easy conversation with the boy, asking the subject of his senior thesis. The student was writing about the College Board examinations. Nader was immediately alert. "Do you think it would be worth it to send a study team after the Educational Testing Service?" he asked. "The College Boards are an instrument of the status quo." He wrote down the youngster's name and asked him to send him a copy of his thesis. Nader asked the student about one of his old professors, a teacher of sociology. "Students don't really like him," the boy said. "He's a guy who was a left-wing anti-Communist, so he has to justify himself, I guess. He's heavy and he doesn't like students." Later, Nader said, "You know the reason they don't like him? He demands work. They don't want that anymore."

Inquiries at Claire Townsend's dormitory, the Princeton Inn, produced the information that she was at a rehearsal for the Triangle Club show. "It's not a good sign," Nader said with a shake of his head, "to come to Princeton and find a Raider in the Triangle Show." A little later Miss Townsend, a slender blonde wearing jeans and a dungaree jacket, returned, and Nader walked across the campus with her to meet Lallie Lloyd.

In the summer of 1970, Claire Townsend was the project director of a team of six girls from Miss Porter's School (one of whom was Lallie Lloyd) who studied conditions in nursing homes. The girls, no one of them—except for a young teacher from Miss Porter's—more than eighteen, produced a heartbreaking report. They took jobs as nurses' aides and described in their diaries the casual brutality with which the dying are treated: an incontinent old woman left in her urine-soaked clothes in front of a television set, the body of a legless man left from nine in the morning until eleven at night because no doctor would come to sign the death certificate. "You know what's really bad," Claire Townsend wrote in an early diary entry, "is that instead of coming up with a crusader wish to help the nursing home problem, I came out last night vowing to commit suicide before I get old." The girls described their experiences, and the results of a summer of research that included interviews with government officials and others in the field of geriatric care, before the Senate Special Subcommittee on Aging.

Claire and Lallie were trained to be insouciant in one of the best finishing schools in the world, and their treatment of Nader is a mixture of comradeship and deference. Nader treats them with prideful affection, interested but teasing, like a godfather. In speaking of a group of rich do-gooders who had contacted him, he could not resist making a toothy jest of the word *socialite* while giving Lallie a sidelong mocking glance. In the restaurant, Claire ordered coffee. *"Coffee?"* Nader said with a look of betrayal. Claire changed to orange juice. She had earlier revealed that her father, Robert Townsend, the former chairman of Avis and author of *Up the Organization,* had given her a Volkswagen; Nader let the news go by with no more than a sigh.

For the girls, last summer was over. They chattered about Princeton and giggled over one of their teachers at Miss Porter's who had recently married. Claire spoke of opening what she called "an honest advertising agency" with her brother when both finished college. Lallie gave Nader a letter from one of her friends who wanted to become a Raider. Nader lived through the small talk with an indulgent smile. Then he described his plans for a follow-up study on nursing homes, to be carried out in the summer of 1971. Neither of the girls was interested. They had summer plans for Cape Cod, and maybe travel to Europe. Nader let the subject die, then walked with them back across the campus, through the dappled light cast by streetlamps shining through the leaves of the elms. After he had left the girls he said nothing more about them.

That night Nader slept in a Princeton hotel with the windows wide open to the damp April chill, and he rose at six-thirty to take another plane. He stopped over in Washington for two hours to do some work, appearing at the departure gate, his arms loaded with a fresh set of manila envelopes and newspapers, one minute before his flight for Minneapolis was scheduled to take off.

While a welcoming committee from Saint Cloud State College, where Nader was scheduled to speak that afternoon, waited with a worried air, Nader hunched over a telephone in an open-sided booth, dialing call after call. Over the public-address system a voice, distorted in the concrete throat of the huge airport terminal, repeated an announcement.

One of the welcomers said, "I think they said there's a bomb." The announcement was repeated again: there was a bomb threat, and everyone was requested to leave the terminal. Nader's welcomers hung back, hesitant to interrupt him. His companion tapped him on the shoulder and told him about the bomb. Nader said, "Just a minute," and dialed another call. People were scurrying out of the building. Nader turned the pages of *The Washington Post*, marking articles with his felt-tipped pen, while waiting for his call to go through.

When he finished talking, five minutes later, he and his companion walked out of the empty terminal, which is faced with enormous sheets of plate glass running from floor to ceiling. Even a modest bomb would have filled the terminal with a storm of jagged glass spears. "That's really conspicuous inefficiency," Nader said, "hot in summer, cold in winter. Where do you suppose we got this system of perverted esthetics?" Outside, being interviewed by an earnest young reporter in a pink dress, he said, "The Democrats have got to get rid of the idea that because a couple of them have staked out claims, ecology is their exclusive issue. Everybody has got to get involved." The interviewer, her hair shining in the pallid northern sunshine, kept glancing up from her notebook at the great glass building fifty feet away, wondering if the bomb would go off. It did not, and Nader did not mention the possibility of an explosion, then or later. For Nader, events are made from words, not gelignite.

Two hours and more away over the prairie, at Saint Cloud State College, five thousand students awaited Nader in another enormous gymnasium. "This gym could be full of radiation, of carbon monoxide, and you wouldn't be able to tell," he told the audience. "You are moving all the time through an atmosphere of silent violence. We have become biologically obsolete to detect these hazards. The law has winked, has turned its face away from this monstrous destruction." He gave his listeners a vivid description of Alloy, West Virginia, where he had never been, and brought them laughing and applauding to their feet when he said, "The Chicago Seven kept twelve lawyers busy in the Justice Department. I've yet to hear of *one* of Attorney General Mitchell's lawyers concerning himself with the Detroit Four. GM and Ford are criminals. This is serious enough to hand over to Vice President Agnew for action—but before he becomes interested we'll have to find polluters who wear beards and sandals."

That evening, back in Minneapolis, he dined on steak in the Holiday Inn and stayed up much of the night, disputing over the soiled dishes and crumpled napkins with Karim Ahmed, the coordinator of the Minnesota PIRG. Ahmed, a thirty-one-year-old Pakistani, is a postdoctoral fellow in the medical school at Saint Cloud State College. He had been inspired by Nader's advance men and practically single-handed had organized a statewide referendum of university and college students. Fifty-two thousand of the state's 90,000 students had voted to have three dollars per year deducted from their student fees for support of a public-interest research group. The referendum result was applied to all students, so Ahmed's work could conceivably produce $270,000 a year for the cause. Nader was alive with plans to exploit the triumph. Ahmed was sated with his effort and wanted to discuss questions of deeper import. He is married to an American. "The U.S. is a very strange place," he told Nader sadly. "All one's friendships are with women, one has no deep friendships with men."

The next day, on a plane for Tulsa, Nader confessed that he had great difficulty relating to Asians. The whole Third World, with its lust for industrialization, is a troublous subject for him. "They should go home from our culture with their eyes opened," Nader said. "They can avoid the mistakes we've made—they've got plenty of what we've run out

of, time. How can you persuade them to use it to make the
right decisions?" Nader thinks that China and Russia, because they have virtually no automobiles, may very well have
saved the earth's atmosphere.

In Tulsa it was almost summer. Nader has no eye for the
seasons, and he gave the flowers blooming by the roadside
only a cursory glance. At an airport press conference, he was
asked if there was anything good in the consumer field.
"Yes," he replied, "there are some good umbrellas on the
market, marbles are still colorful, and a car can go from one
end of the country to the other without the transmission falling out. The problem with cars is not going, but stopping."

At lunch at the University of Tulsa, in a small room off the
student cafeteria, Nader was approached by a young teacher.
"I've done a lot of research in prison reform, going around to
the prisons," the teacher said, "and the prisoners are very interested in your getting involved." Nader gave him a quizzi-
cal look. "They're interested, or *you're* interested?" he asked.
"I can't get involved in that, there are others doing it. I used
to be interested, the prisons have a very interesting press. At
one time I collected all their newspapers. But I'm not your
man." He returned to his lunch.

Wherever Nader goes, he hits the biggest local industry
with a quick left cross. A few weeks before, at a college located in the center of North Carolina's tobacco region, he
had excoriated the cigarette industry—and was rewarded by
a total lack of response. At the University of Tulsa he said, "I
think the Tulsa newspapers are the most radical in the United
States. No others are so staunch in defending the right of the
oil industry to overthrow capitalism." Only an hour before,
riding in from the airport, he had asked the names of the
local papers. His audience of students roared with approval.
"The oil industry," he said, "always wraps the flag around its
loins. An executive order by the late President Eisenhower
costs the consumer 6¢ a gallon extra on gasoline as a result

of import quotas he gave to the patriotic oil industry. The flag shouldn't be a bandanna or a fig leaf, stained with oil. It should represent something decent, something just, something fine." The microphone failed; Nader pushed it this way and that, and said, "If I was as paranoid as the oil industry I'd think that was a conspiracy."

Something about this audience tickled Nader. Despite the lack of a public-address system, he continued speaking even longer than usual. There is a kind of subliminal sexual symbolism in much that Nader says—Profit, merciless and gross, crouching over the trembling nude body of America. On this day, with the warm southern sun shining through open windows, he brought the allusions to the surface, sending ripples of laughter over the audience. "What is pornography?" he asked. "It's what that young man is reading furtively at the newsstand, standing on one foot. There's a Ford ad in a recent *Playboy*. It says, 'We made it hot. You can make it scream.' That's pornography. There was a problem selling male cosmetics to American he-men, themselves created by advertising. But as Madison Avenue does so well, they grabbed it right by the . . . horns." There was a roar of boisterous laughter.

The audience, unlike most others, did not remain responsive. Nader, like a guest led into a monologue by an overcordial host, spoke for more than two hours. One by one, and then in larger groups, his audience began to leave, so that by the time he finished no more than half of the original two thousand were left in the stuffy room. A beautiful girl with long blond hair, who sat transfixed in the second row for the first hour, shining a smile upward at the lectern, finally lost interest; the light in her face went out, and she left limping from her long imprisonment on a wooden chair. Nader was left, in the question period, with a group of about thirty, clumped in front of a sea of empty chairs. He took their questions with as much delight as if the hall were still full.

To the inevitable question as to what sort of car one should buy, Nader gave a new answer with a flash of mischief. "I'm in favor of zero automobile growth," he said, "otherwise known as ZAG."

Nader kept his buoyant good humor later in the afternoon on a quick visit, just before closing hour, to the national headquarters of the U.S. Jaycees. He had always wanted to stop in but never found the occasion; in 1967, Nader was voted one of the Jaycees' Ten Outstanding Young Men, and before that, he confessed, he had been a Jaycee in good standing for a number of years. A young official, who said that he was fast approaching the retirement age of thirty-five that is mandatory for Jaycee employees, showed Nader through the building, draped with flags and mottoes and hung with the smiling photographs of former Jaycee presidents. Before he left, Nader gave his guide a slow wink and said, "I've always felt the Jaycees have all the potential in the world to do something really important in this country." The young man, in shirt sleeves under a huge flag in the foyer, was left to wonder what a wink from Ralph Nader might mean to his organization.

Beyond Tulsa lay more little colleges in Kansas and Illinois—more days of movement, more afternoons of evangelism, more nights of talk. Nader took his next airplane as happily as he had taken the first, four days before. His companion said, "You seem a lot happier, traveling, than you do back in Washington." Nader shrugged. "If the change is going to come, it'll come here," he said, gesturing at the windows of the plane. Under the wings of the jet, the American prairie stretched toward its distant horizon, planted with crops, dotted with cattle; the windows of farmhouses flashed enormous reflections of the setting sun.

Nader did not look out, any more than he had looked down at the lovely flirting girl in the audience at Tulsa. From one of his envelopes he extracted a manuscript and began to speedread. He chuckled and underlined a passage with his Magic Marker. Tomorrow he would have a new statistic, telling us perhaps how soon the human race can expect to suffocate. Outside, beyond a gibbous moon, the stars came out over the Great Plains. Nader, flung through the sky by technology, went on reading, flipping the pages of the document with his big, deft fingers—information his ocean, his mind the fish.

15

Who Will Watch the Watchman?

What am I concerned with? . . . The anal effusions of
a society.

RALPH NADER

The public Ralph Nader, with one foot on the carcass of the
Establishment, may be seen as the implacable in pursuit of
the doomed. But after five years of fame, in which he has
gathered about himself a great coalition of the disgruntled,
he still sees nothing but desolation. The system cannot
change, and it will not die. This truth has made him hoarse.
He is touched, for the first time in his life, by fatigue. "How
long do I have to go on like this?" he bitterly asks a friend.
"I'm squandering time. There are books I want to write,
other things I want to do."

Human beings, electrified by his ideas, push him this way
and that. He dreams of walking away from it all, finding
some quiet place like the library at Princeton where *Homo
sapiens,* cleansed of all its smell and noise, sleeps on the

printed page. Like other good princes before him, he has found that sleeping beauties, once they are kissed awake, demand sex and food and constant reassurance.

This is not the result he imagined, but he is beguiled by his life of sacrifice. "I sit back reflecting," he said, alone in one of his empty offices on a Sunday afternoon. "I say, 'What am I *doing* with my time?' What would a person do in a euphoria—or a Utopia? Was it John Adams who said, I am in politics so my children can be in the sciences, and their children in the arts? That's a very insightful thing; that's a hell of an insight. What am I concerned with? I am concerned with society's wastes, with the anal effusions of a society. Or I'm concerned with the trivia of the automobile industry. If you had to lay out the things you wanted to do with yourself, you wouldn't do this in a sort of quasi Utopia."

The mood does not last long. In the next sentence he is brought back to cheerfulness through the description of a new technique. A few days before, he had spoken to seven hundred deaf students in Rochester. "While I was talking there was an interpreter right next to me," he says. "It was fascinating. They could get the concepts across—like they'd laugh three seconds later than the students who can hear."

Nothing can reconcile Nader to the time lag between the expression of his outrage and the obliteration of its cause. He is never satisfied: the auto safety law was not enough; the humiliation of General Motors is not complete; the newly aggressive Federal Trade Commission does not go far enough.

He is contemptuous of reformers who become so identified with their own reforms as to defend them even after they have turned into abuses. Preserving himself from this weakness, Nader denounces everything—even his own work. He will not speculate about the forces he has awakened in the country. Every time there is a test, it is demonstrated that the "consumer movement" (a term more often used by newspapers than by Nader himself) has little power, for all its mystical appeal. Nader is not interested in intangibles.

Nobody knows what, exactly, Nader wants. Nader always stops short of describing his goal. James Roche of General Motors believes that he wishes to destroy the free-enterprise system and replace it with total control by a government similar to those in the Soviet Union and mainland China. "You wonder sometimes," Roche says, "if Mr. Nader had come along about sixty or seventy years ago, where the automobile business, or where the United States might be today. . . . Mr. Nader doesn't seem to have many ideas about how he can improve [the system] within the facts of life."

Nader does not accept Roche's facts of life. He believes that the whole long process of concentrating the powers of the human race in institutions has been a mistake. Nader thinks that structure of almost any kind is bound to be misused. He is against structure as the dominant force in society. He thinks structure, no matter how it begins, is likely to be employed against the public interest and cites the trade unions, with their humanistic origins and their parochial end, as an example. He dreams of new kinds of power. "We've got to have sources of power that will rise to the occasion," he argues. "Somehow unstructured power, *ad hoc* power, initiatory democracy, whatever you want to call it, is less likely to be abused and more likely to be continually nourished."

This power eludes him. Out of three hundred Raiders, he gains six activists. In each audience of two thousand, drawn by the drama of his ideas, he sees no more than one or two who will give up comfort to follow him. Nader, who has never had an ordinary job or a wife or a child, believes the masses—who are impelled to have all these things—have somehow ceased to be fully alive. Nader, who has hidden from other humans all his life, worries about the way in which intercourse has been machined out of modern life. "Afflu-ence produces diseases, psychological as well as physical," he says. "The destruction of neighborhoods—everyone in his cell. Americans will pay money to observe a square in Mex-ico, where people walk and meet each other. It's fascinating to them."

America is blowing its social germs across the world in a cloud of radioactive waste and industrial pollution. "We can poison the world," he says. He brushes aside the argument that what he does—protecting Americans from hurting themselves in five-thousand-dollar automobiles, preserving Americans from the harmful effect of foods whose very con-sumption is a form of waste—is irrelevant to the general situation of mankind. Starvation and disease and terror exist on the rim of the world, but the future, which is America, will roll over them.

"When I was abroad, and came back, of course I saw that the problems people have here are pale, compared to what malaria does, or leprosy," he says. "That's not the question. In America we are trying to solve a problem that the rest of the world will have. . . . We've got to do what past genera-tions never had to do. . . . Man-made hazards are tran-scending our traditional physiological alert system. We can't taste the mercury in swordfish, we can't smell carbon diox-ide, we can't see hydrocarbons or feel radioactivity from the nuclear power plants. We've got to rely more on our minds, less on our bodies, to signal pain or anger or fear. We have to do something."

Nader is not certain that there is time. "There are real col-lective suicidal tendencies in this country," he says. "It's ex-pressed in our institutions, it's right there to see. There ought to be a clinical psychology built up on institutional in-sanity. They are generally insane or tending toward it. The Russians have the best satire around because they realize it."

He realizes that what he is suggesting is, as he says, a new demand on human nature. He would like to shock the custodians of institutions back to a sense of humanity, as he thinks Mao Tse-tung did in China. "One of the best solutions is to get people at the top of institutions to go through what their victims go through," Nader says. "The coal magnate should work a couple of weeks in the coal mine each year. That was the main thrust of the Cultural Revolution. Mao saw that they were becoming like the Russians—a bureaucracy, remote, elite. He really broke it. It hadn't been done before in history. He was seventy years old when he decided that. He had fantastic sensitivity."

Not only the leaders in America have become remote. Something about this society, Nader thinks, has bled the people themselves of their sensitivity. "Did we have to let two million Biafrans starve?" he demands. "What we're really talking about is what kind of system operates here and how it affects the rest of the world. . . . We're seeing huge disasters— Biafra, Pakistan. You get a few more of these and people are going to be totally callous. You remember how it was? Bandwagons! Americans would send relief. Now an earthquake wipes out forty thousand and nobody cares."

Nader's solutions lead him away from his old methods, which were based on his instinctive distrust of organization. To cure problems caused by structure, he conceives new structures. Mechanisms spring up around him, and despite his illusion that each is a community of free spirits, all are dependent on him in the most rigid of all organizational formulas: one leader conceiving everything, deciding everything, keeping all but the most unimportant secrets to himself. His followers, if they want anything, want more structure. Too much spontaneity, as more than one of them suggests, is inefficient. Nader's young people, hostile to the old authority, crave the new authority of his idealism.

This idealism is not based on a system of ideas, but on a pattern of emotions. Nader's statistics quantify a feeling that something is desperately wrong in a society in which people have received almost everything their politicians promised them—and are still unhappy. Those who have been left out of this colossal delivery of goods and personal rights—the Negroes and the other minorities—are not the class with which Nader is directly concerned. His activity is based on the discontent of the white middle class. His strength, the implied power to disrupt markets and recall politicians, lies with those who can vote and buy and speak as equals. Nader does not stand among a rabble of mendicants, but at the head of an army of the moneyed and the educated. It is a powerful constituency, deliberately chosen.

It has not, so far, been a very responsive constituency, nor is it a constituency with which Nader is truly comfortable. It does not feel exploited, but guilty. Nader's rhetoric, which has something in common with the inspired banality of a nondenominational preacher, gives the constituency some reason to hope it, too, has been punished by the system that has made it the most fortunate class in human history. Nader, attacking sloth—"What are they going to do with the four-day weekend? You can demand a second career from them!"—apparently does not regard himself as another form of entertainment for the people he is trying to rally. But it is certainly possible that that is all he will turn out to be, and perhaps some dim realization of this causes him to react so violently to the cultists who think he should run for President. He is maddened by Gore Vidal and by the Nader-for-President bumper stickers because these invade his control of his role, threatening him with structure.

Nader considers that the time has come to call the constituency into action. His lonely evangelism, followed by the pilot projects of the Center for Study of Responsive Law, the Public Interest Research Group, and the other mechanisms, represented the first stages. The model assembly line for social rejuvenation has been, if not perfected, then made workable. He is conscious of the failures of the first stages. "I'm not at all willing to say that we can't have impact," he says, "until we have six or seven thousand in a city like Washington—and still nothing happens."

The time when he can marshal that sort of manpower is not, he thinks, very far away. "There's no reason, in five years' time, why I shouldn't have four or five thousand professionals all over the country," he says. The professionals will come for the most part from the student movement; they will work out of the Public Interest Research Groups supported by student funds. They will operate as autonomous units, but they will be energized by Nader's view of the world, and they will attack on the basis of his priorities.

He envisages, also, a citizens' movement arising from his study of the Congress. He chose Congress for the first assault because it is the most vulnerable of the great institutions. "That's the major institution that can begin turning the country around that's accessible to the people," Nader says. "If you're talking about leverage, there it is." He wants to monitor each district, each member of Congress, expose everything to public view.

Nader sees things beneath the surface that he thinks should be made visible to the whole citizenry. "It's very interesting how the executive branch makes Congress weak," he explains. "It makes Congress weak by making one or two congressmen potent. That is, they make sure that a Mendel Rivers controls the whole operation. He's very powerful and in return they control him." He foresees the reaction of Congress clearly enough. "Nobody likes to be judged," he says, "so our sympathizers inside Congress are not going to be sympathizers long. Here come the people—that's what it's going to be."

The final piece in the pattern involves a subtle change in Nader's attitude toward institutions. "Instead of looking at, say, the Department of Agriculture as a monolith," he says, "we look for groups inside it that are consistent with the public interest." Nader calls such people "whistle blowers." They would be motivated by one of his central concepts: that citizens who earn their living from organizations, whether in corporations or in the government, remain citizens. They have a higher loyalty to their fellow man than to the organization; betrayal of the public interest, as Nader defines the public interest, is the only betrayal that counts.

If the formula works, Nader expects that some institutions will fall. "How can the Pentagon continue to function if we are going to improve society?" he asks. "Or the Congress? The Congress doesn't know what's going on, doesn't want to know what's going on. . . . You've got to make them *feel* what's happening."

Nader does not know whether American society has the capacity to reform itself. "I don't think anyone knows," he says. "That's a belief that would be just like a hunch, bred from very elemental impulses of pessimism or optimism. That is what we are trying to find out."

Nader himself moves constantly between pessimism and optimism. One part of his mind despairs of the inertia of the people he is trying to reach—television-watchers, Mah-Jongg players, time-wasters. The other part descries a sunlit future in which the citizenry, fully awake, takes affairs into its own hands and breaks up the elite that he believes has all but ruined human existence.

Satan was no more real to Cotton Mather than this elite to Ralph Nader. The idea that government and industry are handmaidens in conspiracy and corruption illuminates almost every sentence he utters. If one believes so profoundly in the devil, one cannot believe except with difficulty in the existence of honorable men. In his passion, Nader has attacked a series of unlikely witches: William Haddon, Edmund Muskie, Abraham Ribicoff. No reading of Nader's evidence can support the view that these men are guilty of doing anything other than the best they could in the light of realities as they perceived them. One of the realities they perceived, of course, was the certainty that nothing they could do, short of abject public surrender to Nader's point of view, would satisfy him.

It is precisely this refusal to compromise, this grim insistence on his own definition of virtue, that endears Nader to his admirers. It is his harshness, more usually called incorruptibility, that gives him such extraordinary power over the imagination of his followers. His personal virtue, which is unquestionable, has been confused with his public role; he is granted a latitude of behavior enjoyed by no one else in public life.

Nader insists that those who act in the public's name must operate in the public view. But many of his own actions that have profound public consequences are carried out in secret. This tendency to do good by stealth goes back to the beginnings of his career. He was a secret adviser to the Ribicoff subcommittee in 1966; he based his attack on William Haddon partly on information supplied from inside Haddon's entourage. He created and manipulated the candidacy of Joseph A. Yablonski for the presidency of the United Mine Workers of America. He pays and controls Gary Sellers, who is also paid by the congressman for whom he works.[1] All these actions, and many others, can be defended on grounds that they were tactically necessary. But each raises a clear ethical question that almost any other public man would be called upon to answer.

Nader is not called upon for explanations because it is accepted that he represents the public interest. In the United States, it has always been assumed that the elected representatives of the people were charged with custody of the public interest—and that the public interest itself was defined by

1. In December, 1971, Sellers revealed his intention to resign from both positions.

the results of elections. There has always been the potential in American society for another dimension of politics. Nader, through his masterful use of the media, which constitute a nearly perfect instrument for the exchange of hyperbole, has moved into that dimension. He has become the first national political figure who has not submitted to an election or even to the public scrutiny of his ideas and his activities. It was the press, not the ballot, that created him.

Nader may be described in the press as "the consumer champion." But the questions to which he addresses himself are political questions. He is calling for a new national policy across the whole spectrum of events, and he has achieved such successes as he will admit through the manipulation of Congress and the executive branch, which are, after all, political entities. In the latest phase of his activity, he is moving away from the cover of consumer issues altogether to make a direct attack upon the nature of a political institution, the Congress. The logical result of this activity, if it succeeds, will be to change the membership of Congress and to overturn the procedures that have governed its actions over a period of almost two centuries.

This is a great deal to attempt outside the boundaries of traditional political action. Nader clearly falls outside those boundaries. He is a revolutionary—in despair over what he regards as a society on the brink of shipwreck, animated by a burning sense of righteousness, endowed with the gift of personal magnetism, and gripped by the ruthless love of an idea. Like other revolutionaries before him, he has the gift of looking back over a series of spasmodic actions and emotional responses, and weaving them after the fact into a coherent philosophy.

These are, of course, the attributes of another kind of human being as well. When Lyndon Johnson signed the Wholesome Meat Act of 1967, he invited Nader to be in attendance. Johnson, with his maddening talent for the perfect gesture, also invited Upton Sinclair. Almost everyone assumed that Sinclair, who had published *The Jungle* sixty-one years before, must be dead. He was, instead, staving off ruin from a wheelchair.

Betty Furness took Nader over to meet the old man. Sinclair tried to struggle to his feet; he wanted to stand up to meet Nader. "I sort of felt," Nader said long afterward, "that two historic consumer ages were meeting—Upton Sinclair and I were together in the White House. Maybe this time, I thought, the work will have some effect."

No one knows what Upton Sinclair thought. Maybe the poet, still alive surely in that old body, felt the ironical truth in his bones: that if technology is a church, as many of Nader's enemies and perhaps he himself believes, then Ralph Nader is its first saint.

A Note on Sources

It is evident that the writer who undertakes to describe the life of a young man must depend almost entirely upon the verbal recollections of those who have known him. Almost three hundred persons have been kind enough to talk to me about Ralph Nader. Many of them have furnished valuable documentary material. In all but a few cases, where the conversation was tape-recorded—or where, as in the case of experienced public figures, it could be assumed that the source was speaking by design—the transcription of the interview was submitted to the source for the correction of factual errors. There were some cases in which I did not accept changes in syntax that seemed to me to detract from the vividness of the quotation without adding to its accuracy. In those rare cases where changes were requested that conflicted with my notes and my clear recollection of the original statement, I have noted the conflict in a footnote.

There is the advantage, in reporting the life of a contemporary figure, that he is available to explain himself, and to match his recollection of events against those of his observers. Ralph Nader has been generous with his time and painstaking in his answers to my questions, and I am very grateful to him.

Nader's written work consists of his book, *Unsafe at Any Speed,* and his magazine articles. I have drawn on these in many ways. Where I have quoted from newspapers and other printed works, I have identified them in the text, and it seemed superfluous to burden the reader with footnotes. The reports of the committees of the Senate and the House of Representatives, where the bulk of Nader's public utterances are preserved, were extremely useful, and I am grateful to the staffs of these committees for making them available to me.

Inevitably, a great deal of material derived from interviews has not found its way into the book. By way of apology to those who were so generous with their time I can only say that the information they furnished has been of great value. Because some of my sources wished to remain anonymous, I refrain from providing a list of names, which would necessarily be incomplete.

I owe a particular debt to the late Alice Glaser, most sensitive of editors, who commissioned the magazine article that was the genesis of this book. My agent, Don Gold of the William Morris Agency, first suggested that the book be written and negotiated the contracts that made it possible. My editor at the Saturday Review Press, Susan Stanwood, has been a model of good nature and the source of much good advice. And my dear and patient cousin, Alison Rees Mabry, turned a chaotic manuscript into an admirably neat typescript.

C. McC.

Index

Successful
Scriptwriters
Handbook